... As good a marine saga as has
There is a hilarious account of a
session with a killer whale! ... he
myths; navigational and environm........
seabirds and animals, and the incomparable coasts ... he has been
touched with the splendour of a great idea carried out.
Sir Alistair Dunnet – THE SCOTSMAN

... Now available as a full-length book, and what an excellent book
it is. Brian speaks bluntly on various forms of pollution and backs
his case up with a wealth of thoroughly researched facts which are
bound to open a few eyes ... He has an excellent turn of phrase, and
I would put his description of the late night Shipping Forecast as
one of the classic pieces of canoe writing ... this is without doubt
the best sea canoeing travel book I have ever read.
Editor – CANOEIST Magazine

This is a book which lovers of Scotland and devotees of scenery, the
environment, wildlife, sea and adventure should not miss ... the
words alone paint the majesty of Scotland's coastline ... a delight
to read ... the reader is drawn into the perils and delights of this
dangerous journey.
Editor – CURAM

A quite exceptionally gifted writer ... a sense of humour and a
strong dash of poetry and romanticism... This is an outstanding
travel book, right outside the run of ordinary sports writing.
JERSEY EVENING POST

Beautifully illustrated, by a perceptive conservationist ... is both
topical and entertaining in its catalogue of evidence of problems
facing the marine environment ... as full of fascination for the non-
paddling reader as for the active sea canoeist.
CANOE FOCUS

... I don't know whether the adventure itself or the story of it deserves
the greater admiration; the combination strikes me as a triumph
– which I hope will have many successors.
BBC RADIO 4 – Book at Bedtime

About the Author

Brian Wilson is a well-known and respected member of the British Canoeing scene, specialising in extended sea-kayaking expeditions and adventure travel. Born in Greenock in 1962, educated in Aberdeenshire and at Edinburgh University, he graduated with an honours degree in Philosophy in 1984. He was twice British Universities Judo Champion, and won the Scottish Superstars competition in 1984.

Having worked with many of the major Scottish conservation and environmental organisations, he is now a freelance environmental contractor specialising in traditional stonework, thatching and vernacular building conservation. His company won the Association for the Protection of Rural Scotland conservation award in 1996 and 2000.

Brian lives near the north-west Highland port of Ullapool with his French partner Marie-Pierre and their daughters Malin, Manon and Nellie. Among his greatest pleasures are unspoiled coastlines, blazing driftwood fires and good books; and his ambitions include paddling, burning and reading his way along many more of the world's finest shores, not necessarily alone.

Brian Wilson is also the author of:

Dances with Waves – Around Ireland by Kayak, Two Ravens Press (2008) ISBN 978-1-906120-21-4
Recreation and Access, in: *The Islands of Scotland – A Living Marine Heritage,* ed. Baxter and Usher (HMSO 1994) ISBN 0-11 4942-43-9

For more information about the author, see:
www.tworavenspress.com

BLAZING PADDLES

A Scottish Coastal Odyssey

Brian Wilson

TWO RAVENS
PRESS

Published by Two Ravens Press Ltd
Green Willow Croft
Rhiroy
Lochbroom
Ullapool
Ross-shire IV23 2SF

www.tworavenspress.com

Third edition.
First edition published in 1988 by The Oxford Illustrated Press;
second edition published in 1998 by The Wildland Press.

ISBN: 978-1-906120-22-1

British Library Cataloguing in Publication Data: a CIP record for
this book can be obtained from the British Library.

Designed and typeset in Sabon by Two Ravens Press.
Cover design by David Knowles and Sharon Blackie.

Printed on Forest Stewardship Council-certified paper by Antony
Rowe Ltd, Chippenham.

FSC
Mixed Sources
Product group from well-managed
forests and other controlled sources

Cert no. SGS-COC-2953
www.fsc.org
© 1996 Forest Stewardship Council

Acknowledgements

Only if a traveller – fully self-contained and financially independent – could drop to Earth fresh from the Heavenly forge, could there be such a thing as a truly solo expedition.

A special thanks must go to my major sponsors, Fox's Biscuits, for sensitive and considerate support. To the companies mentioned in Chapter One I'm grateful for the donation and loan of equipment and food.

I'd like to extend my gratitude to HM Coastguard for weather forecasts, for friendly advice and for keeping track of my eccentric wanderings without a hint of derision, and the Fisherman's Mission organisation whose hot showers and hospitality went a long way towards relieving me of much more than salt and grime.

Many people whose generosity formed part of the story will find themselves on the pages that follow. Others, who merely stopped for a chat or a word of encouragement are too numerous to mention; but for leaving me with a smile on my face and the knowledge of how valuable a casual word of kindness can be … 'Thanks.'

In the typing and preparation of the book I owe an enormous thanks to my mum – whose time and energy spent helping me over the years have never been grudged – and to Deolinda Caldeira – whose help and enthusiasm were happily in no way related to the financial rewards involved.

I owe a great deal to the inspiration and friendship of canoeists who have shared journeys over the years, in particular to Dennis, Faz, Jules and Bob.

Finally thanks to Mrs Thatcher and the DHSS, without whom there might have been no journey and no book.

Foreword

It was in the Intermediate Technology offices, way back early in '85, that I first met the Gentle Giant. He'd come down from his home in Aberdeen especially to outline his dream to canoe around Scotland. In his earlier letter, he'd mentioned raising funds for I.T. by canoeing 'somewhere.' Now the full enterprise hit me.

'What! All the way around?'

'Yup, that's the aim.'

'But ain't that a ... of a long way?' I stuttered.

'Och, a fair few miles,' he replied with a helpful smile, for my benefit grossly understating the incredible challenges ahead.

As all readers of his book discover, that calmness was built on the security of experience. Brian's strength and appeal was that he knew and acknowledged nearly all the different sorts of problems ahead: storms, rip tides, turbulent waters, physical exhaustion, mental fatigue; he knew about navigation, boat maintenance and nights in soaking wet sleeping bags, above all he knew the joys of a Scottish sunset and the hospitality of the crofters. What he didn't know was how far he'd get. Even in the first week out of Glasgow there were a myriad of problems, any one of which would have stopped most people. Within the first month, the rest of us would have gone home defeated. Brian keeps going, he takes the rough with the smooth; each day is a new day.

If I've done my sums correctly then he has packed more than three million paddle strokes around the coast of Scotland into his book. Yet it is much bigger than a story of adventure and streaks ahead of a nautical log. It is a unique personal diary blended in with all the local colour of alehouse punters, shark-hunters, mermaids and many more.

He has also woven in the fresh breeze of environmental awareness. Many of us share his concerns about modern pollutants and misuse of resources. In this respect, we at the charity Intermediate Technology are most pleased that Brian has chosen to raise funds for work which aims towards the efficient use of local resources for the benefit of all.

Ultimately, the beauty of Brian's extraordinary adventure is not only the simplicity and fondness with which he describes the Scottish coast (and the tenacity with which he paddles his frail craft!) but also that it is a rare example of someone setting out into the distant blue, not knowing if they can reach the end, but that they can make a start.

Richard Crane BSc, PhD, FGS, FRGS

Introduction

Blazing Paddles is not so much a book of techniques and jargon for canoeists as an adventure story of a journey which just happened to be undertaken by canoe. Why a canoe? Well, because there's nothing else quite like it. Technically speaking a 'canoe' is a different beast from a 'kayak', but for my purposes the terms are interchangeable; indeed I often merely refer to 'the boat', for in the end that's what it is: a very special boat, but a boat nonetheless.

Similarly, although I have gone into tidal matters in some details, tides and currents are for my purposes largely ambivalent labels. Correctly speaking, the Gulf Stream in Chapter Six is the only 'current' in the book.

In the same spirit, this was not a *purist* expedition. It was important to me to be a self-contained travelling unit as far as possible, and to remain independent of the land or sea support that often accompanies similar ventures, but I was not out to set records for distance or speed. Although the journey was somewhere in the region of 1,800 miles, I remain unsure of the exact mileage achieved, and had to think hard to even work out how many days it took. Likewise, while I am not aware of anyone ever making the journey before, I would not be disappointed to learn that someone had, nor angry if someone duplicated it tomorrow, for 'staking a claim' was never part of the ethos of the trip.

Since I had set no rules, to those who reckon I cheated by using ferries to cross the Minch, I would simply reply that they have missed the point. I had hoped to be able to paddle the Minch – and indeed have done so twice since then – but conditions were simply unsuitable, and taking the ferry was infinitely preferable to waiting endlessly for a good day, or to meeting my Maker in mid-Minch. Safety was a prime consideration at all times.

I am aware that certain passages in the book make canoeing sound unduly easy. It is not. A great deal of training and care over safety are necessary for a solo journey at sea. I carried a wide range of safety equipment, mastered basic 'self-rescue at sea' techniques, and kept in touch with the coastguard – by radio or by telephone – whenever possible. But there is no substitute for experience – knowing when to go and when to stay; understanding the weather and the sea; knowing your own limitations. Batman and Robin used to warn us: 'Don't try this at home – you might get hurt!' but I hope the book conveys a sense of the unique and special experiences available to the solo traveller, and anyone who first arms themselves with adequate training, equipment and experience will not need me to wish them *luck*.

Finally, although controversial, I make no apologies for the comments and observations on environmental issues relating to the future of the coast line and its uniquely beautiful wildlife. One cannot travel on the sea for four months and live in a tent without gaining a heightened awareness of the intricate ecological processes of the sea and shore and those things which are threatening them.

Submarines, supertankers and sea-pollution are issues directly related to my journey, and so earned a place in the fabric of experiences which form this book. But it is also my hope that wider appreciation and more open discussion of the problems involved will encourage those of us who love the sea to exert greater and more effective pressure towards its sane and sustainable management.

Brian Wilson
Glasgow, May 1988

Introduction to the Second Edition

Already it is ten years since the first publication of *BLAZING PADDLES*, the story of a journey which, I realise with hindsight, was to influence almost all of my thoughts, plans and priorities during the decade that followed.

It has been a decade full of change, within which I have evolved from a single, city-dwelling student to a rural-based father of two, who – despite living on one of the finest sea lochs of the north-west Highlands – finds it increasingly difficult to safeguard a place for kayaking in an ever more hectic work and family schedule!

In that same time period, sea-kayaking itself has developed from a fairly obscure sub-sect of a minority watersport, into one of the fastest growing adventure sports in the world. Manufacture and retail of sea-kayaks and associated equipment has become a highly competitive international business; there are commercial outfitters offering kayak tours in many remote parts of the world; and kayaking symposiums and trade fairs are major events.

Happily, despite this great boom in sea-kayaking, there is still plenty of sea-room out there. Unlike the parallel increase in the number of people taking to the overburdened hills and mountains, or to motorised pleasure boating, sea-kayaking seems to be eminently sustainable. The kayak itself causes no erosion, no noise and no fumes, and kayakers in general are not only sensitive to and appreciative of the wealth of wildlife to which our shores and seas are home, but also concerned to support initiatives designed to safeguard the coast from pollution, exploitation and over-development. There are few better platforms than the kayak for coming to know and love the wildlife of our coasts.

Finally, throughout a decade of rapid changes there have also been many constants. The great swell-waves still pile in upon Scottish shores from the wide Atlantic; the tides scour and swish through the island narrows; the seabirds return to their rocky outposts each spring; and the summer flowers still crowd the Hebridean machairlands. Above all the Scottish coastline remains one of the most magical places in the world for relaxation and discovery, exploration and adventure, and the kayak is still the best way I know of to make it my own. It is my sincere hope that *BLAZING PADDLES* will continue to touch the hearts, not just of kayakers, but of all who love the special places where land and sea combine.

Brian Wilson
Ullapool, 1998

Introduction to the Third Edition

A book is at liberty to make its own way in the world; once freed from the aspirations of its author and publisher, it begins a voyage of its own. Passing through many hands, as gifts, purchases, loans – perhaps even as stolen goods – books migrate from shop to coffee-table, re-locate from library to fireside, precipitate from jumble-sale to wobbly table-leg, entirely independent of their makers and minders. Their passage smoothed by word-of-mouth or rave-reviews; sales hastened by mail-order and internet auction; books become fragments of swirling flotsam in the great tidal vortex of readership.

Of course an author may get occasional reports back indicating how his creation is faring – glimpses of it on a bookshelf perhaps, or a publishers' royalty statement – and gain thereby a patchy appreciation of the voyage, but short of fitting books with feedback coupons or GPS tags, the life-cycle of an individual book will forever remain enigmatic and untraceable.

One of my greatest joys as a writer over the years has therefore been to receive letters from readers describing how certain stories or episodes from my books have been important to them, made them laugh, or touched an emotional chord for some personal reason that I could never have foreseen. Accounts of how they listened to it on *Book at Bedtime*, read it in the bath or found it in a bus-station, are like rare postcards from the travels of a long-lost friend. Occasionally I have been amazed at the places it has reached: one note came from a homesick ex-pat reading *Blazing Paddles* in Uganda; and on a recent kayaking trip to a remote island in the Azores, I was astounded to find that BP had in fact got there before me!

Ten years ago, writing the preface to the second edition, I was heartened by how many of the special elements of my *Blazing Paddles* journey remained intact out there on the coast of Scotland. Today, a further decade on, I am concerned by just how quickly, and radically, things are changing. The seabirds which once crowded the great cliffs and skerries are today struggling desperately with pollution, over-fishing and the consequences of climate change. The mounds of driftwood and wooden fish-boxes which once comfortably fuelled and furnished the campsites of a coastal nomad, no longer wash up on our western beaches, having been superseded by generations of polystyrene and bright plastic. And the concepts of solitude and wilderness – which lie at the heart of *Blazing Paddles* – are under threat from the tsunami of miniaturised, digital technology which has rapidly revolutionised adventure travel. True solitude dissolves when we choose to carry a reliable means of contacting (or being contacted by) the outside world. And the idea of wilderness recedes in direct proportion to the quantity of technical bling we choose to bring with us in pursuit of it.

It is my sincere hope that you will enjoy *Blazing Paddles* as this third edition ventures forth, not only as a narrative record – a colourful snapshot of a time which is rapidly passing – but as a portrait of a young man's first low-tech voyage of discovery, floating boldly alone among the seabirds and fishboxes of a very special country.

Brian Wilson
Ullapool, 2008

Contents

For MARIE-PIERRE with thanks
for your constant love and support,
both on and off the water.

'Just Add Water'

'What is it when we're on it?'
'A sort of boat I think,' said Pooh.
'Oh, that sort.'
'Yes, and we're going to discover a Pole or something. Or was it
a Mole?
'Anyhow, we're going to discover it.'

(Winnie-the-Pooh, A.A. Milne.)

'Two thousand miles at sea in *that?* Dae ye think I came up the Clyde in a banana boat?' said the cynical Glaswegian, not quite convinced by my attempts at an explanation. It's one of the most picturesque phrases in 'the patter', referring to the naïve and city-stunned crews of early trading boats, but its origins are lost somewhere in the hazy history of Clydeside. And yet in April 1985, beneath Glasgow's Victoria Bridge, it was inadvertently given a new life and meaning. For my kayak *Natural Crunch*, billed by Radio Scotland as 'a modern marine anomaly', was indeed a 'banana boat'; a kayak of bright yellow fibreglass whose pointed ends curled gracefully upwards in a fair approximation of Eskimo nautical engineering, and in exact resemblance of a great banana. With a ceremonial push it was launched, along with its bewildered Aberdonian cargo, into the Clyde.

Thirty feet above, on the wooden decks of the R.N.R. Clubship *S.V. Carrick*, reporters, T.V. cameras and radiomen fussed and jostled for a view; as far as they were concerned this was the start of a long sea journey around Scotland in the eighteen-foot kayak.

Down at water level an old friend, who had become my self-appointed 'manager' since hearing that a free bar and buffet were on offer, wobbled precariously in a slowly sinking clinker boat, bailing out frantically with one hand and directing me with the other towards a photographic rendezvous in mid-Clyde.

With a flick of the paddle I sent the slender kayak out across the water and swept a wide arc round towards a tiny orange dinghy drifting, apparently, out of control. The dinghy held three overweight photographers in immaculate suits and carrying neckloads of

1

cameras; like stuffed cuckoos in a waterlogged nest they drifted and spun further and faster downriver as they attempted to master the use of the tiny plastic oars. I approached within camera range and paddled in for the first picture, but the dinghy rotated in the wind so that each had to crane and twist to avoid filling the frame with the others' ears and balding heads. A second approach and all was well until a mis-timed pull on an oar sent their vessel and their lenses spinning out on a 180° span of Clydeside. The offending oar floated over towards me and curses echoed over the water like a scene from Jerome K. Jerome's *Three Men in a Boat* – and it's little surprise that next morning's papers displayed my widest camera grin, for it was all I could do to avoid laughing myself into total capsize.

Meanwhile, in the bar of the Carrick, serious journalistic speculation was in progress. Some tipsy representatives of the less reputable press were putting my girlfriend Pippa's mind at rest by explaining that they were only interested in the journey if I was to have an affair with Royalty or get a seal pregnant en route, and suggesting what fun they would have with the ominous name *Natural Crunch* when the expedition hit disaster.

My brother, dressed to pass as a pressman, sat with glass in hand, looking suitably replete, in one corner, and sure enough by the time I arrived the buffet had long since been demolished. Drunken reporters gobbled and quaffed wherever I looked, while I was nudged into a prominent position, decked in sponsors' regalia, and bombarded with questions from a magicube-flashing throng obviously anxious to get the interview on tape and renew intimate professional contact with the bar.

'What do you think of Jimmy MacGregor calling you "a mad heidbanger"?'… 'How can you go "round Scotland" when it's not an island?' One misguided soul even congratulated me on 'winning the Round Britain Yacht Race'!

To a string of questions which lacked any trace of perception of what my journey was to be about, I gave polite and inane answers which were printed next morning word for word. Being the focus of such concentrated attention seemed to bear little relation to the lonely adventure that I was about to embark upon. But accepting sponsorship is never a 'something for nothing' situation and, of course, it could have been so much worse. I had firmly refused

2

the earlier photocall requests to pose, one foot on the kayak like a hunter with a slain crocodile, wearing lifejacket, wetsuit and kilt, and to the accompaniment of a piper on the clifftop! The day at the Carrick was a compromise, a chance to fulfil an obligation to my major sponsors, Fox's, and to publicise the Third World charity Intermediate Technology, for whom the expedition was to raise funds, without prostituting the ultimate privacy of the expedition. Fox's had understood this; the expedition was still 'mine' and the true launch, the following day near Dumfries, would be a private affair untainted by media presence.

In the brief moments of quiet allowed to me as I stripped off the promotion gear in a back room, I thought of the questions that had remained unasked and of what, for me, were the real purposes, reasons and expectations of the journey.

❖ ❖ ❖

Long before the age of fourteen, when I floated my first patched battleship of a canoe down the river with a pair of rusty pram wheels strapped on behind to haul it home again, the idea of self-propelled travel by water had me utterly seduced. Why struggle up and down hills with blistered feet and a 60-lb backpack wearing lumps out of your shoulders, or slog along twisted roads with a loaded bike, when you could pack twice as much gear into a kayak, let the water take the strain, and use the current or tide to your advantage?

Throw in a paddle and a sprinkling of basic techniques and you become a master of a craft which makes no noise, gobbles no fuel, leaves no waste, and whose lightness and shallow draught allow it to travel in waters often too treacherous for larger vessels.

Wearing the kayak tightly like a garment, one sits below water level, separated only by a thin shell of fibreglass from the great sweep of the tides and every smaller movement of the sea. But although fragile in appearance, the kayak well-handled is one of the most seaworthy boats in the world. Its manoeuvrability is unrivalled; a whole range of movements is executed from the hips and knees alone. And with skilled use of the paddle the capsized kayak is righted again in seconds.

As an undergraduate in Edinburgh in 1980 I began my first course in sea canoeing. Wednesday afternoons were spent floundering in the freezing surf of the Firth of Forth or paddling nervously out to the Bass Rock, learning the basics but always with bigger things in mind.

Steadily I accumulated the basic skills, learned to calculate and predict the complicated movements of Scotland's tides, to navigate using map and compass, to Eskimo-roll a capsized kayak and, most importantly, to appreciate my own strengths and weaknesses. Each summer a small group of us headed west for ten days' kayaking and camping among the islands, making sense of all those Wednesday afternoons and of my little-boy's belief that it was possible to travel independently and self-sufficiently, by water.

Long days of paddling among idyllic scenery, Hebridean beaches and island campsites began to work in me to create a strong addiction to the Scottish coast and to the freedom afforded by the wandering sea-kayak. But ten days were never long enough and each year, as my experience grew, my resolve strengthened to launch a larger expedition, perhaps of several weeks' duration.

Back in Edinburgh, Plato, Wittgenstein and Nietzsche shared bookshelf and mind-space with Gavin Maxwell, Neill Gunn and Frazer Darling, and in idle moments the dream evolved until in 1984 I envisaged doing an extended voyage, combining the experiences of several shorter forays, and seeing the Scottish seascapes throughout a range of seasons and conditions. Between bouts of study for final exams in philosophy I took mental refuge in building the journey upon the most adventurous ideas I could conceive. *Why not paddle from border to border around the entire coast of Scotland?* By including the Outer Hebridean Islands I could increase the distance of the trip to over 1,800 miles, almost equivalent to the entire distance around mainland Britain. Deeply scarred and pitted with sea lochs and host to isolated island groups, the Scottish coastline is literally thousands of miles of bewildering variety in seascape, wildlife and human tradition. Within its compass fall some of the wildest of unspoiled beaches, the grandest of cliffscapes and the most notorious sea passages in all Europe: the Dorus Mor, the whirlpool at Corryvreckan, the Butt of Lewis and the Pentland Firth, and coastal obstacles such as the great headlands at Mull of Galloway, Ardnamurchan and Cape Wrath, all increasing in severity as I passed, clockwise, around the coast. Of course, it would have to be done clockwise, sunwise. In keeping with Celtic mythology;

deeds done 'widdershins' always ended in disaster. *And I could do it alone!* All supplies and equipment could be carried in the kayak with no need for land or sea support and virtually no restrictions on destination.

The final concept was of a highly improbable, self-sufficient, solo circumnavigation of the Scottish coast and Hebridean Islands. And at last I was satisfied, for I had created what I believed to be the very paradigm of independence and adventure, the sort of dream one could suck dry for a lifetime. But I had exams to sit and a job to find. I had no money and didn't even own a kayak! There were plenty of excuses for copping out.

And so months went by in which I added nothing to the dream. I passed my finals and life became real. I taught canoeing and archery in Edinburgh, cycled through France with Pippa, dried hops in Kent and worked at tree surgery in Aberdeen. But as 1984 drew to a close I found myself unemployed and with no real desire to follow friends into mortgages, marriages and secure jobs in the city. The current of life had veered off and left me in a stagnant backwater. I was sinking fast into one of those ruts that dominates one's character and crushes all motivation, and which is the biggest danger of unemployment. I had neither the awareness to see what was happening nor the power to reverse it until one morning Pippa put her arms around me and with sad eyes said, 'Brian, you're becoming depressed, stagnant and cynical. It's time for you to DO something.'

And it was as though the elf queen had whispered in the ear of a hobbit for, with the force of sudden revelation, I knew that she was right. Unmarried, unmortgaged and healthy, I was to all intents and purposes as free as ever I would be; and yes, of course, there was a dream to realize. Suddenly, through the love of someone who understood me, the dream was rekindled and I began to throw all my energy into bringing it into being, never stopping to consider whether the aims of that dream were really *possible,* or to doubt my ability to achieve them.

And so began the long months of preparation that lie behind any expedition. The route had to be decided, maps acquired, distances and timings estimated as accurately as possible. What sort of food should I carry? How much would I need? What would that weigh? Essential canoeing, camping and safety equipment would have to be decided on and purchased. A sea-going canoe would be useful.

What would all this cost? And, most importantly, how the hell was I going to pay for it!

There would be physical preparation too, but at least I was fit. I had won the Scottish Universities 'Superstars' contest and taken my second British Universities Judo title earlier in the year. After several months of outdoor employment I had at least a sound basis upon which to build the expedition training.

Before Christmas, using the little money I'd saved, I bought a damaged Nordkapp H.M. sea kayak and channelled more money into its repair. It was a boat I knew and respected for its seaworthiness and storage capacity. Perhaps not as stable nor as manoeuvrable as some boats, nevertheless it 'tracked' well in a rough sea, was fast, sturdy, and light.

An initial run of begging letters to equipment and food manufacturers, in my most humble and persuasive prose, brought an almost unanimous response of 'Dear John's, 'sorry's, and 'No's. I was an unknown quantity in the expedition world – not a household name like Bonnington, Fiennes or Clare Francis – and had no leverage with potential sponsor companies. I began to realise that for newspapers and magazines I had to make the expedition sound as hare-brained and spectacular as I dared; for potential sponsors it had to sound exciting but well-planned and safe.

So a second draft met with some limited success. Each morning I waited for the post to discover what new package, pledge or promise had arrived to improve the prospects of the trip, and as parcels and letters of encouragement started to flow I began to feel, at last, that I had a real expedition in the offing.

Canoe equipment manufacturers Harishok and Wildwater sent their blessings along with vital equipment items. Lendal products donated a collapsible spare paddle to be carried in case of emergency and, for performance testing, Timex sent an indestructible waterproof watch with an alarm which played 'Love me Tender, Love me True' by Elvis.

Damart thoughtfully provided two sets of thermal underwear and Mary Buchanan of Slioch Outdoor Equipment asked for a shockingly intimate set of personal measurements in order to fashion a pair of thermal trousers. The result was without doubt the most fantastic, fleece-lined, curve-hugging garment I've ever possessed!

Aberdeen companies B.P.I., Marconi and Arthur Duthie raised the safety margin of the trip by providing an emergency radio-beacon and hand-held radio on loan, and a veritable arsenal of assorted distress flares.

'What's in a name?' I thought, as I accepted a wetsuit and yet more flares from Aberdeen's 'Sub-Sea Services', and agreed to display their stickers, without superstition, on a prominent part of the kayak.

As the equipment list shrank, my room began to resemble Everest Base Camp. Robertsons of Stromness sent fifty bars of Orkney Fudge with best wishes, and Jordan's Wholefoods pledged five hundred original crunchy bars in three flavours. Things were looking good, there were still maps to be bought, more equipment to be found and a balanced diet for five months to be provided.

Food would be an expensive problem. Hundreds of letters requesting financial assistance had already drawn a total blank; the price of stamps alone would have accounted for a week's good eating. I had to find a source of income, fast.

During January and February I took a job as a night security guard for an oil company office. This gave me time during daylight hours to train, while at night 'on the job' I researched and digested everything I could find concerning the Scottish sea, coast and islands. After two weeks I could afford the forty-one O.S. maps (1:50,000 scale) which cover the coast of Scotland.

I raised my daily running distance to five miles carrying two 3-lb weights, swam half a mile daily and cycled eight miles each way to work. Now the nights consisted of plotting chart information about tidal anomalies and coastal hazards onto O.S. maps and taking page after page of detailed notes for future reference. I struggled to make myself master of a specialist combination of skills, studying navigation, finalising routes and logistics, translating Gaelic place-names, reading up on first aid and meteorology. Each week I stepped up my training; I began aerobic-popmobility and practised, in the kayak, deep-water self-rescue techniques I had seen in a book. But on the morning the company boss arrived early to find his 'security' man flaked out and snoring in the executive swivel-chair, surrounded by maps, compasses and bandages, my expedition income came to an abrupt end and the problem of funding again loomed large.

I began to consider the possibility of 'living off the land' to a certain extent in order to cut food costs. I had experimented with 'wild food' before and began frantically reading anything I could get hold of. Encouraged by Richard Mabey's comments: *'The most complicated and intimate relationship which most of us can have with the natural environment is to eat it ... to personally follow this relationship through, from the search to the cooking pot, is a more practical lesson than most in the economics of the natural world,'* I began to believe that the economics of the natural world were at least more optimistic than the economics of my world.

In teaching archery I had become fairly accurate with an arrow; could I bring down the occasional rabbit? I could drag a darrow-hook for fish, patrol the ebb shore for shellfish, boil seaweeds, fry silverweed and samphire; the possibilities seemed endless. The only problem would be finding time for canoeing! Despite the latest sponsorship donation – vitamin pills from Sanatogen – I had to admit to clutching at straws, but I wasn't going to give up the journey at this stage.

In mid-February I began canoe training, doing twenty-five-mile trips in the Nordkapp and, on camping weekends, cavorting around in the surf at Cruden Bay, north of Aberdeen. The North Sea in February is a cruel place and at the end of a day I'd be unable to button my shirt or zip my fly for cold numb hands, but I was happy. My reactions were improving – I could handle ten-foot surf now easily, and the kayak performed well; the repair was strong. New equipment was given a thorough testing. Stamina was good, strength still growing, but most of all those weekends took my mind off the details and financial problems of the expedition.

❖ ❖ ❖

1985 was the year in which distended Ethiopian stomachs glared from every T.V. set as the developed world at last began to feel uncomfortable at its own complacency. The disasters of drought and famine, and the dramatic pictures which they created, were the climax stages of the polarising trends of an even greater disaster, *modern international economics.* The fast-living, short-sighted production and consumption patterns of the wealthy lead to the ever-greater dependence and alienation of the impoverished and to the ecological rape of the planet. 'The rich get richer and the poor get poorer', but it had long been foreseen by many experts whose advice had gone unheeded. Among them was Dr E.F. Schumacher, an economic consultant to the United Nations and author of the influential *Small is Beautiful*.

The need for emergency famine relief was undeniable, and it became imperative to me to link my expedition to some form of Third World aid. But I was already painfully aware that disaster relief is but an inadequate dressing, applied in panic to a badly-infected wound. Schumacher had pointed out, in simple terms for us non-economists, that famine, poverty and environmental destruction will never disappear until the roots of the problems are tackled in an appropriate way. The people of the rural Third World must be given the means, the know-how and the low-cost, small-scale technologies that will enable them ultimately to work themselves out of the vicious circles of poverty and aid, disaster and relief.

Thankfully today many charities have re-orientated their aid programmes to acknowledge the importance of long-term development in the Third World, but in 1985 I knew of only one charity pioneering work in this area. Founded in 1965 by Schumacher, the Intermediate Technology Development Group (I.T.) were adapting and developing low-cost tools and methods which could be used in rural areas to cultivate, store and process food, pump and distribute water, construct better homes and to safeguard the fragile environment. By its very nature, the work of I.T. was cutting the bonds of economic dependence and setting rural communities back on their feet.

The principle is often summed up with the adage 'If you give a man a fish, you help him for a day; if you teach a man to fish you help him for a lifetime'. The trouble is that he is dependent, for replacement equipment, on your alien technology and skills. But if you can teach him to make and maintain his own fishing tackle, cheaply and efficiently, you will have helped him to become self-supporting and independent. This, ultimately, is what I.T. is about. On 28 February I travelled to the I.T. Offices in London to offer my journey as a fund-raising venture.

'Oh, no, no, NOOO! Not another maniac!' said Steve Bonnist, I.T.'s long-suffering Press Officer. A seasoned sufferer of many expeditions, Steve has Run the Himalayas, Cycled up Kilimanjaro and reached the 'Centre of the Earth' in the amazing publicity and fund-raising company of the unstoppable Crane family; he has climbed two hundred and twenty-seven Scottish mountains in one winter and won the Three Peaks Yacht Race ... all from the confines of a crowded office in Covent Garden! I hesitate to say 'comfort,' for Steve's job of media-hassling, sponsorship-coordinating and press-release-writing on behalf of an increasingly influential charity, makes high mountains and heavy seas pale into insignificance.

'You can't do this to me,' said Steve, careworn and weary from the paperwork for *Bicycles up Kilimanjaro,* but the outrageous schemes of the Cranes had already numbed his better judgement and – despite some initial cynicism – I was soon welcomed aboard the I.T. bandwagon and given the chance to make my journey work for others.

I.T., whose full name would be more suitable to a computer software firm, lacked the emotive appeal of other relief charities. Greater public awareness of the importance of their unique approach to aid and development was therefore, to my mind, their most urgent need. I returned from London convinced that the I.T. linkup was the most worthwhile contribution I could make to Third World aid, and from that point on publicity and media exposure of the aims and methods of Intermediate Technology became an integral part of my plan.

That evening I sat alone in a railway station with a ticket to Aberdeen, drinking tea and enjoying a biscuit. Without really thinking, I turned the wrapper over and scribbled a quick request to the manufacturer for a supply of biscuits. Had I guessed the results of that scruffy note and second-class stamp I'd have probably choked on the biscuit. But when the manufacturers, Fox's, answered my letter, it was not just with an offer of biscuits, but with a proposal to underwrite the whole financial deficit of the expedition.

Fox's, in the process of launching a new health-bar biscuit, wanted an adventurous profile for their product. They had also recently been involved in baking the emergency high-energy biscuits for distribution in Ethiopia by Oxfam and other aid groups, and as such they were wholly behind me in any fund-raising and publicity for I.T. And so, for the tidy sum of £700, a dowdy kayak became the highly decorated *Natural Crunch,* a showground of coloured publicity stickers and an evangelical mission for Intermediate

Technology.

Suddenly, with money available, it was time to think of what *sort* of food to take. Packed space and weight were now the main variables. Fox's had pledged five hundred Natural Crunch Bars which, along with the Jordans' supply and the Orkney Fudge donation, would see me okay for snacks. But there were main meals to consider. A high-energy, nutritious diet would be immensely important to the expedition's success, but space in the kayak was limited.

I estimated that, carrying a few canned items, some cereals, soups, crispbreads and a wide selection of dehydrated and freeze-dried meals, I could pack up to one month's supply at a time in the kayak. I ordered Raven dried products in bulk at a reduced price and made up monthly supply boxes, portioning the food and other equipment out evenly. These boxes – which also contained stove fuel, camera film, paperback books, radio and torch batteries, a change of clothes and the appropriate maps, tide-tables and extra equipment – were sent ahead to my estimated positions for the end of each month of the trip: Oban, Uig (Skye), Ullapool and Thurso.

With the supply boxes packed and consigned to their various destinations I was at last ready to launch, fully prepared, fully fit and self-sufficient for one month at a time. And as I packed the final box with the supplies for the initial stage of the journey, the simple instructions on the dehydrated ration packs seemed to underline my readiness with a peculiar relevance. Over and over again they said 'JUST ADD WATER'.

Flotsam, Jetsam and Me

'Go and tell Lord Grenville that the tide is on the turn;
It's time to haul the anchor up and leave the land astern.
We'll be gone before the dawn returns, like voices on the wind.'
(Al Stewart, 'Year of the Cat')

Smiling nervously, I squeezed into the tiny cockpit. Hours of careful packing, and I'd almost forgotten to leave room for me. Never before had I carried supplies for more than a two-week trip, and even then the load had always been shared out among the members of a group. Now I was carrying equipment for a journey which would span three seasons, and I was carrying food for a month at a time. The edible contents of the kayak had to last until I reached Oban, and my next supply box, approximately three hundred miles away by sea. The price of the self-contained travelling unit was that it all had to be carried by me.

This first attempt to pack, despite what I considered ruthless editing of the final equipment list, had been utter chaos. With front and rear decks loaded in unorthodox fashion and all the items which stubbornly resisted my attempts to jam them into the waterproof holds below decks, the final result looked more like a pack-mule or a double-decker bus than the sleek business-like craft I'd been so proud of. At 400lb it was well beyond the manhandling capabilities of the strongest individual. What if it won't float! I fretted; the only buoyancy in the kayak was the space between packed items, sealed by the water-tight bulkheads fore and aft, and there was precious little of that.

At the edge of the incoming tide on the ripple-ridden Mersehead Sands, I jammed a final four waterproofed packages – along with an old ammunition canister used to hold my camera-tightly between my legs – pulled the spray cover over the cockpit coaming and tried not to think of what would happen in the event of a capsize. Would it roll? Could I free my legs in time to get out?

In stark contrast to the sunny Glasgow press-launch, the real journey began, as it was most likely to continue, alone beneath an overcast sky. Pippa had gone, unable at the last moment to watch me paddle

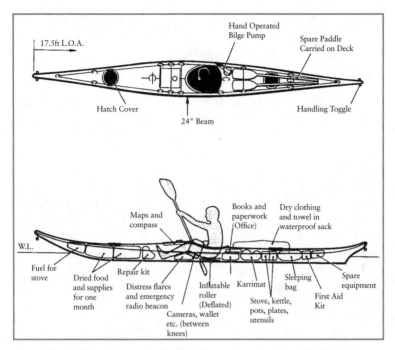

away from her. To my left the disused, unpainted lighthouse at Southerness – one of the oldest in Scotland and built in 1748 to aid sea trade with Ireland and the New World – was my sole onlooker; it felt strangely appropriate.

The Solway at low water is a vast expanse of mudflats and quicksands across which it is possible, with local knowledge, to walk or ride from England to Scotland. But the incoming tides, known as the 'White Steeds of Solway,' are rapid and fierce, reaching speeds of 8 knots, and can be heard approaching by shore dwellers twenty miles distant. The race is fast enough to overtake a galloping horse, and many were the travellers drowned in the 'Sulwath' on a mistimed return from the Cumberland fairs.

Within minutes of sealing the cockpit there was water all around me. Small waves parted across the kayak's bow and sped shoreward; but the boat sat unmoved, only sinking lower into the softening Solway sand.

Now the waves were lapping over the foredeck, and still there was no response from the heavy boat. This was worrying; if it was to carry me across 1,800 miles it would be reassuring to feel it float!

13

One of the publicity stickers, 'S.S.S.: Sub Sea Services,' winked at me wickedly.

I pushed downward with both hands but met nothing solid, leant heavily on the paddle and tried to punt forward; a creak from the fibreglass but no movement. Thinking of the Solway horsemen I began to sweat beneath thermal layers. Oozing mud had already engulfed half the kayak and held it fast while the waves grew, breaking now in my lap. I knew I had to struggle free soon or abandon the boat and wade for shore, so I gripped with my knees and started the sideways rocking motion of a bored child. At last, a movement! With a slurp, the sand and mud released their grip. Just as the kayak began to rock freely, one big wave crashed hard on my chest and the kayak bow surged upward in response. I twisted round and pushed with the paddle to free the stern as the wave passed beneath. And then we were afloat. The inertia of the loaded boat was appalling and I felt the bottom bump sand twice more, but there were four months of determined training behind each solid paddle stroke and nothing was going to hold me now. Never had the kayak felt so heavy; never had it sat so low in the water – but, my God, it floated! And what's more, I was making progress: already beyond the wave-break line and heading west; my journey had begun.

The steady rhythm of paddling, the gentle dripping of water as each blade lifted clear of the sea, the co-ordinated, economical use of the whole body to push the simple craft through the waves, the unusual qualities of light for which the Solway is famous, all helped to erase, for the moment, any worries I had about the overloaded boat.

Clocking miles westward along this coastline of smugglers' caves and low cliffs was what I had yearned for; months of planning and preparation, the stress of publicity, the sweat of intensive training and the obligations of sponsorship disappeared behind me. I was alone, the sea was mine, and ahead ... well, who could tell?

On the first full day I rose at 5.45 am to catch the weather forecast and the best of the tide. Wind dropping, skies brightening and a full Solway tide in my favour, it looked like a good day for progress. I reckoned on an average paddling speed of 4 knots (which may not seem much, but a steady 3 knots would carry you round the world in a year) and, with six hours of tide assistance, a daily distance of twenty-five to thirty miles. However, this estimate was unreasonably proposed under the crazy assumption of meeting 'average' weather and wind conditions, and seconded in the light of a good sleep and an early start. With a few days' experience of the local weather pattern I became accustomed to scaling down those estimates considerably; but it was a pattern 'local' not so much to Galloway as to ME and was to remain with me for most of the four-month trip.

There was much to learn about managing this world of tides to best advantage. You can't efficiently paddle against a strong tidal stream, so that these great longshore movements largely dictated the times and rates of travel. Times of high and low water also played a major part in the cosmic equation, and often I learnt the hard way. Hauled out on a rough shore for lunch, I beached the kayak between dog-sized boulders and went on foot to explore a cave. Half an hour later the rapidly ebbing tide had left the boat stranded ten metres from the water's edge. It took me over an hour to haul and drag it – and not without damage – across the large boulders which were steadily being uncovered by the retreating tide.

Afternoon progress too was halted. This time by the red flag of a tank and artillery testing range which, for two hours at a time, renders Mullock Bay an unpleasant place to be in a small boat. Rather than defy the flag, I hauled ashore and wandered up to the look-out tower, hoping for a cup of tea. The 'look-out' jerked to attention as I entered, but soon dozed off again once he realised that I was not a superior officer. Regular shell blasts shook the tower on its wooden stilts, but the sun streamed in through the open window and very soon I too was nodding off. By the 4 pm cease-fire, the last thing I felt like was taking to the water again and paddling the remaining ten miles to Kirkcudbright, but I had to get beyond the firing range while the flags were down.

The best of the day's weather had now been replaced by a strengthening wind, all along the rough coastline the sea had developed an irregular angry-looking 'chop'. I splashed my face with water, slipped into the kayak, and launched with a push from the rocks. Immediately, I was sprayed with the shredded spume of waves which broke on the deck. Riled, I stepped up the pace, putting an extra push behind every stroke and leaning aggressively into the headwind, but my drowsy afternoon had left me short of energy and I was tiring fast. By the time I reached Gypsy Point the sea was dangerous and difficult with a Force-7 wind opposing a 3-knot tide and the MOD, concerned about deteriorating conditions, sent the Range Safety Launch out from Ross Bay to check on my progress.

I watched the powerful launch heave its bulk towards me through the churning sea and wished I could free my hands to photograph it – but they were fully occupied wielding the paddle to steady the random bucking of the kayak, whose previous inertia meant little to that breaking sea. All I could manage was a wave of reassurance and 'Thanks' before rounding Gypsy Point and gaining the more sheltered conditions of Kirkcudbright Bay. It was 8pm, and the four-hour strain of 'Gypsy' had left me positively knackered. Cold and tired, by the time I'd crossed the Bay all I wanted was to pitch tent, eat and sleep. But with dehydrated rations, before I could eat I had to find water. I thought I had hit the jackpot by camping near a small public toilet block, but found it securely locked. High in the wall a small window was open, so I shinned up a drainpipe and squeezed my tired limbs through the tiny space, dropping head-first to the floor below. I washed the salt from my face and filled my water container in luxury from the chrome tap, but it was a further half-hour before I could summon the strength to climb back out! 'Just' add water, indeed!

Once I had rustled up a meal, changed into dry clothes and pitched the tent, I was more than ready just to flake out and sleep until morning brought a new tide and the need to face the sea again. But according to the regime of expedition flexi-time this was 'administrator's hour'; forward plans had to be made, maps studied, tidal movements calculated and the daily log written before the events of the day drifted off on the ebbing tide of consciousness.

Relaxed and dry, this was also the time for reflection, problem-solving, and assessing the chances of the expedition. I had underestimated the almost miraculous ability of salt water to penetrate supposedly watertight packing and, despite wrapping it in bags, bin liners and cases, much of my gear had become sodden in the rough passage off Gypsy Point. 'Must be more careful!' reads my log after I discovered that my vital *West Coast Pilot* book had got damp. I relayed a message of my position and tomorrow's plan by radio, via a passing fishing boat, to Ramsay Coastguard on the

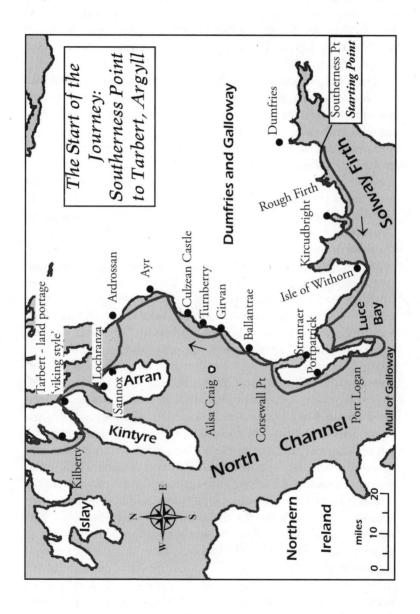

The Start of the Journey: Southerness Point to Tarbert, Argyll

Isle of Man. I carried a Marconi CoastStar hand-held radio in a waterproof case, but the case had developed a crack and the radio too would have to be carefully stowed in poly-bags within the hatches of the kayak. This wasn't an ideal solution, since it would take up valuable space and be unreachable from the cockpit.

'Have I done too much today?' was the next log entry. I had covered only perhaps twenty miles in a long day, but had pushed myself hard in heavy seas for four of those hours in a wind stronger than I'd ever paddled in before.

I made a mental note to take it easier tomorrow, but the seeds of doubt, once sown, sprout quickly.

Could I continue with long, hard days followed by lonely nights for a four-month period, without home and comfort, without Pip? Solo canoeing was as yet new and strange to me. There was no one to discuss the fear, the exhaustion, with, no one to share the planning decisions, no one to relax and forget with and no one else to blame when it went wrong. Apart from football, I had never met a physical challenge that I hadn't, with effort, been able to transcend, but this was another story, a genuine unknown. Among other things it would become a journey into ME, and I wasn't at all sure I wanted to go there! For the first time the scale of what I had undertaken began to dawn on me – almost two thousand miles of dangerous sea and a real possibility of drowning – but how could I back out now? With publicity, sponsorship and the charity involvement, to abandon the trip would require a damn good excuse. For a brief moment I considered smashing the canoe irreparably or injuring myself, and wished I hadn't started at all: I felt helpless, trapped and entirely to blame. This spirit of mutiny was to surface occasionally throughout the trip as a dissenting faction within a basically contented, often euphoric expedition soul. But already I had the germ of the ability to cope with it for on the same page of the log is a reminder that I must 'try to see this attitude as a part of tiredness, weather and a reaction to previous months of tension and stress'. After all I had only been at sea for two days! Nevertheless, I felt very alone.

Waiting for the tide to turn, I hitched a lift into Kirkcudbright where, flicking idly through the paper, I was stunned by the main picture on page 3. Not what you'd expect, perhaps, from the reputable local weekly, but the picture was in fact of Yours Truly! The publicity machine was working its way ahead of me. Time to move on, I thought, as I jogged back to the bay ready for a good day's paddling. A Force 6 wind was forecast and it looked like being another day of limited mileage. But I was less preoccupied with the weather than with the story of a sea-mystery still claiming hot columns in the local press and creating hot-gossip in the pubs, for I was about to enter the 'Manx Triangle'. Only two months earlier the Kirkcudbright boat *Mhairi L*, fishing for scallops in calm conditions and in familiar waters near the Isle of Man, had sunk with the loss of five lives. It was a tragedy which had stunned the community, for no ordinary explanation seemed to account adequately for the boat's disappearance; lack of any radio communication or distress flares suggested that she went down very suddenly and without warning – a strange occurrence under fair conditions.

The talk in the pubs, where the boat and its men were known, was that she must have been pulled under by something very large moving very fast, and in Whitehall there were allegations that the American nuclear-powered submarine – the U.S.S. Nathanial Green – was responsible. It had been seen returning to its Holyloch base under cover of darkness, damaged (missing one propeller), and it was alleged that its crew had been immediately sent back to U.S.A.

The Ministry of Defence, however, stated that there were no submarines operating on that day and that the Irish Sea was not used for submarine manoeuvres as it was too shallow.

The official explanation was that the *Mhairi L* must have snagged and been pulled under by an undersea telephone cable serving the Isle of Man. Scallop boats drag an iron dredge along the sea bed to unearth scallops which are then caught in a trailing net, and a video film taken by naval divers showed that that the telephone cable was indeed looped over this dredge.

However, local unrest and continued speculation seemed justified, for the official explanation was far from watertight. British Telecom at first denied that there were any cables in that area, although they later changed their story. Local people who saw the naval video claim that the cable seemed far too tightly tangled in the nets of the boat, and the Navy can hardly be counted a disinterested party in the inquiry. Furthermore, it is hard to understand how local men, trawling in a known area, could snag on a chart-indicated cable and, even then, how the cable could pull the boat under so suddenly and without warning.

But perhaps the most sinister aspect of all was that the wreck of the *Mhairi L* occurred eighteen miles south-east of the Isle of Man, in a part of the Irish sea (between Antrim, Cumbria and Galloway) known as the 'Manx Triangle', due to the increasing number of boats mysteriously disappearing in these waters.

The 'Secret Submarine' stories – tales of boats being dragged sideways or backwards through the sea at great speed – are fast becoming part of modern fishing folklore. Until recent years almost every fisherman had 'heard of a man, whose brother's boat...', but the stories are getting more frequent and closer to home. In 1982, a French trawler disappeared without trace; the 42-foot *South Stack* from Holyhead went missing in the Irish sea in calm conditions and was never seen again – the coastguard report stated: 'It can only be assumed that the *South Stack* caught her gear in an obstruction and overturned' – and an incident involving an Irish trawler was blamed on a submarine; in 1983 another French trawler was lost with ten men; in 1984 another Irish trawler was mysteriously dragged backwards for three miles, and in 1986 a third French trawler had a similar experience.

Last year the MOD's claim that the Irish sea (including the 'Manx Triangle') was too shallow for submarines was conclusively proven to be nonsense and subterfuge. Mrs Helen Maxwell, mother of one of the *Mhairi L* crew, obtained admiralty charts dating back to 1980 which confirm that the area has all along been used for submarine manoeuvres, and on Wednesday 18th February, 1987, the 57-foot Irish trawler *Summer Morn* was snagged fourteen miles north-west of the Isle of Man and dragged astern for ten miles at 3 knots, the speed of a cruising sub. Eventually the crew were able to cut the nets free, losing thousands of pounds of gear in the process, and a black torpedo-shaped object floated to the surface. It had American markings, and the Pentagon had no choice but to admit responsibility for the incident.

It is now known that the Irish Sea is heavily used by both U.S. and British submarines based at Holyloch and Faslane, and that top secret 'hide-and-seek' games are played out, every day, under the sea off Scotland's west coast. In fact, there are currently more nuclear reactors at sea in submarines than on land in power stations, and many of these subs also carry nuclear weaponry. Russian subs are known to lie at the mouth of the Clyde and also around Cape Wrath, and a Russian service vessel, monitoring ship movements, is permanently stationed off Northern Ireland. But why the dangerous cover-ups in the Irish Sea? To Mrs Maxwell's allegations, a Ministry of Defence spokesman in London responded: 'For security reasons we do not comment on submarine exercises'. But the number of incidents in recent years, proven or not, suggest that British, Irish and French fishermen working around Arran, the Sound of Jura, the Minches and especially the Irish Sea, even aside from the normal hazards of the job, are in constant danger of losing their boats, their expensive fishing gear and ultimately their lives. While fishermen remain ignorant of the sinister manoeuvres deep below the surface on which they sail, they will always be vulnerable to the hazards of silent-running subs, and while those 'security reasons' remain all important, it seems that men's lives will continue to be lost.

❖ ❖ ❖

Between two small islands, I met sudden breaking seas and the full force of the wind. Breaking waves are the greatest threat to the canoeist, promising to tip the boat at any moment and therefore requiring full concentration. Still tired from the previous day, I quickly became quite exhausted by the demands of that sea and was glad to reach the safe haven of Brighouse Bay. Out of the open sea, I could lower my guard, slump against the rear deck packages and, in the bright sun of a wind-scoured sky, appreciate the beauty of the bay. Beyond the bay-mouth, the surge and swell of the sea made the horizon giddily uneven and I decided to 'call it a day' – but it was a pitifully short one.

Immediately ashore a couple of figures had been watching my approach through an ancient pair of naval binoculars. 'The Commander', quite assured of his own stout and rosy importance, welcomed me 'on behalf of Dumfries and Galloway', drumming up pomp and circumstance with a ten-minute history of the Kirkcudbright sea cadets, while his companion, 'Brother Ronald', a Franciscan monk from the nearby monastery at Barcaple, waddled pleasantly towards us along the beach. Brother Ronald's eyebrows, perched at an almost vertical angle, reached fully 90 degrees during his frequent and thorough blinking sessions and did nothing to discourage me from thinking of him as the Mole from *The Wind in the Willows.*

Their sympathies stirred by the morning's newspaper article, and tutting and cooing like eider ducks at my overdramatic description of the wild beyond, this unlikely pair volunteered to save me some effort by carrying the boat above the tide-line. Brushing my objections aside, they did their honest best, but the Commander soon became breathless and complained of an old war-wound in his arm, and Brother Ronald, all of five feet tall, began to grow blue in the face. When I finally intervened to take it over the last stretch myself, unabashed and immensely pleased with their efforts they shook hands with each other, and with me, and wandered back up the beach.

That afternoon I also met Katy and Sandy Sproat, who have the 'Brig House' of the bay, and readily accepted their offer of the use of a caravan for the night. But the hospitality didn't stop at that, and before I left Brighouse next morning, I had been treated to two enormous meals and an encyclopaedic list of possible hospitality-stops covering the entire Scottish coast! Such spontaneous kindness, from people I'd never met before, was to become a regular feature of the journey, but like everything else, was, as yet, quite new to me.

Feeling well fuelled and rested after a comfortable night in the caravan, I launched with renewed enthusiasm. The Isle of Man coastguard had a wind forecast of Force 2-3 with good visibility and sea conditions 'slight'. So I struck out across the wide mouth of Wigtown Bay for the village known as 'Isle of Whithorn'. Crossing the ten miles of open water was a refreshing change; two hours of fast paddling sent the horizons into retreat and, for the first time, visibility was good enough to allow a properly 'orientated' feeling with views across the Solway to the hills of Cumbria, the Lake District and the Isle of Man. It was a good chance to practice compass bearings and scare the submarines with a few cowboy songs:

> *'Then one day ... a tall man came riding from ... the barren lands, that lie... to the north ... of New Mexico.'*

It was one of my greatest regrets that I never learned the words of more songs. Tortured by half-remembered snippets, whose full versions never quite reached the tip of my tongue, I often repeated the same refrain over and over just for the sake of singing something.

> '*He was over ... heard to say, He was looking ... for Billy Gray, A wan ... ted man and ... a dangerous outlaw.*'

At school a combination of embarrassment at my inability to produce the required notes, and boredom with the weekly TV programme that was relied upon to provide us with melodic skills, meant that my repertoire was sadly neglected.

Thoroughly turned off by 'moo-moo-moo's' and poppokat-tapettles's', I pleaded simple tone deafness for years. But alone at sea where tone makes no difference, singing punctuates the breath and does wonders for the paddle-rhythm, and there was no holding back.

> '*No not her ... chosen one! He was a ... hired gun, Wanted Kan ... sas City by the law*'.

Country and Western songs were the only ones whose words came to me with any regularity and rhyme, so, after a couple of rounds of 'Me and Bobby McGee' I arrived at Isle of Whithorn in high spirits, feeling just like the lonesome drifter in an imaginary cowboy film I had christened 'Blazing Paddles'.

I coasted into the tiny harbour on an outgoing tide which beached me coolly at the foot of a ladder, horse-tied the canoe and climbed to the town.

The mid-afternoon sun blazed hot across the deserted main street as I slung my lifejacket, saddle-like, across one shoulder, rolled a cigarette, and narrowed my eyes to the glare. Hearing the echoing canyon whistles of the spaghetti westerns in my mind, I buckled my camera belt around my hips and positively 'moseyed' into town in search of some action. It was obvious that all the other gunslingers had dived for cover, but as I passed the saloon the double-doors burst open and a buxom barmaid nodded me over. Inside I was surrounded, given a drink and distracted by bar girls for over an hour as the proprietress sent an urgent telegraph. Somebody, it seemed, was expecting me. Then the sheriff arrived, flashed his lapel badge and led me, without handcuffs, outside the saloon

... and out of the film set. In the full light I saw that his badge read Galloway Gazette, and above the door, 'Whithorn General Stores'. He thanked the shop assistants for looking after me and we wandered together back to the reality of the kayak journey. Around the muddy harbour at low tide we took some pictures and recorded a short interview. Never once did he call me to draw.

But reality was short-lived in the 'Isle of Whithorn'. I got chatting with a local fisherman, Andrew Scott. On board his boat, temporarily grounded in the harbour mud, we studied his charts of the area and I felt my first twinges of apprehension concerning the Mull of Galloway headland. But the charted rows of swirls and squiggles which denote watery chaos were soon forgotten as we shared our third beer. Relaxed in the mellowing sun, I looked over the boat-side to where the beer supply hung in a plastic bag. The tide was out; the 'fridge' was off, and there, suspended by a rope cradle and painting numbers happily on the boat was 'Walter the Shrink'. Walter had lectured in psychiatry for ten years in London, and had the slight continental accent to prove it, but had opted out on the basis that people were just not ready for what he had to teach. So Walter, working his way to Shetland with his wife and baby, was writing a book on mental health, not for this generation, nor perhaps the next, but aimed at a readership for 'after the holocaust'.

Wow, I thought, and wanted to dig further into this strange mind, but it was early evening and I was anxious to push on around the coast as soon as the harbour tide had risen enough to float the kayak. To reach Westward meant first rounding Burrow Head, the southern tip of the Whithorn peninsula which juts far out into the tides of the Solway. Andrew warned me about the possibilities of rough seas off the point, and Walter threw me a fish. Shaking his head diagnostically he said it was a pity I hadn't read his book! I'd done only ten miles that day and so I decided to have a go, but it was a decision I was soon to regret.

Riding a strong tide, I made good progress for the first hour, travelling steadily onward with the motion of a fairground-carousel horse. But the west wind rose to Force 5 and crumpled the tide like a bulldog's nose giving rise to the worst possible of local sea conditions. As I rose, tottering on each wave crest, I could see ahead to Burrow Head, where the sea became dark and ominous; the troughs were deep chasms and the waves themselves steep-sided mounds which welled up and clapped together with a terrible power. With continuous cliffs along a hostile rocky coastline there was no possible landfall before Monreith, fully eight miles distant, so for two miles I fought hard in the large and breaking swell. Then suddenly, but very definitely, I lost my nerve. Feeling vulnerable and frightened I just knew that any moment soon I'd make a mistake, lean the wrong way and lose the battle. I did then something I'd never done before or since; I turned around and fled back the way I'd come.

Turning in a large breaking sea is one of the hardest of all manoeuvres; to retain stability it is necessary to adapt your balance and bracing points continuously through 180 degrees leaning into gusts of wind first from one direction, then another – and then adjusting to paddle in a sea which is surging from the opposite direction. This turning, and the passage back, took complete concentration and intense physical effort. I sent the paddle thrashing in all directions finding support on crashing white wave crests and firing the boat forward with all the strength I could channel through my wrists. My hands were white and bloodless with strain, and trembled with nervous energy when at last I reached the Whithorn shore where I hauled the boat mercilessly over sharp-edged rocks to camp.

Burrow Head had beaten me and, although I was out of immediate danger, I knew I would have to challenge it again soon. And if Burrow Head was that bad how could I hope to survive the Mull of Galloway? Unanswered, barely acknowledged, this question was to ferment in my subconscious as I gradually drew towards the Mull. Thoroughly dispirited, shaken and tired I was glad of a quick camp and the womb-like security of a warm, padded sleeping-bag; perhaps Walter was right after all!

Over the next three days, high winds and Solway tides conspired to keep average daily mileages below fifteen and gradually to wear me down. But I continued to force progress westwards in short bursts. I took Burrow Head when it wasn't looking, survived 'backlooping' on a steep-sided swell in a Force 8 gale, and crossed Luce Bay MOD range during a Sunday cease-fire. And while I camped snugly among the dunes at Sandhead, on the edge of the Luce Bay 'Danger Area' the Scottish papers – getting progress and weather reports from the Coastguard – wrote of 'Canoeist blown ashore' and 'Sailing into severe weather'.

And so the first week of the trip passed, costing me huge effort, but gaining proportionately little progress in terms of miles. On the other hand I was learning many things. I had improved my packing system and could change into dry clothes, pitch tent and have a brew on all within a half hour of beaching, and began to realise that alone, working on my own timetable, I was probably more efficient. There was no need to take account of the comfort and wellbeing of others, far less their moods and foibles; there was no need to compromise. I was learning to cope with the pressures of being alone and in danger and although my understanding of personal 'ups and downs' was far from complete, it was growing. As I lost count of gale warnings my attitude to the weather changed. No longer was it an invincible 'deity' whose decisions were final. Rather it became a respected competitor in the same game as me; sometimes I'd sneak along inside or ahead of a predicted gale; other times it caught me out, but all the time I continued to learn. Most importantly perhaps, I had become 'tide regulated'.

As the moon's gravitation pulls the sea directly beneath it to a 'high tide', the water on the opposite side of the earth simultaneously rises to high tide due to centrifugal effects. The points midway between these highs experience a corresponding 'low tide', so that as it rotates through a full day each part of the earth experiences two high tides and two low tides. But during the twenty-four hours of that rotation the moon itself has moved part of the way on its monthly orbit round the earth, so that it takes an extra fifty-two minutes for the earth to return to its relative start point. The tides therefore occur exactly that much later each day.

In mid-ocean the tides are simply a rhythmic rise and fall, but on the continental shelf they become a movement of water towards or away from the land. The rising water produces the tide's flood, and the fall is its ebb, and between these are brief periods of slack water. Huge volumes of water pour around Scotland's coast each day to fill and empty (and fill and empty) the North Sea Basin; these create tidal streams. Complicated by islands, sea-lochs, narrows and shallows, not to mention weather, the tidal streams of Scotland are among the most dangerous in the world.

But the streams don't always flow at the same speeds, nor do the tides rise and fall to the same levels, for the sun's gravitational pull is also important. Thus at fortnightly intervals, at first and third quarters of the moon, when the pulls of the sun and moon conflict, there results a neap tide whose range is small and whose streams run weakly around the coast. But at full and new moons (also at fortnightly intervals) the moon and sun are in a straight line with the earth, like a tug-of-war; their pulls co-operate to create an especially powerful tide, a spring tide, which rises higher and falls lower and rushes madly around the coast giving rise to the most dangerous coastal hazards.

The name 'spring' has nothing to do with the season of that name, but comes from an old Norse myth which tells of a fount or spring beneath the oceans which tops up the water level twice a month.

The phases of the moon were long thought by rural communities to be inextricably linked not only to the tides, but to all the most important processes of life such as menstruation, fertility, childbirth, crop sowing and even haircuts! Marriages consummated on a waxing moon would be strong and fertile, but a child or a calf born on a waning moon and a fading tide had little hope. People planted crops and looked for signs of recovery in the sick during a rising tide and a waxing moon. And most of all the full moon was the time for mysticism and superstition, or werewolves and seal-people. Even the seductive and dangerous Scottish mermaids, personifying the beauty and treachery of the sea, have been associated with the moon – ruler of tides – which is represented by the mirrors they hold in their hands.

Time of high water anywhere on the coast, any day of the year can be calculated in relation to high water at Dover by means of tide-tables, and the tidal stream directions and speeds are correspondingly calculated – according to neaps or springs – using the Tidal Stream Atlases. And although I continued to use these I had become as conscious of the tides and the phases of the moon as any werewolf or 'lunatic', varying my times for sleeping, waking, packing, launching and eating accordingly. For not only did journeys have to be planned in coincidence with favourable (rather than antagonistic) tides, but dangerous areas had to be tackled at slack water or neap tides wherever possible, and 'wind over tide' (tides running against a prevailing strong wind) had to be treated with caution. Furthermore, launching and landing as near to high water as possible saved the 'portaging' energy and the boat damage of a lengthy drag, for I still could not lift the boat alone. The southern peninsula of the Rhinns of Galloway extends eighteen miles from the head of Luce Bay to the exposed lighthouse point where a great 'toe' of land reaches seaward, doing its utmost to trip and cause havoc among the tidal waters that thunder by below its cliffs. The Mull of Galloway is a Parliament of tides, a confused meeting of Scottish, Irish and English waters which refuse to live together in peace, jostling for sovereignty in an area restricted and made shallow by the land mass of the Mull. The streams rush around in both directions at up to 5 knots, and the resulting 'overfalls' – water tumbling over itself to produce steep waves very close together – and dangerous races extend far out to sea.

From my camp at East Tarbert I watched the races form white caps on the east side of the Mull during the ebb and die back at slack water. A successful brush with some mild turbulence off Cailliness point had whetted my appetite for action and I was anxious to get to grips with the Mull itself. But as evening fell I remembered how fishermen in the Auchenmalg Inn had casually taken bets on whether it was possible to round the Mull of Galloway in a canoe; the odds in my favour, I recalled, had been low. A group of divers, drying off at Tarbert, gave me beer, hot soup and yet more advice against attempting the Mull in a small boat. They pointed out that I could easily portage across between East and West Tarbert using a narrow isthmus used until the last century, by fisherman, to avoid the fierce currents of the Mull.

The Tarbert isthmus not only separates the great 'Mull' headland from the rest of the Rhinns peninsula; it also marked the final stronghold of the last Pictish clan when, sixteen centuries ago, Niall, Ardrigh of Ireland, made a plundering invasion on the Pictish lands of Galloway. Before his fierce Scots warriors, the Picts were mercilessly slaughtered until, far down on the Mull of Galloway, only one clan remained. As it happened this clan were the hereditary holders of the Pictish secret of how to make strong ale from the heather, mentioned in verse by R.L. Stevenson:

> *From the bonny bells of heather*
> *They brewed a drink lang-syne,*
> *Was sweeter far than honey,*

28

Was stronger far than wine.
They brewed it and they drank it
And lay in a blessed swound
For days and days together
In their dwellings underground.

The proud secret was theirs alone, and was defended to the death; in the final bloody massacre, men, women and children all died as this clan too was annihilated. By chance, however, the Scots warriors found two survivors, a Pictish father and son, huddled beneath a rock on the heather moor, and offered them freedom in return for the secret of Heather Ale.

The father thought in silence then, with lowered eyes, replied 'For the young, Honour is valued higher than Life; but to the elderly, Life itself is more precious. Slay my son to save him the dishonour of his father's betrayal'. But when the young Pict had been bound and thrown to his death from the cliffs, the father raised his eyes, faced the Scots and cried, 'The courage and honour of the young one might perhaps have wavered under sword and flame; but now the secret shall never be revealed!' At that he burst from his captors and flung himself from the cliff to the rocks below, where lay the crumpled body of his own son. And with the last of the Picts died for ever the secret of Heather Ale.

A toothless shepherd had earlier helped me to collect water where a piped spring flowed into a cattle trough. Short, hairy and big-booted, he looked himself like 'the last of the Picts'. For the Picts, they say, were strong, red-haired people with feet so large that in a rainstorm they lay on their backs with their feet in the air like umbrellas. As if summoned by the image, the little shepherd appeared again at my tent bearing beer and eggs.

'Theeth are from my thithter' he said, as though shy of his own kindness, but he was not a man of conversation and disappeared surprisingly quickly back across the fields, leaving me to cook corned beef and beans on a driftwood fire. I drank the beer and studied Tidal Stream Atlases until the sun went down over the bay at West Tarbert. It was a beautiful and tranquil spot, the peaceful ideal tainted only by the knowledge that tomorrow held the first 'make or break' obstacle of the journey. It would be a simple choice: either 'go for it' or portage out, but somehow I couldn't achieve the 'distance' necessary to enjoy the evening, for in that decision lay many meanings for the rest of the journey. Because the obstacles would become bigger, more severe, as I went on, a 'refusal at the first jump' would be psychologically disastrous. But I remembered Burrow Head, the fear and the tension, and fresh worry hung like a choke-chain around my neck. I craved someone to talk it over with and, with the Mull lighthouse flashing a constant reminder of tomorrow's task, I drifted undecided into a troubled sleep. I woke early on a warm still morning to a breakfast of scones and milk left silently in the dewy grass by my Pictish shepherd. Almost immediately the adrenaline was flowing, for something inside me had resolved itself in the night and switched to a definite 'ON'; Come Hell or High Water I was going 'round the Mull'.

High water Dover at 11:00 ... add one hour for British Summer Time ... thirty-five minutes for local tidal constant ... so High Water at Mull of Galloway would be 12.35 ... N-going stream begins just after High Water at Dover ...'

I planned to set off as the tide came up the shingle beach, catching the last quarter of the flood tide to reach the Mull. On the slack period between the tides I could sneak past the great headland unnoticed, and make my getaway up the Rhinns coast on the strength of the north-going ebb.

It was a long-drawn morning waiting for the coincidence of conditions, and as the last hour ran out, checking and re-checking my tidework, I felt as though I was about to enter an exam hall or some other occasion of great reckoning.

At 12.20 I was on the water, and hit the Mull by 12.30. Even at slack tide the surface of the sea was deeply etched with spirals and vortices, both the spoor and the promise of misguided currents, but in a mere Force 3 northerly, wind conditions, so far, were good.

I paddled continuously, always expecting a thrashing mill-race to manifest itself around the next buttress, but the sun shone bright on the water and, craning my neck up the sheer cliff face I watched pairs of Persil-white kittiwakes on their rock-ledges and could have plucked pink heads from the cushions of thrift, so close was I to the cliff-foot in almost ideal conditions. My nervous grip on the paddle relaxed; it had been so easy, and before I knew it the lighthouse lay some distance behind me.

I passed West Tarbert Bay and was just congratulating myself on a successful, if rather anticlimactic, assault on the notorious Mull when I felt the kayak lurch forward, as though suddenly possessed, in the mild turbulence off Port Kemin rocks. The ebb had started. The corrugated surface of the water poured itself northward and the cliff coast began to speed by in the opposite direction. There would be trouble ahead, heavy races and 'overfalls' off the Crammag and Laggantalluch headlands, increasing in violence as the tide strengthened. I braced myself and paddled on, my heart revving on a rich mixture of two-stroke adrenalin and fudge.

The Crammag race appeared from a distance as a stretch of rippling water which bracketed the headland, tailing off northward, unavoidable. The kayak bow struck the first wave and forced itself under. At the push of the paddle it roared into action, its shape and marvellous elastic buoyancy bringing it surging over the crest and down again, handling well and as stable as a bicycle cruising at speed. Soon we were among hydraulic mounds so close together that surfing down the face of one brought us immediately within the shadow of the next. A hard paddle-stroke, a thrust of the hips and up, over and down again at amazing speed. But the kayak was master of its element, responding instantly to the grip of the knees and a flick of the hips to retain tentative balance. Hanging for a stretched moment on one paddle-blade I cut out of the mainstream turbulence to find a slower-moving eddy close into the rocks… Pheew! one down.

Only feet away to my left the main race thundered past at upwards of 6 knots, like a herd of white-maned buffalo or some kind of waterworld rollercoaster. Its sheer violence amazed me, for there can be no more impressive vantage point than directly alongside, at water level, in a flimsy boat.

By the time I reached Laggantulluch the ebb was at full strength. I hit the race with a sickening thud and immediately the vast machine graunched into gear, leaving my stomach behind. For several long minutes I thought of nothing but raw survival as the boat pitched forward and back, nosediving deep into foaming, heaving masses, bucking free and launching skyward again. As the race veered seaward and weakened I rose on a wave to see the shore, now a distant speeding blur. Then turning my bow from the main current I broke free to catch my breath and steady my heart in the eddy stream, and headed shoreward for a well-earned lunch.

31

I was ecstatic, I had conquered the Mull of Galloway, survived the ebb tide races and, for the first time, I enjoyed a surge of confidence concerning the trials that inevitably lay ahead.

That night I landed at the beautiful Ardwell Bay, made camp on a grassy knoll backed by primrose-clumped cliffs and found myself the sole inhabitant of a magnificent white-sand, west-facing beach.

I peeled my salt-crusted wetsuit to the waist and waded into the sea to cool the sunburn on arms and face, for the glare of sun off water can be as severe as snowburn, or worse.

Lying later in the mouth of the tent I cooked a meal and looked out over Atlantic colours in a herringbone sky. The Mull of Galloway conquered, the Solway seemed to have lost its hold on me. The weather had taken a turn for the better and already I was looking forward to tomorrow's paddle – Portpatrick and beyond – stepping up the daily mileage and catching up on schedule. This was the stuff that defeated loneliness and lethargy and, although I was aware that it would hit me again, I was determined to keep it at bay as long as possible.

The distant rim of land to the west was the coast of Antrim and although unable to make radio contact with the Isle of Man, perfect reception from Belfast Coastguard saved me a long trek to a telephone and the new accent was a significant mark of progress. A gentle purring surf told of peace on the Irish Sea.

Strong spring tides still ruled the tidetable; that week they ran 'my way', northwards, in the afternoons, which gave me the mornings in which to eat, read, and break camp leisurely. The weather held fair, I felt my arms burn and my face tighten like a drum in the sun; and with the sun I felt stronger, fitter and at peace with the world. Having eaten through almost half the food, my load trimmed just enough to make me believe that my packing system had become super-efficient!

After Ardwell Bay, Portpatrick was too touristy for my liking and a brief meeting with a 'butch' New Zealand girl, displaying a fine pair of large tattooed arms, sent me hastily back to sea to resume the journey northwards.

At Port Maggie cove, below the Kilantringan Lighthouse, I passed close to the wreck of the coastal container ship *Craigantlet* where she had lain in two pieces since running aground in 1982, after leaving Belfast for Liverpool.

The wrecking of the *Craigantlet* on the Galloway shores gave rise to the local equivalent of the 'Whisky Galore' situation on the Southern Outer Hebrides, for the *Craigantlet's* cargo was a mixed load of clothing, gas masks, industrial spares, toys and vegetables. At least one of its broken containers held the uniforms, equipment and military band instruments of a garrison regiment which was leaving Northern Ireland at the time. Bagpipes and drums started to drift ashore and reports of silk shirts and new woollen jerseys cast up by the sea were vigorously denied by the best dressed and most musical group of coastal farmers and fishermen in the country!

But the *Craigantlet* story had its more sinister side, reflecting dangerous trends in container and tanker shipping around our seas. The crew were safely evacuated by helicopter, but there was immediate concern about the cargo which was thought to contain dangerous chemicals, held in large tanks, most of which were washed ashore within a few days. Scientists discovered that some tanks recorded as 'empty' contained chemicals; others contained chemicals which did not correspond to cargo records, and some of the chemicals could become highly toxic either on mixing with each other or with sea water.

After five days of storm the damaged containers began to leak. The lighthouse keepers were evacuated to Stranraer due to dangerous fumes and it was forty-two days before conditions were deemed safe to return.

Modern container ships are often loaded according to a method known as 'groupage' which can result in the mixing of various consignments and incompatible materials in a formula for disaster. Container transport is also the most anonymous form of sea transport ever used; the freight manifest need not show the contents of each container, which often remains unknown even to the ship's Master. Add to this the tendency to stack containers haphazardly in unwieldy, three or four-tiered loads, and the problem of encountering fast-moving masses of wind-driven water in the major oceans, and it's little wonder that lethal semi-submerged floating containers, the size of family cars or larger, are now a major hazard in all the world's main shipping lanes.

Almost all international trade is carried on in ships, with over two billion tonnes of oil being shipped each year (more than all other sea cargoes put together). This oil trade involves the constant flux of thousands of tankers, some of them up to 400,000 tonnes and carrying 250,000 tonnes of oil, the largest moving objects made by man, seeking ever faster, ever cheaper ways to transport their cargoes from port to port. In Scotland, the Irish Sea, the Pentland Firth and the Firth of Forth, have long been recognised as major tanker shipping lanes, and recent controversy has surrounded the proposed use of the Minch (between the mainland and the Western Isles) as a tanker route.

The Minch area has not been surveyed to full modern standards, only by echo-sounder, and approximately half of British coastal waters have never been surveyed at all. In addition, of the 16,000 wrecks, and parts of wrecks, known to be in British coastal waters we know the exact positions of only 12,500, and the depths of about 14,000. So how safe are our seas and coasts from this constant flux of tankers and container ships?

When the tanker *Torrey Canyon* ran aground on the Seven Stone Rocks in 1967, spilling 100,000 tons of crude oil on England's shores, its Captain had no Admiralty pilot book of the area and had been at sea for a year without shore leave.

How did the *Craigantlet* manage to hit Galloway when bound on the short journey from Belfast to Liverpool? We shall never know. The suspicion that her skipper was drunk was never proven, for as a German-registered container ship, flying a flag of convenience, no enquiry was held by British authorities and the circumstances of her grounding remain officially unknown.

Are these massive ships safer for having computerised radar and other navigational aids? It didn't do the Craigantlet much good. Lloyd's, the ship brokers, have coined the phrase 'Radar Assisted Collisions', and there was even a case of a tanker master whose favourite navigational aid was a labrador dog trained to bark when on a collision course with another vessel!

We cannot be too careful about the safety standards we must demand from the sea-transport industry. Apart from porpoises, whales, sharks, fish and human interests, twenty-three species of seabird regularly breed in Britain, some with populations of hundreds of thousands; over two thirds of the world population of gannets and grey seals breed around Britain's coasts, and in winter British estuaries and other wetlands are home to over half the total number of wading birds in all Europe. A major oil or chemical spill off the British coast could be an international disaster from which the fragile coastal eco-systems and in-shore waters might never recover.

❖ ❖ ❖

In a kayak, closer to water level than any other form of boat, you are continuously splashed from head to waist, and particularly on face and arms, by spume and salt spray. With a long day's sun and breeze, and sometimes even by body heat alone, the brine is constantly evaporating, leaving behind its crystal residue of salt. At the day's end the salt layer can be quite deep, thickly rimming the eyelids, collecting around the hairline and eyebrows and creating marbled patterns on cheeks and forearms.

Not so many years ago the same process was the basis of the important Scottish industry of salt-making. Before frozen or dehydrated food, or a reliable transport network, a good local source of salt was vital to the safe preservation of meat and fish, and place names such as Saltcoats, Grangepans, Prestonpans, and Salt Pans Bay, mostly on the Forth and Clyde coasts, derive from the time when salt was being extracted from sea water on a considerable commercial scale. Wood or peat and later coal-fired pans were constructed from iron sheets near the upper tidal limits on coastal carse-lands. But in some areas such as the long, flat tidal reaches of the Solway, the heat of the sun alone formed salt crusts around tidal pools, and even today at Guerande in Brittany, salt is produced in this way.

Over the four months in my mobile, biscuit-powered salt-production unit I must have collected pounds of the stuff, and often when I came ashore I was able to cook a meal and season it with good, healthy sea-salt simply by leaning over the pot and rubbing an eyebrow. But no matter how hard I rubbed, the other eyebrow could not be coaxed to produce pepper!

I beached at Kilantringan just as an early evening surf was building up, swam the caked salt of the day from my body, changed into my 'evening suit' of thermal trousers and a Fox's T-shirt and wandered down the sand beach in search of firewood. It seemed that the careless tragedy of the *Craigantlet* was still bearing fruit, for between buzzing piles of seaweed the foreshore yielded an amazing collection of junk. Three years later it was still a beachcomber's paradise with toy cars, a whole range of industrial fan belts, car and tractor tyres, perished gas masks and torn silk shirts, as well as the fish crates and boxes always in abundance on an exposed west-facing beach.

Despite my love of that unstructured, wandering existence, method and routine in simple tasks like packing, pitching tent and fire-building were very important to me and I grew inordinately proud of some of my 'systems'. I had developed for instance a simple and effective system of fire-building, making full use of local 'facilities'. To the handles of fish boxes I would tie a long piece of rope (or loop fan belts) and sling it over my shoulder. I could then drag up to three crates, wagon-train fashion along the tide-line, filling them with graded pieces of desiccated driftwood. Into the crate with the smallest kindling I would also throw any dry grasses, bracken, ropes and papers as failsafes to start the fire with. Then I would drag the whole convoy back across the sand to my chosen fireplace, light the fire and burn those crates which I didn't require as a camp seat or table.

Some of the pieces of seasoned driftwood were strikingly beautiful – sun-bleached and sand-scored, wind-worn and sea-carved to form flowing sculptured shapes, tinder-dry and salty. I thought often about the old philosophical problems of aesthetics; could 'natural art' be more than just a quaint metaphor? What place did human intention and expression have in art? Could there be 'art' without an 'artist'? I had worked long and hard over these problems in my Edinburgh room, struggling for a synthesis and understanding. Now, on the beach, there was a new angle on the matter for driftwood art, freed from academic constraints, burns beautifully!

Fire was my companion, my pal. I cared for it and it responded. There was no need for words between us but as I lay on an elbow smoking a tight liquorice cigarette, the fire glowed orange and warm over one side of my face and I passed it tit-bits of broken wood.

'*Oban Fish*'

'No *unauthorised use.*'

Lying in front of that blazing crackling driftwood furnace, my kettle red-hot and glowing, I relaxed and unwound as the sky darkened and the beam of the lighthouse at Black Head began to sweep the night. As the roar of the fire died down I could hear the surf on the beach, fifty yards away rolling pebbles landward up the beach and retreating with a long backwash 'hissss' like hot oil in a pan. It was the high spring tide of a full moon.

Wet, Wet, Wet!

'Small boats are only good for two things ... a wet arse and a good appetite'.

(Kipper House Tales, Forsyth Hamilton)

Mid-May. The canoe lay prostrate on the shingle at Lady Bay, Loch Ryan, dragged just above the tide-line, no higher than necessary. Belly up to shield its cockpit from rain, it looked like a dying sea creature, its chest cavity rising and falling in the last throes of a hopeless exhaustion. The remains of the huge decals, 'FOX'S: NATURAL CRUNCH: AROUND SCOTLAND SOLO: NATURAL CRUNCH: FOX'S', which had decorated both sides of the hull, and which were now the victims of vicious shredding by rock and wave, were peeling off like leprous skin.

Already the gradual wear and tear process had become serious as innumerable forced landings on rough-shingled beaches and rocky shores had taken their inevitable toll. Boats native to these waters, crafted for launching and landing along rough shores, are not only built of heavy clinkered timber but have an iron-plated keel-strip for extra protection. Not so the gentle kayak, which relies on being lifted across potentially damaging terrain. John MacGregor, probably Britain's first sailor/canoeist, and a dauntingly upright Victorian gentleman, writing in 1868, exaggerates the point:

'[The canoeist] can wade and haul his craft over shallows, or drag it on dry ground, through fields and hedges, over dykes, barriers and walls; can carry it by hand up ladders and stairs and can transport his canoe over high mountains and broad plains in a cart drawn by a man, a horse or a cow!'

Never mind 'high mountains and broad plains', shifting my fully-laden boat between camp and shore was already by far the biggest problem of solo kayak travelling!

The portage trolley which I stowed in the cockpit worked admirably with an unloaded boat on smooth, firm ground, but its performance 'in the field' was depressing. Firstly, the weight of the laden kayak was more than the trolley could handle; it made the base press down onto the wheels and the washers pop off under the strain. Secondly, even with the load reduced, and despite having broad plastic wheels, the trolley refused to cope with soft or bumpy terrain. This in effect ruled out most beaches as landing places (as smooth sand tends to be soft, and firm sand tends to be serrated!) and rocky shorelines were, of course, unmanageable. So I tended to search for a sandy beach or grassy shore where I could camp near the water's edge and just drag the boat above the high tide mark as gently as possible. However, in south-west Scotland, soft landings are few and far between, and using the 'drag' method usually left behind a slug-like trail of scraped fibreglass and 'gellcoate'. Already several minor repairs were crying out for attention and, over the last few days, the boat had been leaking at an alarming rate from a small gash in the forward hull.

I lay in the tent that morning, as I had done the previous evening, watching in awe as the big Sealink and Townsend Thoresen ferries steamed up the loch, to and from Northern Ireland at speeds of around twenty knots. I doubted if even a bright yellow canoe would be visible from the bridge of such a boat, and was certain that the radar would overlook me. Besides, they could do very little to avoid me even if they did detect me on screen. So, crossing Loch Ryan around lunchtime, I was taking no chances.

Wearing a bright orange 'Hi-Glo' skullcap, holding my whistle between my teeth, my top pockets bristling with white collision flares – if they hit me they'd know about it – I paddled like crazy across the two miles at the mouth of the Loch.

By the time I reached Ballantrae on the Clyde coast a Force 5 was whipping out of the north and the sea was a mass of white horses as far as the horizon. But ashore, out of the wind, sheltered by a solitary, rusting winch, I munched biscuits and read and dozed in the afternoon sun. At 6pm the tide turned and I was back on the water and bound for Bennane Head, a tricky passage with a considerable race off it during the strongest part of the tidal streams at springs.

The wind was still strong, gusting Force 5 and 6 and an alleged one-knot tide looked like a ragged river in spate, flowing in the wrong direction! The passage was not technically difficult, but in these conditions distance was hard-won in short exhausting bursts, I gradually perfected various techniques of wind-avoidance. A strong wind will raise wave crests and a sizeable swell proportionate to the distance of sea across which it blows unhindered (its 'fetch') and the time for which it blows. But by sinking low in the cockpit these very waves can be used to give a degree of shelter from the wind, at least while in the troughs. In the same way, by keeping the paddle blades low there is less chance of having them blown from your hands.

I began to notice that according to different conditions I was using the paddle in a variety of different ways, as a puntstick on a shallow shore or an outrigger on an unstable sea, as a bat, as a racquet, sometimes like a medieval quarterstaff as I spun from the waist to brace against a wave or to counteract a strong wind-blast. At other times, however, the nearest analogy was Mickey Mouse with his conductor's baton in *The Sorcerer's Apprentice.*

Constant paddling in a fierce wind, with clapotis (reflected waves) and random, confused seas becomes, at length, almost a martial art, a non-aggressive form of essential full awareness and self-defence. Akin to Kendo, the central balance and posture have to be mastered and maintained at all times, while always remaining responsive to 'attacks' from all four main directions. The strength and speed demanded in particular strokes have to be measured and squared with the endurance demanded over a three-hour stretch, while also allowing the flexibility and reserves necessary to counteract the unpredictable wave or wind gust.

On the last reserves of a day's strength and stamina, against an increasingly stormy wind, and drenched with sea-spray, I limped onto Dipple beach.

It was a relief to be off the water and into the eroticism of dry clothes, but camping among plastic and metal debris, on an industrial shore that looked like a demolition site, outside an alginates factory in a grey and persistent drizzle was not my idea of paradise, and I pined for the beautiful bays of Ardwell and Kilangtringan.

Thunderstorms were forecast and, backed by a Force 5 wind, rain lashed the tent all night, rattling the walls mercilessly while the factory farted and belched stinking fumes. I slept little, convinced that at any moment the tent must rip, and by morning my sleeping bag was damp from leaking tent seams.

The wind continued to whistle down the Firth of Clyde at upwards of 30mph and with it the rain lashed the campsite. Undeterred, the alginates churned in the gloom as I settled for falling yet another day behind an already redundant schedule. My log reads:

'Now two weeks since Southerness point and the weather remains unsettled. Conditions at sea atrocious. Well behind schedule and powerless to do anything about it. Suffering great difficulty over the stretch of the journey I'd assumed would be easy. Food and fuel will last another two weeks, but there's a long way to go before Oban!'

I huddled in my damp bag, ate the last of my tinned food, overdosed on Fox's and studied maps, previewing the coast as far as Turnberry.

Next morning I rose early to phone for a forecast. The coastguards were helpful as usual, but unable to arrange anything more convenient than a Force 6. But the wind had at least veered out of the north sector, and tides in the area are gentle, even at springs, so I caught the 10.30am outgoing tide and headed north.

Culzean Castle, perched on a sheer cliff face and standing on its wooded hill, aloof from the surrounding farmland, was almost impressionistic in the roving clouds. Arran's 'Holy Island' showed itself briefly on the north-west horizon. Ailsa Craig, although much nearer, remained invisible. Heavy rain reduced the swell a little, and washed the salt residue from my hair, the rain drops making pockmarks, and the bulging clouds studying their reflected bellies, in the grey sea surface. For a full day I battled along a coast made almost featureless by the colours and weight of the reflected sky, as I fought a Force 6 wind gusting frequently to full gale force. It was the kind of wind that sends even wet hair streaming, flattens your ears back and fills your nostrils with so much air that you have to turn your head sideways in order to breathe comfortably! Several times it almost caught me unawares by changing direction suddenly, but by the end of the day I had stolen fifteen miles. The punishment was a long haul over the tidal flats to camp below the castle ruins at Doonfoot on the outskirts of Ayr.

❖ ❖ ❖

'Can I take your cagoule, sir?' Too tired to collect water and make a meal, I had wandered into town in search of sustenance; high tea at the rather posh Balgarth Hotel was the result. I ordered and waited, but shelter from the wind, a soft seat, the sudden warmth, Richard Clayderman music on the P.A. and the soft buzz of background conversation soon sent me into a deep sleep. I woke to hear two girls at another table giggling, but was compensated by a huge mixed grill, toast, scones and endless tea.

Back at the tent, replete and relaxed, I did my tidework and studied the map as far as Ardrossan. Things looked better on a full stomach. Radio Westsound gave a reasonable forecast for 'sea areas south of the Cumbraes' and even played 'I do like to be beside the seaside'! I folded my map into its waterproof case and, as the rain tapped a light accompaniment to the chatter of the radio, settled down in my damp bag to read Scott's *Talisman*. High tide came at 10pm and so would be back high at 10.30am. I would leave then to avoid any portage problems.

❖ ❖ ❖

One of the beauties of the journey was that I never knew just where I'd find myself next; or who I would be meeting. As I was drinking tea, for instance, in the toilet attendant's bothy by the seafront at Ayr, Maggie, from the women's toilets across the green, perched cross-legged on her seat, announced that a scorching summer would begin next Wednesday. Seeing my sceptical look she assured me that the prediction was based on sound scientific fact – the arrival of a comet which was to clear the air and bring fair weather in its wake. Ever hopeful, I had to agree that it sounded quite plausible until she confessed that she'd read it all in the Sun newspaper. I knew the Sun was fairly reliable as far as tabloid heavenly bodies were concerned, but comets? Perhaps not.

❖ ❖ ❖

It was out there somewhere. Of course it was. Islands don't just disappear; but when I set off from Ardrossan not a smudge or smear of Arran was visible. Not even Ardrossan harbour materialized to reassure me as I headed seaward into the thickest and most solipsistic of pea-soupers. But in the country of the blind the one-eyed man is king, and I had at least a compass-bearing which, transferred from the O.S. map, should take me south-west into

Brodick Harbour, fifteen miles across the Firth of Clyde.

Paddling into such poor visibility, on a glass-calm sea whose surface bore my ripples as its only blemishes, was an eerie feeling. I felt much as a zipper must when it parts the fabric down the back of a silk ball-dress, as the spreading wake of my progress peeled 'off the shoulder' in both directions. It was a milky, low-cloud world in which sense experiences had neither source nor reason; the industrial sounds – sometimes loud, sometimes muffled – at my back must have been Ardrossan, but a sudden dog's bark seemed to come from the sea immediately to my left, and somewhere far away there was the echo of some damn fool singing cowboy songs.

The cocoon of mist, with its sounds that came from nowhere, tended to promote the impression that I was the only thing afloat on the whole of the Clyde, an illusion suddenly shattered when a fishing boat purred across my path and was swallowed up again just as quickly; the Firth of Clyde is a busy shipping area and I must stay alert. But with no objects by which to judge distance travelled, nor any sort of relative movement by which to gauge speed – no horizon, nothing but the water itself – the journey had the quality of a dream in which one struggles desperately and yet gets nowhere. Glancing backward I could see my trail, where the opening zip revealed glassy flesh, dimpled by regular paddle-prints, stretching eastwards beyond visible limit, the fog swallowing each dip even before its ripples had time to disperse.

After two hours' paddling – by which time I should have been well over half way across – a vague and distant shadow appeared. Although it was far below where I'd imagined the juncture of land and sea should exist, it had to be Arran. Another half-hour passed and I could identify Brodick Bay by the distinctive shape of the Arran Hills; Goat Fell and the A'Chir ridge to the north and lower land to the south.

Secure at last in a confirmation of my compass bearing, I perversely decided to change course on a dogleg farther north to Sannox Bay. An hour later the approach to Sannox from seaward was like a Norwegian Fjord. As the mountains came into focus, layer upon horizontal layer, the scene took on a hazy, screen-printed postcard image and there's no doubt that the mist itself was an integral part of its beauty.

Half a mile out from Sannox the ubiquitous Grey Seal Reception

Committee gave me an inquisitive welcome of the 'anything to declare' sort, but very soon I left them behind in the mist. I reached Sannox, a journey of sixteen miles, only three hours after leaving Ardrossan and my longest open crossing so far. The strain on my lower back and the constant weight on the bum had been uncomfortable towards the end, but my arms and shoulders – the power system – had held out well at a steady 5 knots and after a brief land stop I wanted to press on again. Lochranza, only eight miles farther round the Arran coast via the Cock of Arran, became the obvious target.

After almost a full day's lack of visual stimulation the coastal paddle seemed full of beauty and interest anew, for I was unusually receptive to the slightest details. The Arran hills, tumbling steeply to the rocks of a marked 'raised beach' platform and then on, less steeply, into the sea, made an impressive ever-changing scene for a close inshore paddle.

From half a mile off I could hear the whistling whines of common seals, and approached as closely as I could without disturbing them, although the way they slither and plop from their rocky perches into the water always amused me. Once in the water they became the nosey ones and I was subjected to fairly detailed research as they approached in little groups of leopard-patterned heads. To be sociable I tried to copy their exhaling snuffling sounds, but soon came to the conclusion that re-sealable nostrils are necessary for an accurate imitation.

Through perspex-clear water starfish were everywhere visible among the multi-coloured fronds of the sea floor. There were brown laminaria oarweeds, thongweeds and bladdered seawracks, all couched together with smaller, finer red carragheens in a crystal stillness between tides; it could have been part of a vast paperweight on a Brobdingnagian businessman's desk. A defiant gull stood its ground, one-legged on a rock as I passed. In its mouth it held a small pink starfish. Colourless Aurelia moonjellies each wearing four purple reproductive rings, the 'hippies of the sea', floated in the ultimate meditation, pulsing a harmless dance to the rhythm of the sea.

I reached Lochranza thoroughly tired, sinews protesting with every laboured stroke, but knew I had rolled two days' scheduled paddling into one. Despite the massive lapse of schedule, that was satisfying.

Deep into the bay I paddled past the ruined castle on its promontory and dragged the boat out onto the grass at the road verge where the tide, thankfully, was reaching its height.

Lochranza was ablaze! Smoke filled the air and drifted toward the purple hills; it was as though the Vikings had landed ahead of me. On the common grazing ground the villagers were burning old furniture and other junk. I placed four potatoes to bake in a pile of ashes beneath the upholstery of an old sofa, arranged corned beef, beans and cheese on embers at the fire's edge and watched my coffee pot percolate from the phone box only yards away.

Cuckoos sang, swans cruised in the bay and the tide came to within a yard of the road verge. My camp on the common ground looked beyond it all, past the castle, to the distant Kintyre coast across Kilbrannan Sound, the first stage of tomorrow's journey and, despite the comings and goings of youth hostellers from the pub, I slept as though I'd paddled twenty-five miles.

❖ ❖ ❖

The history of Kintyre ('Cean Tir' or Head of Land) is one of the most fascinating of any part of the British Isles. From Tarbert to the Mull of Kintyre it has the distinction of being the longest peninsula in Britain and yet at one time, without either geographical change or fluctuation in sea level, it qualified as one of the Western Isles!

'When is an island not an island?' is the strange question of definition that faced a Scottish king in the eleventh century (1093) as he concluded the first known treaty with a Norwegian King defining their respective territories in a manner which formally acknowledged the Norse domination of the Scottish Isles. King Magnus of Norway was the latest in a succession of Viking invaders who had adventured, plundered and settled their people among the Gaels of the islands and, according to the treaty, he was to be given sovereignty of all the islands off Scotland's western seaboard.

For the purposes of the treaty it was stipulated that an island was any piece of land which could be circumnavigated in a boat with its rudder fixed. King Magnus – known as 'Magnus Bareleg' for he had adopted the wearing of the kilt – satisfied that the wording of the treaty was adequate, immediately set sail from Tarbert to test the definition on his favourite piece of the Scottish *mainland*, the

Kintyre peninsula. When he returned to the narrow neck of land at Tarbert, having all but circled Kintyre, he summoned his men to haul the boat out and across the isthmus to the sea on the far side, while he remained stationed at the rudder, no doubt waving two-fingered gestures of goodwill at the Scottish King and laying claim, at least temporarily, to a substantial chunk of the mainland.

'Neat,' I thought. It was a bit late to claim sovereignty of Kintyre for Fox's Biscuits, but I nevertheless pictured myself as the potential plundering invader as I left Arran, still asleep beneath its morning mist, and crossed Kilbrannan Sound to the North Kintyre coast. Kintyre itself faded in the distance down Kilbrannan to the south, but there were changing views back down into the Firth of Clyde beyond Bute and the Cumbraes.

The Cowal peninsula of Argyll was a patchwork of greens and browns on a low, rugged coastline across lower Loch Fyne and the clear health of the water was spoiled only for want of something other than a dull sky to reflect upon its surface.

❖ ❖ ❖

A target shore never seems farther away than when the strident call of the bladder reveals nature's diabolical sense of humour and timing. The constant pressure of the moulded seat on the kidneys, the massaging effect on the bladder of tensing and relaxing stomach muscles in paddling, the rolling motion of the sea itself and the sight and sound of water in every direction combine to ensure that those last few yards to shore are the most agonising torture. And the occasional cold splash with an icy wave doesn't help either! After minutes which seem like bowel-wrenching hours the shore is at last gained and the boat securely beached, but relief is not yet mine for, as the wetsuit has no conveniently placed fly-zip, a complicated system of clothing must first be combination-unlocked in the right order. First the life jacket is removed (buckles, zip and ties) and the windcheater cagoule peeled off to expose the shoulder strap of the spraydeck while I stomp about the rocks in agony. This discarded, the one-piece wetsuit itself can be loosened and stripped from the upper body (and try doing that with cold, numb fingers!) Only then can I at last take stock of wind speed and direction and relieve myself in incomparable ecstasy.

There were, of course, times when I was caught short while

still several miles from land and far removed from anything that would double as a 'little-boy's room'. Several months of paddling, prolonged sitting and constant damp all combined to weaken the sphincter muscles that control the bladder and it was almost impossible to be stoical for long. Often a sudden cold drenching from a passing wave made the final result inevitable and I just had to 'let rip' inside the wetsuit, inside the canoe! It was a fact of this strange new life but I have to admit that once I'd accepted that there was no alternative, especially on a cold day, I actually enjoyed the delicious warm feeling which spread down one or both legs, and it was no problem to have a quick remedial hygienic dip at the end of the day.

I had drunk perhaps one coffee too many at breakfast and was cutting things a little fine by the time I reached the Kintyre shore, nonetheless landfall was made without mishap. This journey had become a crash-course in the pleasures of simple needs fulfilled – of dry warmth when cold and wet, of basic food when exhausted and hungry, of calm water after a rough passage, and most of all of an unchecked steaming cascade after a stretch of masterful bladder control.

❖ ❖ ❖

At the busy fishing town of East Tarbert, Loch Fyne nestled amid hummocky wooded hills and a brief patch of late afternoon sunshine transformed the scene as I wove my way between fishing boats and yachts of all sizes. Tired and hungry after four and a half hours' paddling and only a brief stop I was beginning to doubt whether I'd be able to complete the portage across land to the West Loch, and raping and pillaging were definitely out of the question! But after a wander around the town and an excellent refuelling on Loch Fyne kippers and trimmings I felt like a Viking again and was ready to resume the day's journey; I'd seen enough of the local 'buzz' and tourists to know that I was keen to move on out.

The kayak, still fully loaded, lay on the mud of low tide, beached near the harbour wall but fifteen feet below street level. The only means of lifting it out was via a steep flight of stone steps. Optimistically I began unloading some of the heaviest gear and all that was strapped to the decks. Then I took a deep breath, placed both hands on the cockpit rim, straightened my back and heaved.

It moved! And so, six steps at a time, I man-hauled it out of the harbour and onto the street, blue faced, sweating and amazed. Perhaps John MacGregor ate Loch Fyne kippers too!

There was still the small matter of the one mile portage to take care of; but wait a moment, Magnus Bareleg didn't have to do his own manhauling. Then the solution appeared – on the corner stood a crowd of small boys. I began to pack stove, tent and other gear back into the kayak hatches but, conscious of the growing interest of the boys, I kept the ammo-box and safety flares out, for their curiosity was my trump card. On my hand-held radio I talked loudly to a fishing boat for a weather forecast and then reeled in my catch, seven sturdy ten-year-olds!

They explored the kayak hatches, read the stickers, sat in the cockpit, played with the bilge pump and spare paddles and at last, when I had attached the kayak to its trolley-wheels, they were almost begging to be allowed to tow it along the road. With mock reluctance, and feeling more like the Pied Piper of Hamlyn than a Viking war-lord, I sat one of them in the cockpit and walked ahead of them the full mile across to West Loch Tarbert.

At the head of the West Loch they showed me the best slipway to launch from. As we sat to share a few biscuits I felt superbly at ease with the world for, well fed and rested, the evening was free and conditions still good for progress.

Paddling down the calm loch, the reflections of a windless evening all around me, was the most tranquil and beautiful experience.

Oystercatchers, cuckoos and the birds of water and woodland were the only producers of sound to rival the rhythmic dip and splash of my paddle. Dip, pull, trickle … twist-dip, pull, trickle … twist-dip, pull, trickle… The smells of the evening were the after-damp breaths of distinct alders, birches and rowans where the north shore was lined with a respectable remnant of native Caledonian deciduous woodland, dense and damp, moss-padded, fungi-studded and decorated with lichens.

Pushing on down the south shore looking for a campsite I was slowed to a halt by a thick tapioca-like mass, my first encounter with a hatching ground of the common 'moon-jelly'. The water was thick with them, my paddles scooping up mounds of tiny medusae of about 10p size as I pushed my way through their pulsating masses. The male jellies shed sperm into the sea, which swim into the females' mouths and fertilise internally. The young swim out of the mouths and settle on the sea-floor as tiny polyps I until the following spring when the polyps grow buds of new jelly-fish stacked upside down like piles of saucers. Eventually each detaches to start its free swimming life. I was experiencing the gelatinous baby-boom results of last year's fertility and the name 'jelly-fish' seemed particularly appropriate for them when seen in this orgy of undulating opacity; I pushed all the harder to get out before they set solid!

Beyond the jelly and another short paddle the wind was getting up and darkness closing in so I chose a sheltered campsite on the edge of the woods which fringed a small bay, stalked a tiny stream for fresh water and settled in for the night. The morning on Arran seemed at least a week ago; I had travelled for twelve hours and covered almost thirty miles ... this was more like it. I slept deeply for eleven hours and woke to heavy driving rain and the bronchial background wheeze of wind funnelling down the West Loch. The forecast was for Force 7 westerly and I knew it would be another day off the water.

I felt helpless and frustrated, compelled to lose another day just when I was beginning to achieve some good distance, for I was still far behind schedule and my inability to accept the 'give and take' routine of the sea and the weather still branded me as a greenhorn traveller. By now I had to think twice about using fuel in the stove and it looked as though food could run low before I reached Oban, still many miles to the north.

I had woken up damp. The sleeping bag was damp, as was the tent and mat, and all my other gear was sodden. It felt as though moisture was soaking into my skin, sponge-like by day and seeping out again by night, but the real reason, I knew, was that everything – including my skin – was by now heavily impregnated with salt. Salt, being hydroscopic, tends to attract and absorb any airborne moisture and, in the humid maritime climate of the west coast, my equipment and I had about as much chance of drying out as the sea itself!

The sleeping bag now housed the emigrants from a colony of mildew which had outgrown one of the tent walls. I had developed a painful form of nappy rash on my back and groin and my feet – permanently soggy, white and wrinkled – were no longer like feet at all, 'more like anaemic prunes,' as I wrote in my log. It was a mild form of trenchfoot. Chaffs and scrapes on knuckles swelled like miniature volcanoes, and painful gouges under each arm, steadily abraded through paddling in a wet salty tee shirt, were not healing but getting deeper. In addition knees, elbows and lower back began to exhibit the audible creaks and tangible stiffenings of chronic rheumatism.

It was a day for map and tidework, and for making a big fire to save fuel, dry some clothes and shake me out of the doldrums. There was no beach of combustible debris this time, but a short search revealed the ubiquitous fish boxes and the woodland behind my camp yielded enough rotten and dead wood to fill three boxes, along with the horse-shoe shaped 'tinder fungus' which grows on birch trunks. All was soaked by overnight rain, but I was getting the hang of this game and soon had the kind of roaring furnace I called a 'one-match-wonder'. The rocks behind the tent formed a natural hearth and chimney which channelled the heat outward to where I had hung my wet clothes on ropes to dry.

I tried to close my mind to the ants and other insects driven frantic and often roasted alive as their stable worlds were committed to the flames; but a good fire, like a hot shower, is a great restorer of lapsed spirits and soon I was sitting on my cagoule drinking hot chocolate on the edge of the dank velvety, Druidic woodland, almost waiting for a tangled moss-grown Merlin to step from behind a lichened oak.

Earlier I had seen some giant blue wolf-mussel and oyster shells on the shore and knew there must be some substantial beds nearby. There was also a wealth of seaweed and I waited eagerly as the tide turned 'from soup to salad' in a matter of hours. Then I gathered a few handfuls of large mussels and roasted them on the embers of the fire, and fried up a pot of shredded dulse. The mussels, though fresh, meaty and delicious had so many little pearls that I was unable to chew them properly for fear of breaking a tooth, and the seaweed, though palatable, was tough and bitter and would have benefited from a more thorough boiling. But it was a satisfying meal nonetheless, and took the pressure off my supplies temporarily.

The loch flowed, wind-driven, towards the sea showing a 2-knot current where, according to the pilot guide, there ought to be none. The clouds too had scudded all day from east to west but only now, towards evening, was there any vague promise of a little sunshine. On the rocks at the littoral edge, rippling sea-sounds filled my ears, the breeze blew over me and the first of an evening sun gilded a highway across the steady flow of the West Loch.

The Islay ferry rumbled past and in its wake the sounds of the wind and lapping water, and the small voices of the waders kept back the silence. Fragile and delicate against the persistent roar of the elements, the piping cries of oystercatcher and sandpiper expressed an unequivocal belonging and lent a sense of peace and permanence to what, for me, was still largely a scene of conflict, transience and seductively veiled danger. To the extent that I saw its beauty and wholeness in terms of their usefulness or hindrance to me, I remained an observer's distance apart, a stranger.

Out on the loch white horses testified to the strength and vehemence of the prevailing wind in a less sheltered spot, but by tomorrow I hoped to be able to begin moving northwards under the shelter of the coast, eventually through the notorious Dorus Mor tidal stream and onward to Oban. The challenges of this section were far from over yet.

At ten next morning I was packed up and away, but after only an hour I was forced off the water again, having done little more than cross the narrow loch. Even that modest effort had been a harrowing experience as a full gale, concentrated by the tunnelling effect of the lochsides, howled down from the north east. There was no point in going on.

I pitched an emergency camp in the bay at Ardpatrick; the only sheltered spot being among the rhododendrons on spongy marsh where my tent poles sank slowly in the already rain-saturated ground.

Again I had been frustrated in the hope of making progress but this time I was more philosophical about it, using the day to re-seal the seams of the tent, to patch a leak in my spray deck and to place a bivvy bag beneath the tent ground-sheet to reduce seepage and the overpowering smell of the stagnant marsh. Scallop shells beneath the tent poles gave them a broader base and stopped them sinking. Perhaps there was hope for me yet.

Despite horrendous winds the sun shone all day and I walked off in search of a phone. The single track road which leads to Kilberry was infested with adders, Scotland's only poisonous snake, basking off recent dampness on the sun-warmed tarmac, and as I had no thick socks to protect my ankles from a bite, I carried a handful of small stones to disperse them from my path. Rolling the pebbles, marble like, at the sleepy snakes and watching them wriggle into the grass verges became a great game and we meant each other no harm.

Enjoying a day of walking in fresh winds and sunshine I became quite weather tolerant. I thought of the thousands of people being held up in their precious daily routines by the London Underground strike, and remembered a Scottish Tourist Board advert I'd seen on one of the London trains: 'The only high flyers are eagles and ospreys. The air smells of pine trees and heather, not traffic fumes. And money is the farthest thing from your mind.' Yes, I was in that mythical-sounding land, and all I had to contend with were the wind and the sea, dwindling food and fuel supplies and a soggy campsite – I could handle that for a little longer!

That evening as I cooked a meal and played my whistle by a fish-box fire, three real white horses grazed among the rough grasses and flag irises of the West Loch shores as, almost simultaneously, the wave crests died away. A strange coincidence, but it meant that tomorrow I could move.

I left the West Loch in the grey calm of early morning but within a half hour was forced to put ashore again; the boat was shipping water rapidly. On the small Eilean Traigh at Ardpatrick Point examination revealed a six-inch gash in the hull, not the result of a collision but almost certainly caused by rough landings and launchings. Emergency first-aid was needed so I set up the petrol stove to dry the fibreglass around the gash and plastered it over, clinker-style, with fabric tape. I also heated the tape and moulded it into the wound as far as possible but, unable to dry the boat properly, I knew that this cursory treatment was unlikely to hold out even until Oban.

However, temporarily watertight again, I pushed on up the Knapdale coast feeling good just to be moving, and determined to make some distance. Loch Stornoway, Port Mor and Kilberry Bay, with their fine sands drifted past on my right. Lochs Caolisport and Sween were still obscured by the same mist which hid Jura and its peaks from sight, but Gigha to the south was a template screen-printed upon the morning sky.

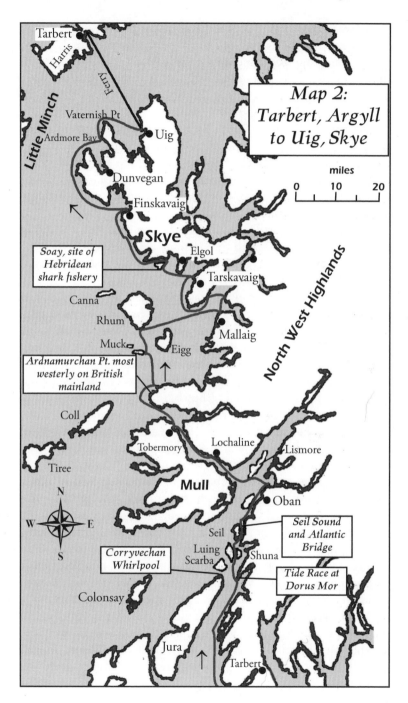

Tarbert

Harris

Little Minch

Vaternish Pt
Ardmore Bay
Uig

Ferry

Map 2:
Tarbert, Argyll
to Uig, Skye

miles

0   10   20

Dunvegan

Finskavaig

Skye

Elgol

Soay, site of
Hebridean
shark fishery

Tarskavaig

Canna

Rhum

Mallaig

Muck

Eigg

North West Highlands

Ardnamurchan Pt. most
westerly on British
mainland

Coll

Tobermory

Lochaline

Lismore

Tiree

Mull

N

W ✦ E

S

Oban

Seil

Seil Sound
and Atlantic
Bridge

Luing
Scarba

Shuna

Corryvechan
Whirlpool

Tide Race at
Dorus Mor

Colonsay

Jura

Tarbert

Between the Point of Knap, the northern promontory of Loch Caolisport, and the 'island' of Danna at the mouth of Loch Sween lie the strange and beautiful MacCormaig Isles. Like stepping stones they stem an area of strong tidal streams causing powerful eddies and a tide race of four knots which isolates them from the casual visitor.

As I approached Corr Eilean, second largest of the group, many potential trouble spots were visible on the water surface. The beginnings of a rip stretched between Corr and Eilean Mor, but in the absence of wind to oppose the tidal flow and aggravate conditions I was able to land on the island and climb its cliffs for a scenic lunch of bread and mackerel.

Then it was on past Danna and up the sound of Jura to Carsaig Bay, a pleasant paddle with the sunshine coming weakly through, and great views of herons fishing in the narrow passages between the islands on the approach to the bay.

On paddling into Carsaig I was hailed by the crew of one of two large yachts anchored in the sheltered bay. They produced a large mug of tea and some biscuits and handed these down to me as I rose on a wave. My attempts to consume these while bobbing up and down, without a spare hand to man the paddle, trying at the same time to describe bird life in the narrows, provided great amusement for the whole crew. But I didn't spill a drop and was soon heading for the sands of the shore to find a campsite.

After a meal of dehydrated chicken and a can of lager, courtesy of the yacht, I unwrapped my 'office' and began to study the strategy for tomorrow's assault on the Dorus Mor or 'Great Door'. As the main funnel for the huge volume of tidewater which passes between south-west and north-west Scotland, the Dorus – the channel between Garbh Reisa and Craignish Point – is one of the most notable tidal features on the west coast. With a tidal set of up to 8 knots on the east to west flood it can be absolute bedlam during any sort of opposing wind, for the presence of several small islets creates a shallow and uneven passage, and in the space of three miles are found numerous eddies, races and heavy overfalls.

The Dorus Mor cannot be avoided by a boat heading north for Oban without taking a wide and impractical detour out to the far shores of Jura (and Jura presents yet other problems). Indeed in 1820 Henry Bell's Comet, the first steamship ever to go to sea, making passenger runs from the Crinan Canal, was wrecked in the Dorus tide race. Despite a speed of six knots and a large square sail rigged to supplement engine power the Comet was no match for the strength of the Dorus rip current and was driven against the rocks where she broke in two. No one was killed, but the aft portion was swept away and lost. The detailed notes I had taken concerning the hazards of the Dorus Mor throughout a full range of tide and weather conditions made it obvious that a safe passage could be achieved, but it was a passage which demanded the utmost care and respect, and would require careful planning and accurate timing.

By the time a definite plan of action had begun to form in my mind, its equal and opposite reaction had lodged in my nervous stomach and I felt ready for a pint. Over the hill at Tayvallich the inn was dominated by the plummy tones of yacht charter crews, and there, in pristine oilskins, sailing smocks, yellow wellingtons, denim caps and seaworthy briar pipes, were the two crews from Carsaig Bay. It was a hard-drinking crowd and whenever I opened my mouth to speak they had another pint down me, so that finding my way back to my camp, on a night in which all cows were black, was no easy task. Gathering bumps and scratches I tumbled down slopes and through brambles, but felt nothing until the following morning despite the fact that all night long a war of beer cans, vegetables and finally distress flares raged in a Trafalgar-type battle between the two charter yachts out in the bay.

I woke with vague memories of the offer of a cooked breakfast on board *Sileas*; and sure enough as I paddled out, tied alongside and climbed sleepily aboard, the smell of bacon, mushrooms and eggs was already rising.

With the strength of a good breakfast inside me I was on my way by 11am, hoping to reach Garbh Reisa and the Dorus Mor, six miles north, on the last eddies of the south-setting ebb tide and to hit the main problem area on the turn of the tide, thereby sneaking through the channel just ahead of the strongest part of the flood stream which began just after high water Dover, at 12.30 pm.

To be caught unawares in the main westerly stream in full flood could be disastrous for it runs, like a freight train, between Coiresa and Reisa an-t-Sruth of the Dorus Mor to the Gulf of Corryvreckan, four miles away across the Sound of Jura, where it becomes part of one of the most horrendous whirlpools in the world. According to an ancient Rutter of the British Isles, the precursor of Admiralty Pilot Guides, 'Correbreykin' is 'a depe holepoole quhairin if shippis do enter their is no refuge but death onlie'.

I knew from the previous year's trip that Corryvreckan was in fact navigable, but it certainly wasn't the kind of place to end up unintentionally!

I made good time up the Knapdale coast and in fair conditions crossed the channel to Garbh Reisa, cornerstone of the Dorus. The surface of the sea all around bore the embryonic surges and spirals of small eddies and the dying phase of the ebb-tide rips. Weird dome-shaped upsurges, up to twenty feet in diameter, welled to the surface from great depths and at one point rose directly beneath me boosting me two feet higher and causing me to sprint forward in reflex. The kayak zig-zagged in response to the tidal confusion in the area and seemed to be getting nowhere. But the south-going stream forms a west-going eddy which in turn flows north along the shore of Garbh Reisa island until the flood stream begins. So I headed for this and was borne without effort to the north end, the 'business end', of the island.

It was now 1.30pm; the tide had turned and the flood began to tear north and west. Leaving Garbh Reisa behind I took the bit between my teeth and reached out for the centre of the Dorus, where the water was already stacking itself into streams running at different levels in various conflicting directions, causing turbulence and great hydraulic piles where they came into contact.

I saw the whites of the grey eye of the Corryvreckan Gulf as the flood started to operate in the whirlpool's centre. I remember reverting to the stiff, staccato paddling rhythm I use when frightened, and making a conscious effort to calm down, but before I had time to evaluate the situation, or my chances of a safe passage, I was juddered sideways for several hundred yards, churned in an arena of white froth and then spat from the danger area towards a tranquil eddy on the Craignish coast. It was all over in minutes. A pause for lunch and a climb to the top of the Craignish peninsula allowed the relief to sink in, and I studied the development of the tide race. It was as though something heavy, but invisible, four hundred metres wide, was pressing down on the water in mid-channel. A definite hollow had formed and water from the fast streams which poured around the dip also tumbled into it from all sides.

The water within it swirled around anti-clockwise like a huge natural jacuzzi; the flood had reached full strength. I congratulated myself on my timing, gave the kayak an appreciative pat and paddled out from Craignish. Minutes later a red-sailed, thirty-foot ketch came sizzling through the Dorus, extremely quickly, extremely undignified and SIDEWAYS! Out from Garbh Reisa the wind filled her sails and she pulled slowly away from the stream which hurtled on towards Jura and Corryvreckan.

The weather remained overcast, but the wind was very slight so I had the edge for speed over two large yachts as I headed for Shuna Sound on what remained of the flood tide. The yachts tacked east and west, hoping to pick up a stray gust, but I surfed forward on a regular swell at upwards of five knots.

I made only one stop, on Shuna, to empty an alarming volume of water from the leaking kayak and continued to carry with the tide, passing Torsa on my left and entering Seil Sound with Ardmaddy Bay to my right. Just outside the bay I saw a movement in the water – a sea-otter. Moving closer I watched it rolling and corkscrewing, sucking the webbed skin between its fingers and the bib of fur on its chest after what seemed to have been a recent meal; a lovely encounter to round off a successful day. Although no longer openly hunted in Britain the otters have been badly affected in recent years by coastal and river pollution to the extent that the north and west of Scotland are their last strongholds in Britain and, even here, to see one is a rare treat.

The channel between Seil and the mainland narrows and is spanned at Clachan by the famous, definitively humpbacked, 'Atlantic Bridge', once the only bridge from the mainland 'across the Atlantic' to an island. The sea channel at this point is so narrow that it gives the impression of being a small river; short of tasting the water, only the presence of seaweeds and thrift reveal that it is in fact a salt-tide flow.

I pitched the tent on the turf by the bridge and boiled a quick meal, using the stove freely again in the confidence of being at last within a day's striking distance of Oban. For once I was in agreement with the stoical John MacGregor who, showing an uncharacteristic sign of weakness, said:

> '... *If you are tired of the water for a time, you can leave your boat at an Inn – where it will not be "eating its head off" like a horse; or you can send it home, or sell it, and take to the road yourself, or sink back again into the lazy cushions of a first-class carriage, and dream you are seeing the world.*'

However, only the first option had any attraction for me. The inn at Clachan, formerly 'Tigh an Truish' (the 'House of Trousers') has historic associations with the days after the ill-fated 1745 Jacobite Rebellion when the bagpipes were declared a weapon of war and the wearing of the kilt was outlawed; the kilted inhabitants of Seil, Luing and Easdale Islands, before crossing to the Argyll mainland, would stop at the inn to don pairs of trousers kept there for that purpose.

Inside now the fashions were different and before long I was joined once more by the dripping oil-skinned figures of my yachting buddies, now anchored at Poll Dobhrain (the Otter's Pool) on the far side of Seil Island. The heavy rain, recently started, had given them a sympathetic picture of me camped in misery and dejection somewhere down near the Dorus Mor. They had underestimated the speed of a kayak on a favourable tide and were so inspired to find me there ahead of them that after several pints were forced my way, breakfast invitations were again forthcoming.

Over a second magnificent cooked breakfast in the homely below-decks of *Sileas* we were discussing heroic hopes for the day ahead, when the radio blurted out '*Securité, Securité, Securité*', the emergency warning of the coastguard, '*Imminent Gale, Force Nine, Westerly, Hebrides*'. Well, it was the excuse they had been waiting for. The wellies were kicked off, books and crosswords unearthed, and pipes lit; 'no one's daft enough to go out in that'.

But I had neither a crossword nor a pipe, and, besides, reckoned that in the lee of Clachan and Kererra Sounds, and the mountainous shelter of Mull across the Firth of Lorne, my passage to Oban should be reasonably safe. Repairs to the kayak had become imperative, and I needed to re-stock at Oban, so as the flowing seaweed at last swung north at about 2pm, I slipped quietly into Clachan Sound and began the shallow paddle northward.

Beyond Seil the water was exposed to the west and became a little choppy, but there was still considerable shelter from the full gale which could be seen busily rearranging grey cloud masses above Mull and in the Hebridean waters beyond.

Four times in ten miles I had to stop and empty the kayak which was now gushing water from several fractures and from the major gash in the forward hull. On my legs it felt like the inside of a damaged submarine in a war movie, and as the intervals between baling sessions became shorter I began to wonder whether I really would reach Oban or sink first. John MacGregor and I had another tiff:

'*The covered canoe is far stronger than an open boat, and may be fearlessly dropped into a deep pool, a lock or a mill race, and when the breakers are high in the open sea or in river rapids, they can only wash over the deck of a canoe, while it is always dry within.*'

I could see what he was getting at, but could have wrung his smug Victorian neck as – at last within sight of Oban, and with water sloshing about inside the boat, increasing the weight and confusing the balance – I made a final sprint, dodging ferries and fishing boats to cross Oban Bay and camp beneath Dunolly Castle ruins.

Oban is the main sea port and tourist centre for the Hebrides, but I was not there for a holiday, or even a rest. Acutely conscious of losing valuable time, I would have paddled out again next morning if I could, but there was a list as long as my arm of things to do, and the sooner I started the better.

First I had to collect my supply box, unload the kayak and send used maps, film and redundant equipment by post to Edinburgh. Then I would tackle the repairs, despatch progress-postcards to friends and sponsors, arrange a local press interview, visit the coastguard station to inform them of my plans for the next section, reload the kayak with the new supplies and finally head up the Sound of Mull in an attempt to get back on schedule. Such a tall set of orders themselves threatened to consume another week!

The kindness of the Templeton's store manager was a great tonic. From the butcher next door (who 'owed him a favour') he commandeered a van to deliver the fifty-kilogram supply box to my camp, and sent me on my way with a freshly cooked chicken, stuffed with bacon, still warm and smelling delicious! Back at the tent I devoured the chicken with bread, gazed absently across the Firth of Lorne to Mull and Lismore, and relaxed with logistic problem number one solved. For a short time the world looked significantly brighter.

After lunch, however, I opened my box and, like Pandora, was immediately faced with new problems and fresh worries. Four weeks' supply of dehydrated and freeze-dried meals, one hundred Fox's and Jordans' biscuit-bars, ten Orkney Fudge, 3lb porridge, rice, noodles, lentils, fruit and nut bags, tinned fish and meat, all had to be accommodated somewhere in the kayak. There were batteries for torch and radio, six paperback books, nine O.S. maps, fresh T-shirts, camera films, toilet rolls, three litres of stove fuel and various other odds and ends which would keep me self-sufficient until the next pick-up at Uig. The north end of the Isle of Skye seemed at that moment a fantasy target indeed.

This miscellany lay strewn over the turf, protected from the wet ground by outstretched bivvy bags, and positively defied me to transfer it into the limited space in the kayak. It was a holiday-suitcase situation, but you can't jump up and down on a fibreglass kayak to flatten the load; not, at least, if you want it to carry you for another 1,500 miles. My nerve cracked and I spent the early afternoon ruthlessly selecting clothes, books, maps and equipment that could be discarded. Everything that had not 'worked its passage' in the past month, or would not foreseeably become essential, had to go. I kept only one towel, one T-shirt and one set of underclothes; I would do all my cooking in one small pot, and all my eating from one small bowl; and by discarding an egg-carrier, a water bottle, spare torch, binoculars (somehow full of sea-water!) – the list went on – I again achieved the anorexic cargo that would furnish the bare bones of a viable expedition.

Then I turned my attention to the kayak itself. It lay upside down on the grass above the shingle beach, exhausted and crippled. The last vestiges of the Fox's legend clung doggedly to the hull in jagged emphasis of the 'down and out' appearance of the boat. All that remained readable was the centrepiece, 'In Aid of Intermediate Technology', like a heroic epitaph, for in comparison to the hull itself the stickers had enjoyed a gentle passage!

By autopsy an eight-inch gash in the cutting edge of the hull stood out as the main wound, its edges failing to meet by over an inch. Since this had been caused by gradual abrasion, rather than a single knock or tear, it was obvious that the area immediately surrounding the gash would also be paper thin and ready to give at the slightest pressure. In fact the whole backbone area, from the forward edge of the bow to the trailing skeg, was severely worn and weakened. The 'gellcoate' covering was chipped and flakes of fibreglass were exposed like raw flesh all along the surface of the rockered keel. Three stress fractures also revealed themselves, one beneath the cockpit where the seat exerted extra pressure on the hull, and one under each of the bulkhead inlays. Some serious surgery lay ahead.

I spread my repair kit on the ground – fibreglass matting: resin, 'gellcoate', catalyst to harden these, sandpaper and various tools, the most sophisticated of which were a sheath knife, a fork and a toothbrush!

Ideally, I reasoned, the whole keel must be strengthened and rebuilt if the same situation was not to recur in the next week, but this would require tools I simply didn't have access to. So I was determined to do my best on a simple but thorough 'patching' job, and resigned myself to having to perform repairs regularly and frequently for the rest of the trip. Reaching Skye seemed increasingly unlikely.

To perform an efficient fibreglass repair all materials must be bone-dry. This looked like another hopeless ideal, but I set to work with my damp towel and petrol stove anyway. Just then the roving cumuli ruptured and within minutes the kayak, the repair kit and myself were wetter than ever, and I finally admitted the futility of trying to perform major fibreglass surgery, with limited tools and limited experience, in the open air in Scotland. I lay back in my tent as my little world ground gradually to a saturated halt and wondered if it was all a bad dream – or a TV cigar advert – and thought of a remark made to me by an American girl: 'The only problem with Scotland is that it doesn't have a roof!'

My only hope now was to find a fibreglass repair workshop within portage distance of the kayak. And so I wandered, disconsolately, through the rain to downtown Oban, where the streets were deserted in the aftermath of the 'Great Oban Raft Race'.

The fishmonger directed me to Currie's boatyard where, in a dark shed, amid the sick bays and nautical debris, I found Donnie Currie pouring over his accounts. He confirmed my fears that, despite the

yacht and dinghy boom, no one in Oban repaired fibreglass and
that I should take the boat to one John Hodgson in Connel, five
miles north on the shores of Loch Etive.

It was too far. I would have to do my own makeshift repairs
and reconcile myself to a leaky trip for as far as I could get before
the boat collapsed. My spirits took another tumble and I headed
for the Fishermen's Mission and a hot shower.

Clouds of steam and endless torrents of scalding water flushed
away stale traces of aggravation and frustration and dispelled the
incipient rheumatics of recent cold, damp days. By the time I was
drying myself with a clean, white Mission towel, my problems were
temporarily forgotten.

Then began a strange stream of events. George Simpson had just
come off a two-week cruise around the islands, survived the recent
gales and, like me, was weather-beaten, unshaven and exhausted.
His shower having a similar restorative effect we started chatting
and established that his sister lived only a hundred yards from my
home in Aberdeen. This coincidence noted, and a brotherhood
formed by hot water purification, we agreed that people in Oban
had been known to drink upon a far less worthy excuse, and hit
the town with enthusiasm.

Aulay's bar was filled with the euphoria of the Raft Race.
Everywhere I looked there were 'Russ Abbot' look-a-likes, pink-
haired 'Scotsmen' with T-shirts, kilts, braces and paintbrushes for
sporrans, all completely legless and celebrating their team's third
place as though it were the World Cup.

My story, as told by George, who now had a couple of drams
in him, made me an object of unrivalled novelty and an extra
excuse for another round. Soon everyone was buying me drinks
and, although I tried to do justice to this generosity, there came a
point when I had a pint in each hand, two pints lined up on the
bar and another three waiting in the tap! These I could not forget
because the barmaid had both a sense of humour and a memory
like an abacus and never lost tally of my progress.

Bill from the boatyard, who had just won a bet as to who had
the 'shairniest paws' in the bar, leant heavily on my shoulder and,
in a brief moment of lucidity, diverted my pursuits for the second
time that day to John Hodgson of Connel. He then turned back
to the crowd and slurred, 'My wife is a better lay than any other

woman in Oban'.

'Aye, so I've heard!' came the reply from another wit. Alan Law, who introduced himself as 'Law of the Jungle', teaches geography as a sideline, occupying himself more seriously with poetry, folksong and drinking. Diver, sailor, cyclist, he and his wife Jan had met while canoeing, and George's increasingly eloquent rendering of my story had attracted another sympathetic ear.

A small group of us drifted into song in a corner of the bar, and since the others couldn't remember the words, I found myself singing most of 'Farewell to Tarwathie' alone. (To those who know me this will suggest that I was also making a brave attempt to reduce the strain on the barmaid's abacus!) Then Jan Law arrived with Alan's guitar, and she and Alan agreed that if I had problems in getting the kayak to John Hodgson then they would transport it for me.

Suddenly everything seemed to resolve itself; all I had to do was call Hodgson tomorrow, then contact the Laws and my problems were over; I hoped that by morning I'd remember all this!

I woke next morning with a head problem, still wearing clothes and cagoule, and only half into my tent. Somehow I'd found my way over the rocks in complete darkness, although there was a sheer drop into the Firth of Lorne only six feet from my tent! On the phone John Hodgson sounded hopeful and suggested that I move in with his family while he worked on the boat. The Hodgson place at Dunstaffnage was a menagerie of ducks, hens, geese, dogs, bees and a donkey. The workshop was neatly ordered but the yard was strewn around with the carcasses of half-stripped cars and boats, among them plenty of fibreglass jobs waiting for attention.

John's wife Jenni, who already knew of my journey through working as a coastguard auxiliary, made a delicious chilli before going on night duty. John began on the kayak almost immediately and worked through to midnight, stopping only for the occasional coffee. After a couple of beers and a chat it was the early hours before I crept into bed where their three-year-old son Jamie muttered about horses all night in his sleep. It was a struggle for me to get up at 9 o'clock but as I could hear John had already started work on my boat, I made the effort. Feeling guilty about his good-natured dedication, and a breakfast of home-laid eggs, I began to look for some way to help out. Jenni was in the process of decorating so, to allow her some sleep, I painted a ceiling and stripped some wallpaper, and by mid-afternoon John had finished work on the kayak.

Small, lean and thick-bearded, John to me represented one of the craftmasters of Norse mythology, and his work matched the image perfectly. With a newly moulded monofibre and fibreglass backbone, and 'gellcoate' coverings, the boat would be stronger even than before. His attention to detail was meticulous and I'd swear the boat looked better than when new.

Next morning, after a duck-egg breakfast, I packed the canoe. Jenni hard-boiled some more eggs for me to take away, and at 2 pm John and I carried the loaded canoe down to the Etive shore. I was glad he refused payment for what he had done, for how can you pay adequately for true kindness and hospitality? Jan Law turned up to wave me off and even joked about coming with me in Alan's old sea-kayak, but it was 'Goodbye' to everyone, and to Stage One of the journey.

I was now over two weeks behind schedule, but the boat, which had so nearly come to permanent grief, now bravely showed a condition fit to challenge the future, and I resolved to find a better system of launching and landing. The next stage would take me to Mull, around the turbulent Ardnamurchan peninsula to the Small Isles, on to Knoydart and so to the Isle of Skye; over three hundred miles of coastline and several islands to visit. But I had a fully loaded boat and a renewed appetite for the sea with which to face the challenge. It was Tuesday the 28th of May, almost a month to the day since I had set off from Southerness.

' ... Malin, Hebrides, Minches ...'

'It is not the frail beauty of the moon,
nor the cold loveliness of the sea,
nor the empty tale of the shores uproar
that seeps through my spirit tonight'.

('The Heron', Sorley Maclean)

'Rockall, Malin, Hebrides, Minches, Bailey'. The shipping forecast for sea areas around the British coast has a poetic appeal similar to that of the rhythmic doggerel of playground skipping jingles. *'Lundy, Fastnet, Irish Sea'*. They trip off the tongue of the velvet-toned broadcaster like psalms to the sea-gods. Yet for the prospective mariner, or land-bound sea-dreamer, such apparent nonsense holds an evocative significance far outranking any visual-aided weather forecast. *'Forties, Cromarty, Forth, Tyne, Dogger'*. For this strange procession of sounds is constantly emphasising the island status of Britain, describing a clockwise roll-call of our inshore waters with *'Faeroes, Fair Isle, South-East Iceland, Viking, Utsire'*, summoning visions of distant shores. What seafarer can deny the powerful nostalgia stirred by the names of coastal stations such as Tiree, Royal Sovereign, Malin Head, Boomer and Mumbles? Perhaps the success of the fishing fleet lies in the balance, or the next leg of that carefully planned yacht trip, for very few modern Gullivers will venture far without the security of a forecast. Furthermore, much of our weather being 'maritime' – influenced by the proximity of the sea – the shipping forecast is the most detailed and relevant to the isolated inhabitants of our northern and western seaboards. In short, for those in whose lives the sea plays a significant role, their daily shipping forecast becomes as compulsive as the city man's morning paper, an item which governs the routine and pace of the working day.

As far as I was concerned it was the one essential external aid to planning the next day's exploits in the appropriate sea area. There were of course alternative sources of meteorological sooth, such as the recently established 'Marineline' service, a recorded telephone forecast regularly up updated for inshore waters. At times when I was able to reach a telephone, this service proved adequate, but it was slightly less comprehensive, and significantly less poetic than the shipping forecast, and dotted the 'I's on 'irritation' with its insistence on concluding the most foul of forecasts with a cheerful, computerised version of 'The skies are not cloudy all day'!

Sometimes it was pleasant to get a personal forecast from the coastguard, and indeed after several days' isolation the thrill of a chat with a husky female auxiliary was worth a lengthy jog to a telephone kiosk. So distracted was I on these occasions that several weeks passed before I discovered that their information was being gleaned second-hand from the Marineline service.

The nightly shipping forecast comes on the air just before closedown at exactly thirty-three minutes past midnight. What could be simpler than catching those few words of wisdom each night before curling up to sleep? But practice was never quite perfect. With an early morning start and a hard day of sea air and exercise behind me, by 10pm I would often be tucked up, well fed and snug in my sleeping bag; that's when the nodding would start. Reading helped to prolong wakefulness for an hour or so, and a mug of strong coffee might enable me to complete my tidal calculations for next day, but despite all the good intentions in the world, by midnight I would be truly struggling. '*Only half an hour to go*', as I strained to concentrate on the news of the outside world, but around 12.15am there would follow a selection of light music. More often than not this would be a gentle classical piece, carefully tempered to unwind the Great British public before bed. Then at 12.30am, if I was still in the game, preceding the shipping forecast is the signature tune 'Sailing By', three minutes of the most deviously soporific lullaby ever devised. That usually finished me off, and I'd sleep soundly through both the forecast and the national anthem until woken by the persistent vacant 'bleep' of the radio's triumph.

❖ ❖ ❖

Camas Bruaich Ruaidh is a shingle bay seaward of the famous tidal Falls of Lora, at the mouth of Loch Etive. Although rendering it liable to possible confusion with hundreds of once delightful sheltered inlets on the Scottish coast which have been annexed by the cancerous spread of aquaculture in recent years, it is referred to locally as 'the fish farm bay'. It was here that I took leave of the hospitality and friendship of Connel and set my paddles out across the agitated waters of the Firth of Lorne. A strong northerly wind soon questioned my resistance to recent days of inactivity, excess alcohol and lack of sleep, but it felt good to be back on the water and I was confident, if not in my own resilience, at least in the restored health of the damaged kayak. 'Ideally', said John with a bearded grin as he launched me from the bay, 'the Gellcoate repair should be given several days of dry warmth to cure properly'. But I was anxious to make up for lost time, had already accepted too much of the Hodgsons' hospitality, and couldn't face another egg – be it duck, goose or platypus – for a week or so!

It was a bright afternoon and wind-stirred anvil clouds threw roving shadows on the western slopes of dusty-looking mountains in Appin and Argyll. Ahead, under denser cloud, lay Morvern and the hills of Mull; Jura, to the south, skulked behind a persistent veil of rain.

I was bound for the Sound of Mull, a narrow, steep-sided, twenty-mile passage between Mull and mainland Morvern which, with its ancient associations with the Lords of the Isles, is perhaps the most romantic in the west, issuing at Ardnamurchan Point and the gateway to the Northern Hebrides. Tidal streams run strongly in the Sound of Mull creating several fierce 'races' through the shallower water to the south and west of Lismore island. One such race is known in Gaelic as 'Bun nam Biodag' (dirk), for its waves are reputedly as sharp and keen as a dagger. Southwards, where the channel is wider and the waves less steep, the race is called 'Bun Mhor Somhairle' – The Race of the Great Somerled – after an ancient leader who gained possession of these southern isles in the first stage of a tactical bid to regain control of the Hebrides from their Norse overlords.

Taking the narrow passage between Lismore and Eilean Musdile, defying the ebb tide and a northerly wind funnelling down the Sound, I was tossed uncomfortably in an area of confused eddies before crossing the small standing waves, which marked the entrance to the Sound. Satisfied that the worst of the turbulence now lay to the south, I crossed the Sound to beneath Duart Castle, ancestral home of the Clan Maclean, and allowed the tide to carry me northwards, eventually re-crossing the Sound to pitch camp at the Morvern village of Lochaline.

Lochaline has an international reputation for the quality and quantity of sand excavated from tunnels beneath the village, and it was at the entrance to the mine that I made a hasty, late-evening camp. Industrial debris lay all around, and an unfortunate crane had toppled into the shallow water at the ferry pier. Thick cloud obscured the view up the loch towards the Morvern hills and I was at a loss to know how the area merited its name, which means 'the beautiful loch'. Next morning after heated protests from a mine-official over my choice of campsite, I felt even less desire to linger and dodged neatly out from the slipway as the early morning ferry from Mull steamed towards me through the narrows. I must admit to cutting prudence a little fine and could almost hear the murmurs of relief from the line of waiting passengers as I emerged unscathed from beneath the boom of the toppled crane and opened a welcome gap between me and Lochaline. I hardly suspected then that it was a gap which was to close within a year, to find me living at the head of that same Loch and striding the Morvern hills in search of eagles, divers and alpine plants as a warden for the Scottish Wildlife Trust, and I have never trusted first impressions since, for Morvern revisited is surely one of the most beautiful and friendly peninsulas of Scotland.

I reached Tobermory through the narrow channel between Calve Island and the Mull shore to land on a small sand beach below the main street of the town. As the metropolitan 'capital' of Mull, Tobermory has a colourful picture-postcard appeal, and rejoices in a full spectrum of garish hues along its sea-front. A bus-load of tourists were leaning on the railing of the main street to supervise my arrival and, as I beached the boat beneath a panel of blankly staring faces, I half expected a row of score-cards to be raised in judgement.

With a fair idea of how 'E.T.' must have felt I snatched up my ammo-box and ran off in search of the local radio station which, I was assured by Fox's P.R. agents, was keen to do an interview. An hour later, puzzled and tired, and with a much improved knowledge of Tobermory, I gave up and phoned Jo Smith in Yorkshire, who checked her files to find that 'Oops, sorry, its STORNOWAY that has the radio station, are you anywhere near there?' Well, I reasoned as I shuffled back to the beach, they would sound similar to a

Yorkshire lass, but it was to be over a month before I reached Radio Nan Eilean in Stornoway!

Meanwhile I assumed residence at a derelict boathouse to the north of the town and started a driftwood fire using a tattered copy of Playboy which someone had jilted. With no tent to pack I would make an early start, for tomorrow held a special challenge, and I hoped that the evening sunset which gilded Tobermory Bay also heralded a settling of the weather.

By 7.15am I was skimming out over a silver morning tide with the weather looking encouraging for a rounding of the great headland of Ardnamurchan, a massive peninsula, scantily clad in threadbare green and dividing the northern and southern island groups. Indeed so far does it project into the sea of the Hebrides that it is the most westerly of any point of mainland Britain. The name, meaning 'Headland of Sea-Nymphs' or 'Headland of Great Seas', refers to the foul tides that have made it

'more notable in aspect and more terrible to mariners than any other headland between Cape Wrath and the Mull of Kintyre'.

(Gazetteer of Scotland, Vol I.)

The remnants of a large swell stirred by recent gales in the Atlantic broke with unexpected violence on the exposed coast, booming loudly in cave and blow-hole as if indicating contempt for temporary lulls in weather and those who heed them. But there was no serious turbulence and on rounding the point the lighthouse pointed, like a white-gloved finger, towards a panorama of islands across cobalt Atlantic waters. Before the sun was at its zenith I had reached the deserted shell-sand beaches of Sanna Bay and as it promised to be a hot, dry day, I pitched camp early with a privileged view eastwards to the Moidart hills and northwards to the Islands. These were the 'Small Isles' of Rhum, Eigg, Muck and Canna, with the Cuillin Ridge of Skye just visible between them, and would be the next diversion on my path northwards.

Unloading my camp gear onto a high grassy knoll I watched a cow and her calf wander to the tide-line to inspect the kayak, then go knee-deep into the turquoise water to cool off, and I was happy, for the only footprints on the beach other than my own were cloven.

The tide being on the retreat I had no qualms about leaving the kayak on the beach and the warm breath of the grassland soon drew me into a contented snooze. On waking to the song-flight of a meadow pipit I became aware of a small man walking slowly towards me across the dazzling sand. There was a woolly hat, beneath which crept wild strands of sandy hair, bare feet peeped from below baggy corduroy trousers and I thought with approval, 'here's someone who's life doesn't revolve around his clothes'. I was right, for it wasn't ten minutes before he had removed them and sat by my camp grinning in the sunshine, as naked as the seals on the beach! This was Dr Stan, naturist and troglodyte. For a large part of the year he wanders the finest areas of Scotland climbing and often living in caves. He explained, in explicit detail, that he was preparing his preseason, all-over tan before heading south to a favourite nudist beach among whose fraternity those who sported the slightest marks of any covering were regarded as part-time voyeurs.

Stan fetched water for a brew, and my canoe gear dried out completely for the first time since April, as we shared lunch beneath a beating sun and pondered the hardships of a wandering lifestyle. By mid-afternoon a handful of people had arrived on the beach, one of whom, an attractive woman in her mid-thirties, became the target of Stan's unique brand of evangelism. I lay back and allowed the sun to dispel the rheumatic effects of accumulated salt and damp, and I swear that steam rose from my bones. It seemed that everyone but Stan and I was dashing back 'somewhere' to work on Monday.

Even knowing that I was behind on my schedule, I selected the illusion that I had all the time in the world and marvelled at the psychological influence of a change in the weather pattern. Low pressure systems are appropriately called 'depressions', an area known for its absence of weather is known to sailors as 'the Doldrums', but there was an anticyclone over the Hebrides, an area of high pressure, and I was high with it.

Next morning Stan arrived early bearing farewell gifts of sugar-free peanut butter sandwiches to save me having to make lunch. When I saw him again, over a year later, he brought me a jar of that same peanut butter; the only additive was nostalgia. The sun had returned – and my map of this area still exudes the lingering scent of sun-oil – but a light breeze ushered me northwards and I crossed the six miles to the Isle of Muck in well under an hour. On the pier at the picturesque Port Mor I ate Stan's sandwiches and watched the tide desert the small harbour; it dries out at low tide, making Muck one of the more isolated of the small isles for the ferry cannot berth here and must moor offshore. But despite access problems Muck has, through the enlightened ownership of the MacEwens, stemmed the tide of depopulation that has beset many Scottish islands. In the eighteenth century eight per cent of Scots lived on islands; today less than one per cent are full-time islanders. On Muck a population of around thirty people is maintained by crofting, lobster fishing and running a small guest house and with a small boat for mail, freight and charter-use, there is, if not quite self-sufficiency, at least an independence from the fickle favours of tourism.

One crofter, Bruce Mather, explained that he was also the local coastguard auxiliary and the island's woodturner/craftsman. He had left his job as a tax inspector in the city and created what seemed like an enviable niche for himself on the island, until he confided that his present commission was to produce two thousand wooden light-pull handles! But island life has an antidote to monotonous tasks in a way that city life could never have; later that year BBC television showed Selina Scott sweating enthusiastically at a Muck Ceilidh and clambering gingerly aboard the boat of the barefooted and fiery-haired laird, Lawrence MacEwen.

Conditions were still good when I left Muck heading northwards again, past the cliffs of Grulin on the eccentric Isle of Eigg, to the grim precipitous bastions of Rhum. The crossing took a full two hours, but they were idyllic hours during which I revelled in the sheer physical presence of this highly unusual collection of isles. Often, I had gazed at the congested group from points on the mainland and, having learned to distinguish their forms, had long dreamed of wandering independently among them. Now I was approaching the most majestic of them all, 'Rhum of the Ridges', almost entirely surrounded by cliffs varying in nature according to the parent rock, and seeming to offer little prospect of a landfall other than the main settlement at Loch Scresort, for the sea here is seldom still, even in the gentlest weather.

But my eye was drawn by a 'bealach' or intersection of two

concave mountain slopes, to a tiny inlet where a crystal waterfall cascaded over a rocky ledge into a deep sea-pool and a storm-beach rose steeply from the sea in a rock-fringed bay. This was Dibidil (deep dale). My deck-map showed a hut, which I then spotted among the browns and greens of the hillside; both the possibility that it might be some sort of bothy, and the ever-present dictatorship of the bladder persuaded me to attempt the difficult landing. A storm-beach of unstable boulders-with the dumping surf and undertow which attends such places-is never an easy option for coming ashore.

The entire beach occupied an area of perhaps six feet in width with steep, undercut cliffs on either side and vicious canine boulders restricting the landing even further. There was little scope for artistry and after several unsuccessful attempts to run the bows securely but gently aground, I found the slope of the beach too severe and hastily back-paddled to avoid damage. There was only one alternative: throwing my ammo-box clear of the waves I leapt from the cockpit and grabbed the kayak by the bow rope, hauling it uphill with the 'swash' before tumbling head over heels backwards down the beach to land in the surf, a decidedly undignified, sodden, chuckling lump.

With a little patience and grace on my part it could probably have been avoided, but I felt my bladder must have been glowing neon-red by then, and besides, my sunburned shoulders welcomed the dip. At the back of the beach was a wall of rock which had to be scaled, and my gear hauled out on a rope, but Dibidil bothy lived up to my greatest optimism: it was clean, comfortable, deserted and sported hammocks of fishing net. Cuddled in the corner of Askival (2,659 ft) and Ainshvall, it afforded spectacular views over the water of the Small Isles to Eigg, Muck and Ardnamurchan, and across the Cuillin Sound to Skye, with fresh water within a stone's throw of the cottage. Somehow, and it remains a pleasant mystery considering the range of obstacles between us, I was able to contact Oban coastguard on my hand-held radio set and to report safe landfall; this done I could relax for the night.

It has always seemed anomalous to me that Rhum – forty square miles of mountain and glen with five peaks above 2,300 feet – which once supported a population of over four hundred, should be numbered among the parish of the 'small' Isles. And as night fell on Dibidil I began to doubt the appropriateness of its being annexed to any 'parish' whatsoever, for Rhum – often mist-shrouded for days on end-seems to hide a dark and brooding pagan soul which defies the 'advances' of civilization. The jagged horseshoe ridge of its mountains and glens, named ten centuries ago by the raiding Norsemen, lends to the island an aura that is beyond the simple Christian dichotomy of Good and Evil; if any one place is a proper setting for the ancient tales of Gaeldom it is the silent acres of Dibidil, in the moon-shadow of Askival, where the cascade of the deep valley plunges into the sea below the hut. The bothy itself, a former shepherd's hut, is haunted by the ghost of a young woman from a ship wrecked in the bay at Papadil (dale of the priests). She knocks at the door in a state of distress, with dripping hair and sodden clothes, though there be no rain outside nor puddles where she stands barefooted. Her cries for help for the survivors of the wreck would bring the most sceptical occupant to the door of the hut, whereupon she quietly and forlornly fades into the darkness. She had struggled three rocky miles across the slopes of Sgurr nan Gillean to Dibidil, but her body was never found. That night was my first in a hammock and, unaware then of the possibility of a second dripping visitor to Dibidil, I slept soundly and dreamlessly.

In the mid-1820s, four hundred crofters were 'cleared' from Rhum to be replaced by the relentless hooves and scouring mouths of eight thousand sheep. In later years, under different ownership, the intensive grazing pressure was continued as Rhum became a deer forest, a 'sportsman's Shangri-la'. The natural scrub cover and native woodland of the island were indiscriminately burned, and was unable to regenerate under such heavy grazing. Eventually there was little left on Rhum but barren moorland and bare hillside, and within twenty years the island was capable of supporting only fifteen hundred sheep and a hundred and fifty people. In 1957, now with a population of only twenty-eight, the island was bought by the Nature Conservancy Council as a National Nature Reserve. As an eccentric use of public funds this purchase was severely criticised; but the N.C.C. case was well founded, for Rhum was highly representative of the entire West Highland situation. Here was a finite portion of impoverished land, with a superb range of geology (especially evidence of tertiary vulcanicity and glaciation), altitude and aspect, where it would be possible to conduct long-term experiments into complex ecological relationships within a fixed boundary. Since then Rhum has become famous for the work done on red deer husbandry, rehabilitation of wasted land and the replanting of native trees-all highly applicable to mainland problems.

Recently, after an absence of over sixty years from Scotland, another victim of clearances in the interests of sheep, the sea eagle or 'Erne', has been tentatively reintroduced from Rhum, and several pairs now breed elsewhere in Scotland. I was lucky enough last year to see one of these great birds, larger than the golden eagle, and await news of their future with fingers crossed.

The morning sunshine highlighted several anomalous green pastures on the wind-blasted mountain tops. These, wholly unique to Rhum, are due to the presence, in huge numbers, of Manx shearwaters or 'Fachachs'. Rhum has both the largest and the highest colony in the British Isles, for although it is a true seabird, the Manx shearwater nests on the mountains of Rhum above fifteen hundred feet – in burrows! Flying in under cover of darkness, in the hour before midnight, to avoid the clutches of the island's golden eagles, each bird is mysteriously able to locate its own burrow amongst thousands of others. From the region of these burrows, and from deep within the holes themselves, at nights, may be heard the most eerie and unsettling of bird calls – the throaty chuckling and shrieking of the Fachachs. There is a marked correlation between shearwater breeding sites and the occurrence of the Norse word 'troll' (e.g. Trallvall on Rhum, Trollkarp in the Faeroes etc.) and it has been seriously suggested that it may have been the strange subterranean mutterings of the Fachach which gave rise to the original Norse legends of Troll.

Throughout the day – which was so hot that I spent much of it immersed in a pool above the waterfall – the troll-birds rafted and fished offshore. The lonely, squeaky-gate call of the golden plover reached me on the breeze from the upper slopes of the glen and several stags still in velveted antlers, grazed close around the bothy. A grey wagtail picked at grains of rice I spilled on the grass, and it would not have been out of character with Celtic folklore if one of these creatures had suddenly uttered some profound words of wisdom. I saw no one all day and, in the cool of the evening, descended the rockface to pack the kayak for the long crossing to the mainland at Mallaig next morning. Although the sun had long since disappeared over the shoulder of Sgurr Nan Gillean the light and warmth showed little sign of fading and, as the rosy pink of evening grew, the island of Eigg across the sound floated contentedly like a misplaced prop from a desert-canyon movie.

The eighteen-mile crossing to Mallaig was to be my longest open-water commitment so far; I would pass close (within three miles) to the southern tip of Skye, but hoped not to have to make landfall until I reached the mainland coast. It was a mental and physical wrench to leave Dibidil, into whose landscape and character I could so happily have dissolved, and to head eastwards for the bustle and clamour that is Mallaig.

I took a compass bearing for Mallaig, invisible across a hazy expanse of ocean, and set off wearing sunglasses and little else; the possibility of sunstroke crossed my mind several times, but never lodged.

Three squadrons of sabre-winged shearwaters (about thirty birds in each) made alarming display flights at breakneck speed towards and over the kayak, each from a different corner, mixing and passing through each other as they met. Some, travelling at about two feet above water level, barely missed the bows of the boat; others, more aptly named 'shearwaters', actually skimmed the waves with their wingtips, in a 'flypast' farewell. Four miles out from Rhum a lone puffin, that comical parrot of the sea, bobbed lightly on the rising swell.

The morning sun glared painfully back at me from the slight ridges of sea which rose beyond the shelter of Rhum and I had to narrow my eyes as my paddles blazed rhythmically into ever more open water. Two hours went by before Mallaig itself was visible on the eastern horizon; it was a Sunday and the ferries and fishing boats were in harbour. With Mallaig as yet eight miles away I was a tiny speck alone, remote and exposed among the massive dreamy rock sanctuaries of Rhum, Eigg and Skye. I lay my head back on the rear deck and stretched, watching the tiny puffs of cumulus drifting, as I too was drifting towards the mainland hills. Two miles off Mallaig I picked up a 'following' sea and rode casually into harbour on a succession of small rollers almost exactly four hours after leaving Rhum.

It was obvious why the sea around had been empty, for it seemed that the collection of hulls, booms and masts must comprise every yacht and fishing boat on the entire west coast; since the coming of the railway in 1901 Mallaig has been one of the most important west coast fishing ports and the main ferry terminal for Skye and the Inner Hebrides. Feeling extra buoyant after my crossing I wove my way slowly through this colourful collection as they bobbed and glinted in the afternoon sun, answering friendly waves and shouts from all sides. Apart from the memory of the year I'd found a box of eighty filleted kippers in this harbour, the image that was strongest in my mind was that of the Eskimo on the T.V. advertisement who paddles into harbour for his pint of a well-known lager; and apart from rubbing noses with the barman, I followed the image to its logical conclusion as soon as the kayak could be whisked up the slipway on its trolley. At the hotel on the hill I ate pear-sponge and custard as a six-pointed sunburst silhouetted the islands and gilded the highway of water I'd followed that day. Gazing furtively back at me from the toilet mirror was a curious fellow with a rough-bearded, sun-leathered face encrusted like a tequila glass, with crystallized salt.

Who was this grizzly Mr. Hyde? I bought him a couple of pints and was happy in his company.

Leaving Mallaig, my aspirations for the day were to reach Sandaig on the Sound of Sleat, immortalized as 'Camusfearna' in Gavin Maxwell's Ring of Bright Water, which probably did more for the Scottish tourist industry than any official body. This meant heading northwards for sixteen miles across the wide fjord-like sea lochs that flank the peninsula of Knoydart, popularly billed as Europe's last true wilderness area because of its inaccessibility and the severely testing conditions offered by its savage peaks.

The weather was due to break and the wind rose steadily as I crossed Loch Nevis, which yawned into the depths of Knoydart. Before I reached the Knoydart shore the sea had become a heaving, steep-sided swell, chopped short and white by the hatchet action of the brisk north westerly. I winced inwardly as waves broke regularly over my head and chest, gradually chilling as the icy water penetrated the neck of my wetsuit, and knew there would be no respite until I reached the lee shore, three miles across the deepest sea-loch in Europe and shrouded in spindrift. The wind reached Force 5, gusting to 6, and it was a gruelling battle to make any progress at all. The combined effect of repeated drenchings and a strong wind rapidly led to a situation of profound chill and sluggishness until I knew that a concentrated burst of energy and power was the only safe alternative to retreating fast to the Mallaig shore. At last, drunk with weariness and trembling with nervous tension, I reached an unknown bay on the ragged Knoydart coast where it was possible to shelter enough to rekindle warmth and feeling in my hands. By virtue of a sponsorship donation I carried an apparently endless stock of Orkney Fudge bars which I was accustomed to treat as instant-energy fuel; I knew just how many 'squares' were required for 'x' hours of steady effort, but in an extreme situation I was still capable of devouring like a dog, an entire bar of twelve squares. Today, as I write, I feel queasy at even the thought!

I continued to skirt the Knoydart shore, fighting doggedly through a steep grey sea whose momentum as it broke on my shoulders was more than enough to knock the breath from me. I had to find landfall soon, for one small mistake in a sea like that and, with reserves of strength depleted, I could be in desperate trouble. At the next bay a rough shingle beach and the wall of an ancient ruined chapel provided adequate shelter for a makeshift camp and, as the storm beach held more than the average quota of fishboxes, I soon had a roaring fire going and life seemed rosy again.

When my hands at last denounced their long accustomed 'hook' shape I peeled off my wet layers and wallowed naked in the warm smoke of the fire, postponing for a moment the simple luxury of the dry clothing that I always carried on the rear deck in a waterproof bag. The comfort and relief of my thermal trousers, woolly jersey, thick socks and dry shoes was almost erotic and I jogged off round the bay to aid circulation.

Fishboxes in various states of disrepair were strewn along the south-west facing beaches, and on the promontory overlooking the Sound, bearing much resemblance to a Pyrenean villa, was a sheep-shelter carefully constructed from nailed fish boxes. Out in the Sound the seas were frantic, the deep ocean blue contrasting strikingly with vast flocks of 'mermaid's sheep', dazzling whitecaps as far as the eye could see; and two small fishing boats toiling hard made little headway against the wind-whipped tide. I was surprised to see what looked like snow on the hills of Skye until it struck me that it was not snow but the gentle cirrus clouds of the morning, plastered by the wind down upon the shoulders of the peaks in a mantle of white; it was a novel effect on me and merited several photographs.

Back at the chapel, sheltered in a bed of tall flag-irises, I demolished a six-course meal catching occasional brief glimpses, in the evening light, of an otter among the rocks of the littoral edge. I flicked absently at the sheep ticks which crawled over my face and ears, but which seemed to have stopped taking root in me. Perhaps I was no longer appetising because of the salt in my skin; I hardly knew whether to be relieved or offended!

❖ ❖ ❖

It is strange to think that the meaning of a word might to some extent depend upon a factor as volatile as the prevailing weather conditions, but for certain words this is in fact the case. In common parlance 'later' is one of the most ambiguous and non-specific terms; 'see you later' and 'sooner or later' might refer to next week, tomorrow or just a few hours. But when the wind reaches 40 knots and a gale warning is issued by the Meteorological Office, the same word assumes the precise and dogmatic meaning of 'it will arrive in over twelve hours' time', just as 'soon' means 'in six to twelve hours' and 'imminent' means 'in under six hours'. The late night shipping forecast gave a 'Force 8, later' for the Hebrides area, so by 8.30am I was packed and on the water-a dramatic departure from my normal routine for I had sacrificed breakfast in order to reach Skye before winds in excess of yesterday's fun made it impossible to cross the Sound of Sleat. Misty views of the Knoydart mountains unfolded at my back until I was looking down the gaping barrel of Loch Hourn ('Hell') where, deep within its steep-sided domain, a fierce squall was already raging. The worst of the weather was as yet impaled on the barbs of Knoydart and, forging now southwards along the Sleat coast of Skye, I was racing to gain distance before it caught me. It was a private fantasy of pursuit and escape that I have long used as an aid to stamina on a monotonous slog. There was a useful 'following' sea and I felt the tiredness temporarily leave me as the unmistakable 'Sgurr' of the Island of Eigg came again into view after two days' absence. But, fearing to push the fantasy too far, I made an early camp among the beds of irises and cushions of thrift on the soggy foreshore of Armadale Bay. Cold, damp and aggravated by the midge clouds which rose from the masses of seaweed cast up by the tide, I shivered in violent spasms as I unloaded the kayak. The carnivorous hordes were anxious to dispense with formalities and to make more intimate acquaintance as I peeled off my wet gear, so I took immediate refuge in the tent and dried off by the warmth of the petrol stove which was already cooking my hot-chocolate drink. It was a miserable campsite and, with a large spring tide and a low atmospheric pressure, the backing of a gale force wind brought the sea to within feet of flooding the tent while I lay, almost disinterested, and watched its approach.

It takes a lot of experience to recognize a morale slump before it hits; all I knew that night was that, deflated and damp at the end of a grey day, I missed more than usual having someone to snuggle up to. But next morning enthusiasm was notably absent. The prospect of another hard day on the water, the thought of leaving a warm sleeping bag to don a pile of chilled, sodden gear, and the residual rheumatic stiffness of kayak fatigue, did little to foster a seafaring spirit.

It was one of those mornings which would have convinced the ancient philosophers of the separate identities of Mind and Body, for, will as I might, that Body just plainly refused to respond for over an hour.

The target for the day was Tarskavaig, fifteen miles around the southern tip of Skye. I telephoned the coastguard for an update on the weather, but the best he could offer was a Force 6 westerly; bad news. I reported my destination and was on my way at 10.15am. It was a day I was lucky to see the end of.

During pre-expedition preparation, intensely aware of the vulnerability of the canoeist alone at sea, I had realized the importance of the bodily reserves of energy known as stamina, and many hours of specific training had been devoted to developing these latent reserves. I had to be confident that in an unexpected situation I would have the extra strength necessary to meet the challenge, for there would be no one else there to throw me a line. The principle is similar to that of the long-distance motorist who carries a spare gallon of petrol beneath his seat: the total amount of petrol in the car is still limited, but he knows that if the regular tank is depleted due to irregular circumstances, he is not thereby rendered helpless. This is a distinct psychological advantage, but the main problem in the physiological equivalent is that there is no petrol gauge!

Round the southern tip of Skye and heading northwards, strong winds and walls of grey water were still the bane of progress and, in the constant struggle I felt my strength wane with frightening rapidity as if the tank had sprung a leak.

After several cold drenchings I found myself suddenly unable to regain warmth, a worrying symptom which suggested I was already on the 'reserve tank'; and I made my way hastily inshore to the first small inlet that offered the possibility of rest. Of this bay I remember very little except sitting on my lifejacket in the lee of some rocks and eating cake and cheese, for almost instantly I fell asleep. Waking within minutes, frightened at this strange condition, I spurred myself on again in a daze. But conditions on the sea were severe and testing. Every movement brought the need for an urgent response or reflexive support-stroke, for there was no regularity in the vicious chop and lash of those waves. Within a half-hour I had hauled out on the rocks again, closer to exhaustion than I had ever been. Given the strength to haul the kayak off the rocks and above the grasp of the rising tide I'd have camped there for the night, but my immediate thought was for shelter from the wind and, although the midges were out, I was very soon asleep again. I woke with the tide around my ankles and was vaguely aware that I must be suffering the accumulated effects of several days' exhaustion.

Shivering violently and unable to stop yawning, my mind kept returning to a particular 'goodbye' cuddle with Pip at Dumfries, and the thought of the obligation to continue and complete the expedition – another two months of lonely exertion and fear – seemed a terrifying burden. As Pippa's sad smile returned I became quite emotional and the salt was washed from my cheeks.

Anyone familiar with basic first-aid will have begun to recognize the early symptoms of hypothermia or exposure. Fatigue, cold and prolonged mental stress on the sea were ideal breeding grounds; the lethargy, emotion, shivering fits and the irrationality of carrying on when I should have stopped, were all classic symptoms of the condition and I ought to have been aware of the warning signs. It is the place of every expedition leader to be constantly alert for signs of exposure and exhaustion in his team; similarly, it is the duty of the solo traveller to monitor his own condition to the same extent, if only because there is no one else to keep a watchful eye on him. However, slow mental functioning and irrationality are also symptomatic of the same condition, making it very easy to overlook the classic symptoms in oneself. Of course once the symptoms are identified, further exertion should be avoided at all costs, for further loss of deep-core heat will lead to unconsciousness, heart and respiratory failure and eventually death. But irrationality gained the upper hand and, with the tide rising fast I felt I must find a better place to land. I got back into the boat, pushing myself over the rocks, through the shallows and into the open water once more. The wind had increased and the tide, disregarding my predictions, had neglected to change direction and was still against me. After perhaps fifteen minutes of tossing, almost out of control in demonic frothing waters, a brief clear thought reached me: I had absolutely no chance of reaching Tarskavaig, still three miles to the north, and this was no place to be in an eighteen-foot kayak. I was dangerously near my final limit, where survival is as tenuous as the fine axis of balance; the shock of a capsize would have sent me into a deep and permanent sleep. The panic of sudden realization sent me surfing erratically into the rough storm-beaten backwater of Inver Dalavil cove.

With the critical wisdom of hindsight I realize how lucky I was to survive that crazy situation in which I had taken advantage of a limit never intended to be fully tested at sea. I had disobeyed all my own tenets of safety and approached the fine distinction between luck and disaster. Paradoxically, I emerged with a greater understanding of my own physiology and reactions to extremes which would be valuable at later stages of the expedition, but I firmly resolved to abstain from pushing my luck in future.

Ashore, there was nowhere to pitch a tent, but an excellent cave offered a comfortable alternative. Exhaustion held me in sleep for over twelve hours, but it was a sleep troubled by feverish dreams, the interpretation of which required no modern Freudian or Jungian training. In the first I had been captured by a secret army of desperate men who were torturing me by branding names and labels on my body. Those names, now so familiar to me – Fox's, Harishok, Lendal, Wildwater – were those of the companies who

81

had provided the expedition sponsorship which led to my feeling of binding commitment. In the second dream I stood in a boxing ring, representing Fox's biscuits, never having boxed before and faced with the less than cheerful prospect of fighting Barry McGuigan for the World Title!

I awoke next morning to a dripping roof and the curious gaze of several large Highland cattle who seemed to have a proprietorial interest in my occupation of the cave.

It is a strange feeling to lie down and sleep knowing there is not another human within many miles of rock and sea, and there is something primal in waking up in a cave surrounded by horned animals and using weather and tide as criteria in the decision on how best to spend the day. It seemed a Rip-van-Winkle of a sleep had cured my dangerous pessimism and accumulated fatigue and, under the duress of finding fresh water to prepare food, I hoped to reach some place more suited to being stormbound than the present one. Expressing grateful thanks for the hospitality of my bovine hosts, I seal-launched from the rocks, and headed toward Elgol and the incomparable Cuillin ridge.

Sharks, Midges and Maidens

'The old hunchback lived all alone
In a cave down by the sea
And stocked his fishbox kitchen
With fools like you and me.
He wore one golden earring and
Grew seaweed in his hair.
Though no one had ever seen him
We all knew he was there.'

('The Hunchback of Gigha', R. McTell)

I sat on the pier at the village of Elgol eating biscuits, deeply entranced by the magnificent Black Cuillin ridge where shredded remnants of cloud hung like fleece on a barbed-wire fence, but pursuing a train of thought which in a strange way seemed suddenly insistent. Elgol had been in the news earlier that year in connection with a tragic accident at sea in which a retired Public Relations Officer from the National Coal Board and two brothers from the area were drowned, ironically while collecting peat for fuel. The capsized boat and a stray oar were later recovered by Tex Geddes, a well-known local fisherman, and it was to Tex that my thoughts now turned.

Five miles to the west of Elgol lies the tiny island of Soay (a common name in the Hebrides given by the Norsemen to small islands, often close to larger islands, on which sheep or goats were grazed), which had become the centre of the Hebridean shark fishing industry in the mid-1940s.

Contrary to popular belief, several species of shark are to be found in Scottish waters, and of the thirty-six 'requiem' or flesh-eating sharks known to consistently attack humans worldwide, several occur around our coasts. Some, like the thresher, mako and hammerhead (which has been encountered as far north as Aberdeen) are occasional strays from tropical waters. Others, like the large Greenland shark (sometimes over 7 metres long), which eats anything up to the size of a seal, are fortunately only rare wanderers from deeper offshore waters, seldom coming inshore. The blue shark (4-7 metres) is a regular visitor, and the porbeagle (3-4 metres) is present for all twelve months of the year, hunting in packs and often coming very close inshore in search of salmon and mackerel.

By far the largest is the thirty-foot basking shark or 'Cearbhan'. At one time great numbers of these plankton feeders migrated into Hebridean waters during the summer months along with the shoals of herring. As a service to fishermen, who suspected them of causing damage to nets, hundreds of these great sharks were rammed each year by cruisers, and their wasted bodies washed up on beaches with the soft gills decayed to leave a narrow 'neck', giving rise to many sea-monster hoaxes. But each basking shark contains a great quantity of edible meat, and a huge butter-coloured liver yielding over five tons of vitamin-rich oil; this oil was the prize sought by the shark hunters.

Gavin Maxwell, in pre-*Ring of Bright Water* days, bought Soay and pioneered the shark-hunting venture with Tex Geddes, an acquaintance from his time in the Special Forces. Tex, in his late twenties at the end of the war, was a formidable character with a violent temper and an affinity with the bottle, having already led 'a short career of dangerous and highly paid professions' as a lumberjack, boxer, knife thrower and rum-runner in Newfoundland. Maxwell was dead, but Tex, I believed, still lived on the island which he had bought after the demise of the shark project. He would be an elderly man by now, I thought, and perhaps not keen on visitors, but I set my mind on meeting him and began to form plans for paddling out to the island that evening.

The sun came out and warmed Elgol pier where a boat was moored, and two fishermen worked steadily somewhere behind me. I had an idea they were loading plastic fish boxes but was too intent on the scenery, and my thoughts, to take much notice. Then the sound of wellington boots approached me down the jetty, and a gruff old voice bellowed, 'That's an awful THIN boat to be travelling about these waters' – an allusion to the kayak which I'd dragged up on the beach – 'chust look how FAAT my one is!' Startled, I gave some weak conversational reply and was invited on board the M.V. Petros for a cup of tea. Petros held several crates of wriggling pink prawns, graded for collection and transport to

Europe where they would fetch better prices eaten whole than sold locally as scampi.

My fisherman was an anomaly in himself, mid-sixties, perhaps, with rotting teeth parted by voids, but with a clear-eyed, far-sighted stare. A cossack fur hat rode a corrugated brow above a flattened broken nose and he sported a greying orange beard like the hair of a fox-terrier. Gaunt and by no means tall, he was yet broad-shouldered and agile, the overall impression lying somewhere between Ivan the Terrible and Popeye. I drank the lukewarm tea and asked where he had come from. 'Soy' (Soay) he said, pointing to the island so recently in my thoughts.

'Then maybe you know the old shark hunter called Tex Geddes?' I asked hopefully.

'Aye,' there was a pause, 'that'll be me!'

Within the hour another prawn-boat arrived carrying Tex's son and partner, John. I helped to unload the boxes of prawns and drag them to the pierhead, loading coal and wood for the island in their place. As I passed Tex on the pier, weighed down with a sack of coal, I joked about having to work pretty hard for a cup of tea on Skye. At this he became suddenly apologetic and announced 'I'm going to give you permission to visit the island of Soy. What do you think of that?' I said I'd been thinking of going there anyway, but then realized that he was actually proposing to *take me* there!

With the kayak on Petros, hitching a lift Hebridean style, we were soon steaming for Soay, two little boats crossing wide loch Scavaig where the Cuillin peaks bear down like the cavernous jaws of the sharks which once frequented these waters. One could almost hear the echo of 'Muldoan!' – the Hebridean sharkers' wild call – ringing still from the walls of rock. Only then did I notice, with a sudden flush of appreciation, that Tex's second fisherman was in fact an attractive young girl in her late teens.

Biddy Harman had answered a magazine advertisement to come and work on Soay and, despite the southern accent, was as much a part of the fishing scene as a wellington boot. She worked with the best of the men, tying on and off ropes, hauling fishboxes and mentally tallying the average prawn-price per stone.

Banter across the two boats' radios concerned the suspicion that they had been sold short over their haul of prawns and Tex maintained a steady stream of invective that likened the most honourable of fish salesmen to J.R. Ewing of Dallas. 'Jesus had disciples who were fishermen,' said Tex in righteous tone, 'but you never heard of a disciple of the Lord who was a fish-SALESMAN!'

Halfway to Soay I was asked to stop whistling in case I summoned up a strong wind – didn't I know it was fatal to whistle on a boat? ('I whistle all the time on mine' – 'Ah but that wee thing disna' count.') And on the subject of wind, a notice read, 'No farting in the wheelhouse – fine £100': facets of a steadily unfolding character.

We steamed into Soay 'harbour', a narrow inlet on the uninhabited side of the 3,000-acre island, and anchored the Petros. Tex refuses to have a decent pier built for fear of rats coming to the island from moored boats, so Biddy rowed us ashore and a place was suggested where I might later put my tent up. I'd been promised a bath and a meal (in that order), so, with the midges in hot pursuit, we made a dash across the island along a path to Camas Nan Gall, beautifully wooded with silver birch and rowan and smelling strongly of honeysuckle, rhododendron, and wild, 'garlicky' ramsons.

I was introduced to Mrs Jeanne Geddes, on whom, I'd been led to believe, rested my hopes of a meal.

I still found it strange to be introduced as a minor celebrity, especially by someone like Tex whose claims to adventure vastly outranked my own, but a copy of the Oban Times lay open on the kitchen bench with a photo and article in a prominent position: *'Oban Refuge for Storm-Weary Canoeist.'* Oban already seemed such a long time ago.

Despite the lack of substance in Tex's suggestion that Biddy should 'scrub my back', I had a wonderfully scenic bath, in brown peaty water, in an upstairs bathroom which overlooked Elgol and Sleat across miles of open sea; I had forgotten that water could be warm! After a good meal there was activity in the bay, for the tide was at last high enough to unload the boats. It was taken for granted, despite protests from Tex – who was known to all as 'the old chap', and played on the 'ooald' aspect when it suited him – that everyone would be on the beach to help; unloading something or other is a regular occurrence since all supplies – wood, coal, food, furniture, machinery – came to Soay by sea.

John and his wife were there with their two wild-looking flame-haired kids. Pleasant and uninhibited, they looked me in the eye and spoke as if they'd known me all their short lives. Indeed the ease and relaxed fashion with which everyone accepted my presence pleasantly surprised me. In all there were seventeen people on the island and with so much labour it didn't take long to unload the goods which were relayed to the beach by dinghy from the prawn boat. The 'black sheep' of the island is Lawrence Reed of the Austin Reed tailor family. Anyone of independent means is looked upon differently in a community which has long been dependent on hard work and co-operation for breadline survival. 'He doesn't farm, he "gardens"', said Jeanne scornfully, for having survived the island evacuation and rebuilt a community the Geddeses were particularly sensitive towards issues involving the viability of the island. But Mr Reed had recently published a valuable book on the history of Soay, and may have at last justified his existence in the eyes of the crofters.

Between loads from the dinghy, everyone (and numerous dogs) squatted down in the shingle of the beach and chatted and smoked. Tex, as ever, was giving the 'I'm an old man' routine and trying to get a cuddle from Biddy 'to keep the cold from his bones', but just as he was about to embark upon a graphic explanation of 'what happens to a man when he gets old' the dinghy returned, laden with planks and spars of assorted sizes and lengths. These were dumped carelessly at the top of the shingle beach and, suspecting that the evening dampness would cause them to warp, I took some care to stack them all neatly and flatly, keeping different sizes together. Tex noticed this and explained to the kids why it should be done this way; at that point I think I qualified for a bed for the night and was initiated into the existence of Tex's private 'den'.

Tex's den must be the most fascinating single room I've ever set foot in, and I could have spent days browsing through the curios that littered it. But 'littered' is the wrong word, for this little room, no more than twelve feet square, was immaculately varnished in knotted pine panelling and floorboards. There were neatly fitted bunk beds with cupboards below, a ship's clock and barometer on the wall, old brass 'crusie' lamps and a tiny skylight window – for all the world like a film-set from the 'Onedin Line'. The obligatory brass objects included propellers, or 'screws', from the old shark-boats and a tiller polished to reflect countless memories. A vicious six-foot harpoon-barb, souvenir of those adventurous days, hung above the roll-top desk where Tex's autobiography *Hebridean Sharker* had been written. Among the collection of books, I found what I'd expected – a copy of Maxwell's *Harpoon at a Venture*, signed and dedicated to Tex and Jeanne. As for Tex's own book, all I could discover was a tattered old copy, much thumbed, but far from being on display, it was, he told me, out of print and he was unable to get a new copy even for himself. Biddy, Tex and I sat in the half-light in basket chairs rolling cigarettes, drinking home-brew from bottles and chatting about shark and whale hunting. Tex, a different character within his own retreat, played a cassette of Beethoven sonatas, and I began to realise just how alien had been my first impressions of this man, gleaned largely from Maxwell's early books. Far from the brutal greed of the bounty-hunter, the indestructible Highland hard-case, he had seen, in the abundance of the great basking sharks around Soay, the chance to regain viability for the island in times which brought depopulation throughout the Hebrides. Enhanced by the evening's talk of big game in Hebridean waters, Tex became the epitome of the Old Man of the Sea (and Hemingway, too, had a place on the bookshelf). Here was a man who had carved a long life from demanding environments, and who had been stubborn enough to remain on an island pronounced unviable, its inhabitants evacuated to Mull in 1953. The Scottish Office had protested over his determination to remain on the island after the withdrawal of the steamer link with the mainland, but Tex reminded me of the story of 'Noah's Ark and the MacNeil of Barra': when invited to join the throng on board the ark, MacNeil replied, with unequivocal independence, and floodwater around his knees, 'Tell Noah the MacNeil has a boat of his own!'

There were many questions I would like to have asked about his past, his writing and especially his dealings with Maxwell, but I was a guest, not a reporter, and saw no way to exceed the limits of friendly curiosity, for to do so would have introduced a formal one-sidedness to the chat. Besides, I noticed that the islanders had found it unnecessary to subject me to the usual barrage of questions about my trip, and I was grateful. Information gathering, then, was limited to what perception could dredge from the deeper currents of an all too shallow and brief encounter.

After a good breakfast of brose and scrambled eggs, and much prodding on Biddy's part to get 'the old chap' into gear, Biddy and

Tex went off in the rain to castrate a bull-calf; I left this alternative world and headed into low cloud bound for Lochs Scavaig and Coiruisk among the Cuillin hills.

◆ ◆ ◆

'Round Cuillin's peaks the mist is sailing;
The Banshee cries her note o' wailing,
And my blue een with sorrow are weeping,
For him that will never return, MacCrimmon.'

It was on just such a day that the Banshee of the Cuillins might have lamented for the last of the MacCrimmons, legendary Pipers to the Clan MacLeod, for as I entered the chasm of Loch Scavaig the mist was indeed 'sailing' at around a hundred feet. Where yesterday had stood the domineering sentries of Gars Bheinn and Sgurr na Stri, now steep barrier slopes rose from the sea and vanished in swirling grey cloud. Squalls from the mountains played havoc with the confined area of sea, making bracing and balancing difficult on the final approach to the inner recesses of the loch. With the mist obscuring the peaks it was easy to become lost among the islets and bays of Loch Scavaig, and the magnetic influence of the Cuillin gabbro renders the compass untrustworthy. Unable to find the bay I was searching for, I camped instead near the waterfall where the short river from Loch Coruisk meets the sea, a dramatic site surrounded on three sides by sheer mountain walls and on the edge of the sea loch called Na Cuilce.

After a heavy downpour the force of the waterfalls running off the gabbro cliffs increased dramatically and their thundering growl carried across the loch to the tent where I sheltered, catching up on the log of my visit to Soay. The wind had veered now; the incoming swell was checked by a group of islets, and in the clear, calm water of Loch Na Cuilce, seals and porpoises gambolled beneath the increased power of the freshwater falls. Sitting on a rock between showers, in the changing light of an overcast evening, looking over this scene was a sublime experience. I took out my whistle and competed, with the double-echo, for the attentions of the Banshee; and, in her absence, gathered an audience of seals who treaded water below me in curiosity, their plump bodies just visible in the shadowy depths. It was well known to the old fishermen that the 'Selkies' or Seal People loved music and could be attracted by certain tunes, or by tears shed in the tide; so I played all the seal-tunes I could remember, but as the wind dropped the midge hordes increased by the minute. The hardest aspect of solo travel in Scotland must be that the appetites of these formidable predators are not shared among others but become focused on you alone. Under pressure I developed the inverted plaza mentality of going into the tent when the rain stopped, and venturing out again when the renewed fall reduced midge numbers to a manageable level. Midge repellent varies in efficacy with different human metabolic types, but then so does susceptibility to midge attack, and most brands are just bottled promises. Indeed I have seen a leaking tube of repellent gel swarmed black by midges as though they were addicted to the stuff.

There are one hundred and thirty species of midge on the Scottish islands, the most common being *Culicoides impunctatus* and *C. obsoletus*, both of which, although equipped to pierce the hides of sheep and deer, find human blood extremely palatable. I studied one individual closely as it drank its fill from my arm. It was a precise and delicately formed creature, but much greedier than I'd imagined until I remembered that, for egg-laying needs, only the female midge bites! And, as if in retaliation for my sexist thoughts she produced an itch out of all proportion to her size. Like many a lass before her, she drank so much that her body visibly swelled and changed hue from black to deep purple. In fact she doubled in size and I was astonished that she was able to fly away. Since she had already done her damage I let her live, but, for the itch that developed, I later believed she deserved a painful death. And on the subject of painful deaths, it was an old Highland torture to tie your enemy out on a still, humid night, stripped to the mercy of the midges, where he usually died, not of loss of blood, but of raving dementia.

There is no way to eradicate the midge 'problem' without extensive draining of the breeding sites, clearing tons of tide-wrack from around the shores and massive spraying with insecticides, which would destroy the physical beauty and delicately balanced ecosystems of the coast and wetlands of the Highlands and Islands. Dragonflies, whose favourite prey are midges and mosquitoes, help to reduce numbers, as do the carnivorous plants of the bogs such as butterwort and the beautiful, outlandish sundews, all of which would be adversely affected by any indiscriminate spraying or drainage policies.

The best method of personal protection is smoke, dense and dirty smoke, so at the nearest bay I bundled some driftwood together with a piece of 'drift-rope' and slung it over my shoulder like the 'poor man' who came in sight 'gathering winter fyoo-oo-el'. With waste-paper, wet heather and the rope, I soon had a roaring one-match-wonder going and was pleased with myself, as all the wood had been sodden. Simple triumphs. The resulting smoke drove our friends far away, and probably tarred my lungs into the bargain. Next morning, I awoke to weak sunlight through the rain, highlighting the colours in the heather, lichens and grasses and reflecting silver from the wet gabbro of the rock faces. Having sought refuge from the rain and from my wonderful furnace, all the midges were inside the tent! Quickly donning my wetsuit and working carefully beneath the flysheet, despite midges in my hair and eyes, I packed up camp. It was time for making tracks again.

I paddled out past the seal skerries where one group, in the strangest of contortions, seemed to be lying on the surface of the water. Only when they eventually wriggled, peristaltically, almost copulative, off did I see the fronds of umbrella-weed which indicated a shallow, submerged reef. As the tide rose, the seals had inched closer together on the highest point of the skerry in an attempt to stay dry as long as possible, heads and tails held high prolonging the sunning of uplifted whiskers and tails, and I was sorry to have been the usurper of such gloriously vain optimism.

It was an uphill struggle against wind and tide. Several times, but for the thin cord which attached it to my wrist, the paddle would have been whipped from my hands which became painfully raw from the cold and wet. It seemed a rather drastic solution, but at last the relentless 'itch and buzz' of midges was gone from my ears and hair in the baptism of wind and spray; it felt clean and exhilarating and deep breaths were at last free from tiny intruders.

Cumbrous breakers gathered and crashed on the notorious Sgeir Mhor reef which marks the exit of Soay Sound and guards the approach to Loch Brittle beneath the great headland of Rubh 'an Dunain. On this rampart in ancient times stood the long-sighted MacAskills, 'legendary watchers o'er the sea' and hereditary 'Lieutenants of the Coast' to the Clan Macleod of Dunvegan.

91

From this vantage they were able to give advanced warning of approaching storms and of impending attacks by the powerful and colourful Clan Ranald whose galleys assembled among the waters of the Small Isles. Even from the sea below the cliff there were views of the cloud-heavy peaks of Rhum, the great cliffs of Canna, and a new perspective on Eigg; and the skies cleared briefly to reveal a convoy of silhouettes on the far horizon – the Outer Isles.

About the west coast of Skye, the Scottish West Coast Pilot has this to say:

'Some of the wildest and grandest scenery ... weather can be pretty wild and grand too, and no yacht should venture out off the W. Coast of Skye unless its crew are confident of their ability to cope with heavy seas, strong streams and tide-rips, and to stay at sea if the visibility closes down at an inconvenient moment.
Ports of refuge are sheltered but widely spaced, usually separated by headlands with severe races off their ends; these get progressively severe towards the north.'

Despite the ominous forecast of Force 8 north-westerly gales, a cheerful English family launched me from Glenbrittle campsite with a handshake, a push and a 'bon-voyage' wave, and sent me bobbing off like a 'pooh-stick' on the considerable swell that remained from previous days; I was borne at speed, with only a semblance of control, along rugged inhospitable shores where stacks and pillars had been wrenched from the black basalt cliffs. The swell broke savagely upon the skerries at their base: grey explosions of sea launched themselves upwards to a height of twenty feet or more, becoming suddenly aquamarine with bold white fringes as the light penetrated the spray. It was a fascinating game to tempt fate by paddling as close to these geysers as possible without being drawn into their catchment area, and the resulting shower of spindrift was refreshing, but for almost ten miles there was nowhere I could have made safe landfall.

Three hours of steady progress along a dramatic sequence of Wagnerian ramparts brought me to the fragmented stacks and storm beaches of Talisker Bay, where I hauled out on the boulders for a photo-stop, for it suddenly seemed obvious that the full glory of West Skye was created to be seen in foreboding weather. The wind rose; I mentally matched the 'Anvil Chorus' to the scene before me, and the surf piled steadily into the bay; the gale was on its way. In fact by the time I'd snacked on biscuits and fudge, the surf had doubled in size and was roaring upon the shingle in vast ordered ranks of snarling fifteen-foot combers. Afraid of becoming stranded at Talisker, for the surf continued to grow, I packed and launched as soon as possible, punching clumsily but determinedly through two large waves and feeling the shock and misery of their cold fingers reaching down my neck. Shaking the spray from my eyes and pushing further forward I was suddenly blasted apart by a third monster wave whose height I could only guess to have been over fifteen feet.

When I Eskimo-rolled the kayak upright I was facing shoreward again with all the adornments of my deck strewn around the churning surf; the elastic deck lines had been torn off and it seemed I was lucky to have remained in the cockpit with a firm hold of my paddle. Frantically I set about gathering maps, books, flares and compass – all thankfully waterproofed and buoyant – before they were engulfed by the strong undertow from the steeply shelving beach. Shipshape again, and taut with adrenalin I tried once more, reversing through two heavy breakers and taking a third and fourth squarely on my head and back. These had the effect of knocking me breathless, tearing one hand off the paddle-shaft and tipping the kayak forward onto its nose. To avoid being carried back to shore by the surf I now had to throw my weight astern and keep back-paddling frantically until several more such waves had passed over me, and although I eventually reached the area of unbroken swell, I was so exhausted that I had to rest for several minutes with my arms on deck, unable any more to lift the paddle. Although the wind never quite reached the dreaded Force 8, progress was hard won that day against the relentless western seas: three and a half hours' hard paddling to Talisker, followed by my surf-battle and a further two hours of heavy slog to Loch Bracadale where I hauled out at the first place, Fiskavaig, that offered a level shore and a sheltered camp. In weary, cynical mood, I felt that 'Fiskavaig' must surely have been Gaelic for 'knackered'.

The award for the most spectacular coastal scenery, and for my finest single journey so far, had to go to the next ten miles of coastline along the Duirinish peninsula, known as 'MacLeod

Country'. Out past the islands of Tarner, Harlosh and Wiay and around the salient headland of Idrigill Point, beneath the two flat-topped basalt hills known – ever since a spectacular banquet – as 'Macleod's Tables', I paddled between three magnificent rock stacks. Towering to a height of almost two hundred feet like the basalt equivalent of the Statue of Liberty, they bear a striking resemblance to Victorian women in bustle skirts.

Although collectively called 'Maidens' they are assumed locally to be a mother and two daughters, and the skerries at their feet have long been known as a favourite haunt of mermaids. The Maidens are thought to embody evil spirits and have reputations as the wreckers of ships, although a local smuggler known as Campbell of Ensay, who used the skerries for his 'false lights', luring unsuspecting ships ashore, may have been eligible for a share of the blame.

Ostensibly to photograph the Maidens and the fantastic cliffscape ahead, but not unwilling to shake the fin of an accommodating mermaid, I contrived a difficult landing upon the Black Skerries. Although it was a clear, bright day, a heavy swell still manifested itself in wild force on the sharp rocks. After only ten minutes of mermaid hunting the skerry was almost submerged; each wave engulfed a little more rock than its predecessor before receding in a hiss of white foam. It was necessary to 'jump' into the cockpit as the wave receded – not easy, for it is a snug fit – and to paddle quickly clear of the rocks as the next wave lifted the kayak, fixing the spraydeck only when well out of harm's way, for the force harnessed in each wave was more than sufficient to dash the fragile hull fatally against the teeth of the barnacled skerry.

I spent the next hour awed by basalt cliff buttresses punctuated by stacks, arches and delightful geos where waterfalls tumbled into turquoise sea-pools, an eloquent retort to the bickering assaults of the ocean.

Towards the day's end the weather deteriorated quickly and, rounding Hoe Rape and crossing Moonen Bay (Bay of the Fairies) I watched the sea become frenzied off Neist Point where a jabbing swell and white-capped waves indicated the beginnings of a serious tide race. From the safety of Neist Point I watched the race develop over the next two hours; aggravated by wind-against-tide it grew to ferocious proportions and looked quite unmanageable. All night long, as the wind and rain lashed my little tent, I planned and plotted the tides and slept very little for worry over the necessity of getting around that headland. I rose early, but waited for slack tide before crossing the eddies and swirls which mark the site of a dormant tide race, and then headed northwards, against the tide, to Loch Dunvegan. Unexpectedly, I found a north-going tidal eddy close in by the cliffs of Glendale and Dunvegan Head and had crossed the loch, a distance of fourteen miles, in under two hours. Any tidal assistance was always a bonus, but to move so easily against the main stream is an unexpected boost, and I teased myself about the wasted worry and lost sleep of the previous night.

Pippa was there to meet me on the beach at Ardmore Bay, but I was in a sorry state. I had to remove the wetsuit immediately, for the salt-rash on my inner thighs had become so severe that I was unable to walk, and prolonged paddling in a damp cotton tee-shirt had caused it to carve deep cuts under my arms. But the bay was superb and, on a still evening, we sat on the cliffs above a classic double arch and tried to recite the names and order of the Outer Isles whose shadows floated on the far horizon. The 'Little Minch' looked tame and inviting in the sunset glow and we watched the rising backs of a pod of pilot whales at the mouth of Loch Dunvegan.

The next part of my journey involved crossing the Little Minch to the Isle of Harris in the Outer Hebrides.

This was a crossing of twenty miles, over one of the most unpredictable stretches of water; an ambitious solo journey, but quite within range if only the weather would hold.

Next day was the kind of scorcher that, even in the Hebrides, has you believing that the sun will last for weeks, so I treated it as a rest-day in preparation for the crossing and spent it lounging around that gorgeous bay with Pip. But in canoeing, if you offer fate a loophole it will surely accept, and so was wasted my one chance of crossing the Minch. Over the next few days cyclonic winds reached Force 8, the cloud base dropped and it rained pitchforks on Ardmore Bay.

Each morning I woke and considered making a dash for Harris, and each day it began to look more hazardous. I had repacked the kayak with another month's supplies and was ready to take advantage of the first window in the weather; it never came. While Pippa remained we made friends with a young bullock, explored Trumpan churchyard and Lady Grange's grave, frequented the Stein

Inn and joked about how badly I smelt, and how my sleeping bag had begun to go mouldy.

At night a ghostly bleating from above the tent was a snipe drumming wind through its tail feathers and, remembering the closing line of a poem by a friend in Connel, I thought 'Stormbound's what I don't mind being most.'

But Pippa had to leave and, in a new loneliness, I became aggravated at falling even further behind schedule, pinned down by gales and now extremely worried about the Minch crossing.

My friendly bullock rolled on the tent and buckled the aluminium poles, and in desperation I decided that, come wind or weather, I would move next day. If conditions were feasible I would tackle the Minch; if not, I would battle through the Vaternish tide race to Uig. It was in the new lightness of heart produced by positive resolve that I visited Portree, the island's main town, where, walking down the main street I found myself standing, staring at the outside of a craft shop. In my present state of indecision, and strongly aware of the force of natural co-ordination, I must have stood and gaped for several minutes without realising just what I was looking at, but the name of the shop was TIPPACANOE! That settled it, tomorrow I would head up the Skye coast to Uig and take the ferry across the Minch to Harris, but at that moment I needed a strong drink.

And so ended the second stage of my journey. With fresh supplies, new maps and tidal directions and a clean tee-shirt, the world of the Outer Isles lay ahead of me. Their fierce seas, desolate beauty and spectacular beaches represented an integral part of the expedition, the romantic challenge of authentic wilderness canoeing, and wilder sea passages than I had yet encountered. There had been times in the last month when this had seemed an impossible goal, and one that I could have shied away from without fear of reproach or criticism, but now I felt that the entire history of my canoeing development had led me to this point.

Machair and Traigh

'*I am forever walking upon these shores,*
Betwixt the sand and the foam.
The high tide will erase my footprints,
And the wind will blow away the foam.
But the sea and the shore will remain
for ever.'

('Sand and Foam', Kahlil Gibran')

Leaving Loch Tarbert, out past the islands of Scalpay, Scotasay
and numerous tiny islets, brought me again into waters
with wider horizons. Looking east, twenty miles across waters
traditionally guarded by the mischievous 'Blue Men of the Minch',

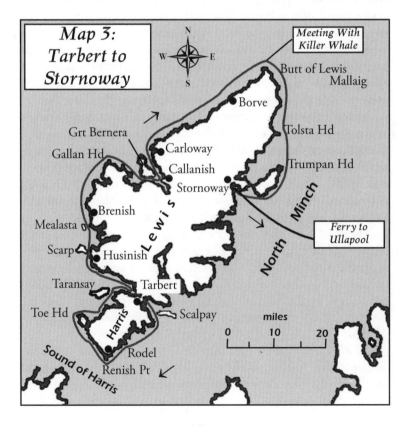

Map 3:
Tarbert to
Stornoway

Meeting With
Killer Whale

Butt of Lewis
Mallaig

Borve

Grt Bernera

Gallan Hd

Carloway

Callanish

Tolsta Hd

Trumpan Hd

Stornoway

Brenish

Mealasta

Scarp

Husinish

Lewis

North Minch

Ferry to
Ullapool

Taransay

Tarbert

Toe Hd

Harris

Scalpay

miles

0   10   20

Sound of Harris

Rodel

Renish Pt

and far beyond the enchanted Shiant Isles, Skye was still visible on the horizon, and a little late afternoon sunshine brought pleasant warmth to the east coast of Harris. The month of June was drawing to a close and, forging south past Stockinish Island, I was aware of many developments in my paddling since April on the distant Solway. I had become as intimate with the boat as with a long accustomed lover; I responded to her slightest movements, and she to mine, almost before they were consciously made. Through her subtle translations I learned some of the secret language of the sea, and developed a greater awareness of that frontier of land and sea we call 'the coast', an environment which had, in a special way, been ours, for almost two months.

Power came easily from shoulders, arms and abdomen and I felt stronger and fitter than ever before. A new capacity to plod on at an economical pace, a 'fifth gear' if you like, meant that mile after mile of sea passed almost effortlessly below the bows until, dodging out of a tide that was bound for the Sound of Harris, I sought haven in a small inlet called Finsbay.

As it dipped over the hills of the west, the sun's low angle highlighted fragments of the Archaean rock which protrudes all across the threadbare blanket of moorland which forms the hummocky moonscape of East Harris. Carrying my water bottle I wandered a winding track, flanked on either side by tiny lily-decked lochans where lapwings whirred and oystercatchers 'peeped' and the remains of the traditional blackhouse dwellings stood as barns beside the modern Harris croft houses. Built in weathered stone and heather-thatch, with no sharp outlines to oppose the wind, and rafters of driftwood twisted by the sea, the blackhouses look as though part of the rock-strewn land itself.

The land here was never rich, with soil too scant and stony to bury a body, and yet it was along this barren and soilless east coast that the population was concentrated by nineteenth-century landowners so that the rich pastures of the west could be stocked with sheep. Bright patches of green, or rich flowers, today mark the sites of lazybeds or 'feannagan' and send the imagination galloping through time to unearth the hardships and injustices that faced the island crofters after the clearances; for despite their name the creation of lazybeds involved a massive effort for a meagre harvest. Small patches were rimmed with peat turves, and the hollow filled with seaweed, sand and dung, all carried on the back in creels. Each patch of soil, to raise a sheaf of oats or a bucket of potatoes, had to be literally created by hand, but it was a method of survival that was to continue until the advent of convenience foods, deep freezes and a money-based economy on the islands.

Independently of archive and history text, the tradition of Hebridean hospitality has happily retained living substance, so that soon after approaching the little croft at the head of the bay with my request for a gallon of water I was seated by the fire at the kitchen table of Mrs Catherine Ross.

Her 'you'll be staying for a cup of tea' was more of a forceful suggestion than a statement of 'second sight', but Hebridean 'tea' equally deserves a place in immortal folklore and is not to be missed, for the reference of the word is far wider than on the mainland. Within minutes I was tucking into homemade scones, oatcakes and several mugs of strong, hot brew under the jealous gaze of Bobbie the labrador, who could apparently see no reason why such service was denied to him.

The homely chat and kitchen warmth began to make me drowsy and I was concerned that the kayak should be hauled securely above the incoming tide; but I was only able to leave that croft by accepting a bag of fresh scones and butter and promising to let Mrs Ross know when my journey was safely completed, for until that time she would not sleep for worry. 'It's a good thing you're not married – and it's sorry I am for your poor mother!' Smiling, I made my way back to the tent, my hands warmed by the scones only slightly less than her kindness had warmed my heart; but it was not 'kindness' that I ate so gratefully for breakfast next morning.

Outside the shelter of Loch Finsbay a heavy swell began to trouble me as I headed towards Renish Point, the southern tip of Harris. An increasing south-easterly from the Minch, and decreasing visibility, made the five-mile journey to Rodel a hard push and by the time I reached the shelter of the small harbour my lungs were heaving.

The Presbyterian Sabbath had dropped a shroud of silence and inactivity on Rodel and it would have pleased me to 'call it a day' and make camp, leaving the Sound of Harris until conditions in the Minch were more settled, but with the tide at an advanced ebb the sea was unhappy in the little harbour and broke heavily on the rough, bouldered bays. Landing would have meant damage to the kayak, if not also to its occupant, so after a snack and a breather in the lee of a small islet I opted for an exposed dash around Renish and into the Sound.

Beyond Loch Rodel the large and random waves of the Minch were bottlenecking at the entrance to the Sound, curling threateningly and snarling white at the caps. Negotiating the restricted passage between the Point and the various islets and reefs which lie offshore in that heaving sea was for all the world like riding a rollercoaster, with the proviso that the responsibility for avoiding those needle-like rocks remained firmly in my own hands! Around the point and the sea was now surging from behind. *Lean forward. Steady. Move WITH the waves. Whoa! Keep off those rocks!* In poor visibility, among dangerous reefs, with cold and fatigue growing, you can't fight that kind of sea with impunity for long, so I hauled out at a small, shingled inlet. Although only three miles from Rodel, I had at least reached the Sound of Harris; another significant corner had been turned and tomorrow, weather permitting, I would head towards the open Atlantic. Mist obscured North Uist and the islands south across the Sound, but I could still see the Minch piling up and breaking at the windward bottle-neck through which I had so recently passed. With tomorrow's timing in mind I sat on the rocks above the Sound and tried to interpret the flow of the tidal streams. Not a particularly rewarding study! It seemed that different streams were flowing in opposite directions at the same time. Furthermore, where these streams met there were whirlpools and overfalls which appeared and disappeared without regular pattern. Despairing of this practical investigation I consulted the Admiralty Pilot Guide Book, always a guru in times of doubt; however it only confirmed my confusion: ' ...In the Sound of Harris tides defy concise rational explanation.' Despite a night of rough weather and a pessimistic forecast, blue skies and light winds welcomed the first day of July. I climbed a knoll and ate breakfast looking out across the Sound to the uninhabited islets of Killegray, Ensay and Pabbay, breeding haunts of the huge Atlantic grey seals, the 'Ron Mor', the biggest land animals in all Europe. Bleached cumulus anvils were reflected in the reformed body of water and I no longer sought concise rational explanation for it was to be a day of constant beauty, sunshine, and one of the best day's canoeing I'd ever had.

At full tide I watched a solitary cruising shark make its way westward and marvelled at the sheer size of it, the largest fish of northern seas. The distance between the first dorsal fin and the yawing tail must have been twenty-five to thirty feet, and its bulk greater than a bus, I guessed, before it submerged with the slow sinking action characteristic of the sharks. Using pieces of a broken wooden ship-mast as rollers I eased the loaded kayak across the rocks and into the water, following the shark out past the Carminish Island group. It was an easy morning's paddle with none of the delinquency of yesterday's seas; the novelty of sunshine and calm water continued to amuse me, and the white beaches of Killegray and Ensay winked through a water-level haze as I pushed through the Sound, Atlantic bound.

Taking advantage of the continuing warmth I stopped for an early lunch at a bay of soft sand beneath the distinctive bulbous promontory of Toe Head. The seal islands of Shillay and Coppay had joined the panorama, but over lunch I was preoccupied with the name of the beach, Traigh na *Cleavag*, and thought it would be a good name for a nudist haunt. Then a short walk across a narrow neck of pasture-land opened, to the north, a view which hit me with sledgehammer effect and almost reduced me to my knees with its blistering perfection. It was a cameo image of Hebridean paradise, that incomparable combination of deep blue water, shading shoreward into aquamarine, fringed by lightning-white surf on beaches of a hue of gold that was almost pink. Never had I seen anything so right. A series of such beaches stretched north, like an ornate golden bracket, to the Hills of Harris, now hazy in the sun's reflection, and the Island of Taransay framed the view to the west. The deep green of the Machair, with its carpet of clover, buttercup and tormentil, added a final dimension and completeness to the scene and I was in love all over again.

I turned and ran back to the beach across the machair, clover-heads catching and pulling between my bare toes, for before I could become part of that scene I had to bring the kayak around wide Toe Head.

Even on such a profoundly calm day, there were the first signs of a true Atlantic swell. Lumbering regular breakers arched their backs and vented brief lives against the island shores with powerful explosions of spray which told of the stubborn power source always latent below an ocean whose surface showed barely even a ripple. It was my first taste of the restless Atlantic, almost forty million square miles of water representing thirty per cent of the earth's water-cover and extending north-south for 13,000 miles, half the earth's circumference, where some of the worst storms of which nature is capable are born. Between here and the east coast of Canada I knew there was nothing but two thousand miles of open ocean, across which many early Harris emigrants, forced from their land, set off, but never arrived on the other side.

It was a pleasure to be able to run the bows up on sand without fear of damage to the fibreglass and my eighteen-foot companion was dwarfed by the sheer extravagance of Traigh on which we eventually alighted. After several journeys to ferry essential gear I had established a camp high on the Machair with a view across sweeping dunes to the island of Taransay.

Here was isolation, 'true solitude without a policeman', and in a primal response to the seductive qualities of sun and sand (and perhaps an unacknowledged memory of 'Dr Stan') I removed my salty clothes and relaxed my legs and shoulders with a loose jog along the beach followed by a baptismal plunge in the Atlantic. As the cold brine eased my aches and chaffs and soothed sunburned extremities I reflected on what had been a day of success and beauty such as I had seldom, if ever, experienced. All the time of my growing up on the east coast I knew that somewhere there had to be a place like this, and that some day I'd find it: the far western seaboard of the Outer Hebrides. I found it to be everything I'd ever dreamed it might be, and vanished into its welcoming smile, with a slight inward apology for leaving it so late.

◆ ◆ ◆

On the seventh day of Creation God discovered in his waistcoat pocket a handful of islands which he'd meant to place somewhere in the South Pacific. Rather than break the rule of Rest on the first ever Sabbath he threw them randomly to earth where they landed, and remain to this day, in a straggling group fifty miles to the west of Scotland.

This local story carries the flavour of reverence for the Sabbath and perhaps more than a hint of sarcasm for the neglect the islands have experienced over the years – for the more cynical crofters claim that HE still doesn't know where they landed! – but it also points to a recognition of features which at times make the Hebrides seem far from Scottish. Vast populations of invertebrate marine life in the fertile seas to the south west of the Hebrides give rise to the enormous drifts of white shell-sand which form the great sweeping Traighs and countless idyllic small beaches throughout the isles. There are places where tropical plants and palm trees flourish, and turtles and coconuts come ashore courtesy of the Gulf Stream, and in the rare periods of warm weather it seems that Scotland and the cold North Atlantic must belong to another hemisphere.

For me what underlines this fantasy is the presence in the Outer Isles (also on Coll, Tiree and rare parts of the mainland) of the unique sandy pasture habitat known as Machair. The Machair proper lies beyond the beach and the dunes where peat, seaweed and animal matter combine with mineral and shell sand to give a fertile sward of grasses and low-growing perennials such as clovers (red and white), buttercups, vetches, orchids, lotus, bedstraws, eyebright, milkwort and wild thyme. In summer the smells and colours of the wild flowers are quite amazing; it is the last stronghold in Britain of the rasping, elusive corncrake, and there is even a distinct sub-species of bumble bee which has the wonderful title of *Bombus jonellus hebridensis!*

But in many areas the Machair is under serious threat. When the stabilising influence of the marram grass is undermined, dry sea winds soon gain mastery and the sand is easily dispersed. Rabbits are a problem for this reason, but more frequently the dangers are man-made; overgrazing, ploughing and the pressure of wheeled traffic and caravans on the Machair must be avoided if we wish to preserve this fragile piece of misplaced tropical paradise.

❖ ❖ ❖

The weather-edge of the Atlantic is a true frontier where conditions can change with alarming suddenness. 'From the west comes the grey wind, the wind of sighs and sadness,' which can bring dramatic weather from the Atlantic in a matter of hours. I awoke to find that high winds and low cloud had replaced yesterday's serenity; someone had stolen Toe Head and Traigh Scarista had become a mist-shrouded battleground of crashing surf and spume. My gentle turquoise ocean was now a seething slate-grey wilderness and both the surf and the wind that drove it, continued all day.

I decided to pass the day in an adventurous and novel way, and as the water warmed on the petrol stove I lathered my face for a shave. Halfway through this rare operation I had an unexpected visit from two strangers, teachers on holiday from Edinburgh. They seemed unabashed at having to converse with that half of my face which was slowly emerging from the froth, and indeed only when I had excavated the whole ME did they resume their walk; the suspense had surely faded into anticlimax. So I waited until they were long gone before streaking across the beach for another dip in the tumbling surf. Luxury was being able to jump into a clean sea one hundred yards from the tent, with a brew on the stove to come back to. I took great delight in jogging around starkers to dry off, for again I was confident that there was no one for miles around.

Just then I became aware of a distant buzz, and within minutes a bright orange helicopter, like a massive dragonfly, sauntered down the Sound of Taransay, parallel to my beach and extra-low because of the mist. So close was it that I could discern distinct figures within and, forgetting my vulnerable state, I returned their cheerful wave with everything I had. Only later, with the radio news, did I discover that there were celebrated visitors to the Isles that day; *'Prince Charles, Lord of the Isles, and Princess Diana landed in Stornoway this afternoon before proceeding to Harris and North Uist by helicopter'!* I had to laugh when, months later, a friend mentioned that he thought Diana seemed to have acquired a certain maturity recently.

As the tide ebbed I followed its path to where a group of sheep had gathered on the edge of the vast tidal flats which stretch from Scarista to Toe Head. At full ebb it was a curious sight to watch this group set out across the wet sand, confident in their purpose of reaching fresh pasture on the far side, nibbling nutritious tit-bits of seaweed along the way.

It was shearing time on Harris and instead of a matted yellow-brown, many of the sheep sported close-cropped stubble of dazzling white. Each had been newly painted with the indelible dye that serves as a flockmark. In normal practice a flock might be marked with a red stripe, a blue flash or in some other distinctive way, but it was typical of Hebridean ingenuity and humour to produce at that time, a group in bright red, white and blue; a tongue-in-cheek patriotism was being expressed by means of an animal which is nowadays so often kept solely for the government subsidies it brings to the islands; the Royal visit was being fittingly acknowledged. For my part I'd begun to distinguish a plain sheep from a pretty one and rapidly came to the conclusion that I'd been watching them too intently for too long.

❖ ❖ ❖

The shape of a wave and the nature of its breaking are largely a function of the wind which gives life to it and the curve of the beach on which that life ends. The surf dumped heavily on the steep lower section of the beach; there was a gradual accumulation of mass before each crest curled rapidly over and the whole ridge came roaring down in total collapse, booming like a cannon as air was trapped within its break. The violence of a dumping surf and the undertow created as the water sluices beneath the oncoming waves can make launching a small boat a hazardous proposition, so I resolved to be up early to launch with the gentler breakers on the level section of the beach at high tide. At 6am, however, bullying wind and rain persuaded me to roll over and go back to sleep. When I woke later and eventually broke camp the surf had reached its most critical height and was thundering down upon itself with a destructive abandon more than sufficient to crush a fragile fibreglass hull.

Several attempts to launch failed miserably and much energy was wasted before I was able to break through the surf – backwards – and I was quite exhausted as I began to paddle up the coast. For two hours I paddled in a heavy swell which held an implied force of frightening scale, shooed on from behind by a sharp, wind-driven rain, five miles to the beaches of Luskentyre. Probably the most famous in Harris, these scimitar curves of sand which stretched in every direction were a fierce wilderness in the face of the salt-laden spray that howled in from the sea that day. As I sheltered for lunch in the dunes at Traigh Rosamol, the high, rocky north end of the island of Taransay emerged briefly from the mist and then was gone.

All along the steep shore of West Loch Tarbert I dodged beneath frothing clifftop cascades which plunged from out of the low cloud base and, despite the weather, it was a spectacular approach to the isthmus at the Harris capital whose eastern side I had left five days ago. The wind reached Force 5 overnight and the tent leaked at the seams from torrential driving rain. All my gear, including the sleeping bag, was again damp from the saturated air of recent days and, with no immediate prospect of drying it off – thinking particularly of the flourishing mould on my bag – I packed it up wet. By late morning I was heading for the island of Scarp.

With a strong and constant wind from behind, it was good fast paddling out of the West Loch, pushing forward – almost surfing – on a predictable running sea; and several waves drenched me, breaking impatiently over my back despite my frantic efforts to keep pace. The tiny Soay islands and Taransay (now four miles south) absorbed much of the ocean's wrath, but such swell as remained was breaking badly off the salient headlands and, beyond the protection of the islands, produced a quartering effect on the boat. This gives uncertain handling and unpredictable surges, but I was coping well, reacting quickly and instinctively making the minute adjustments of balance necessary to compensate for awkward assaults of sea or wind. In fact I went into automatic several times, snapping out of it at one point to realize that I'd been in a trance, singing and whistling in a rough sea, for over half an hour! And yet these were exactly the kind of sea conditions that used to scare me rigid, where I expected to capsize any moment. The kayak was leaking badly, through the worn fabric of the spray deck which was constantly chaffing between my lower back and the cockpit rim, and soon became pig-headed in the literal sense as each lean was exaggerated by the shifting ballast effect of several gallons of sloshing water. I followed the rollers into Govig Bay where I found sand and shelter, took the chance to empty the kayak thoroughly and, having already covered a good ten miles, declared an official lunch-stop.

Earlier in the day I had seen a small pod of whales out towards the Taransay Glorigs, a group of spume-lashed rocky islets to the west of Taransay; now as I explored the beach I assumed that the grey shape on the foreshore must be a stranded baby whale. But when I reached it I found, not a whale, but a common porpoise, not stranded but dead. It lay amid the thongweed at the morning's high-tide mark and blood ran fresh from its mouth which hung open in the cheeky half-grin typical of its kind. Blood also ran from the tail end where the flukes had been cleanly severed. There were no signs of the slashing violence of a killer whale or shark attack and I assumed that this fellow must have tangled with the anonymous propeller of a fishing boat and, without the propulsion and control provided by the muscular tail, had been washed helplessly ashore. It was the first time I had been so close to a porpoise for, despite the name, they are not as common as they once were, and I was fascinated by the myopic, unassuming eyes, the oozing blowhole and the almost P.V.C. feeling of the skin. Along with it on that beach I felt kinship and sympathy as I imagined the hopeless struggle of its last hours; something had gone from the day and left a porpoise-shaped void.

But we weren't alone for long before some wild young Hebridean girls came whooping and screaming over the hill and, immune to my sentimentality, displayed a far more practical attitude by kicking and slapping the porpoise before deciding that it was an ideal bench-seat from which to pass giggling Gaelic comment on this strange man and even stranger boat which had arrived on their beach.

Another launch, another struggle, but after bouncing the next headland in a buoyant, dry boat I surfed into Hushinish Bay. North of Hushinish is a wilderness of mountain, moor and loch and the map showed Hushinish to have the only telephone I might reach for several days, especially if the weather closed in; my radio was useless in such a hilly area. On landing, however, the locals informed me that the kiosk had been withdrawn by the G.P.O. six weeks ago, and a young woman charged me a pound to make a quick 'all's well' call to the coastguard. I felt little desire to remain in 'civilization' any longer than was necessary, so I stocked up with fresh water and rode the surf around Hushinish Point and into Caolas an Scarp, the channel between Scarp and the Harris shore. How convenient, I thought, to be able to choose your dwelling space according to your degree of unsociability at a particular time!

The beaches on Scarp itself, flanking a little stone pier, a graveyard and some empty crofts, looked inviting, but only half a mile across the Sound at Traigh Mheilein was a spectacular stretch of golden sand backed by high dunes, machair and hills, and I was aware of no inner strengths that would allow me to pass this one by! It was in landing at deserted beaches such as this that I really

107

appreciated the fantastic opportunities provided by the wandering kayak, for the nearest land-track ends at Hushinish; here would be isolation enough to suit the most anti-social of moods. Even without a clearing in the weather there was a balance of natural beauty that I found supremely reassuring, but the cloud cover did break around early evening and a brief shaft of sunlight sent me scuttling across the beach for a dip before preparing my meal.

From my camp on the dunes above the beach I watched the flood tide push through the narrow Caolas an Scarp and the evening cloud thicken to the west of the island. The inevitable oystercatchers were already on wave patrol, strutting along the tide-line in a red-legged clockwork frenzy with outsized clothes-peg beaks. When a child draws a perfect 'M' in the sky he is drawing not a gull but an oystercatcher for sure. I could have watched their comical antics for hours, but whenever I ventured onto the beach or along the dunes they would break into abject panic, flying wide circuits with rapid wing-beats and a high-frequency 'peep-peep-peeping', landing with none of the gliding surefootedness of the gulls, but with a little trot like a man alighting from a moving bus. This same nimble trot is used to great purpose on the sea's edge to avoid either losing an outgoing wave or being swamped by an incoming one. From a distance it appeared that they had some all-consuming passion for the scientific investigation of the sea's edge; from a closer vantage I found that of course it was a 'consuming' passion for as the tide brings the sand-burrowing worms to feed near the surface the oystercatcher advances and, using that garish orange beak like deftly handled chopsticks, extracts a worm delicately from its sandy lair. Sometimes they even flushed the sand from the worm with a little shake of the morsel in the oncoming wave before re-swallowing it and retreating –all with the feet still dry!

At the north end of the beach was the head of an oystercatcher chewed off at the neck – probably the work of a fox sneaking up on a sleeping bird – and thereby emphasising the size and strength of the beak. In fact my feeling was that I'd found a beak with a head attached! It is a valuable tool, also used to snip open the muscle that closes the shells of cockles and mussels to the extent that fishermen in some areas consider the birds unfair competition! I found, indeed almost stepped into, several nests placed, as is the bird's custom, on the most open and vulnerable pieces of shingle in the area; two contained the remains of recently hatched eggs. Walking back to the tent, sinking to the shins in soft shell-sand, I picked up a plastic fishbox to use as a seat, filled it with some items from the boat which lay on the strand contented, and climbed the dunes to my grassy plateau.

From my fishbox pew I was able to watch a pair of gannets or solan geese fishing the tide-race at the north end of the Caolas. These were fascinating, collapsible diving birds, fully grown with jet black wingtips contrasting vividly with the ivory-white bodies and nicotine-yellow heads, and it almost seemed as though some frivolous creator had applied mascara to those deep-set eyes. Although not circling as high as I've seen them do in the past, their diving technique was second to none. But if they were not swallowing their catches below water, then they were extremely unsuccessful, for I never saw either to emerge with a fish.

Before the days of echo-sounders fishermen were often able to detect the presence and size of a shoal of fish by the antics of these birds which, far from being inconspicuous, can be seen from a long way off. It was even possible to tell the species of fish present, for a replete gannet, too full to take off from the water, will regurgitate the contents of its stomach when prodded persistently with an oar! With no such devious and practical purpose in mind I spent pleasant hours watching for sheer entertainment until the northern channel filled and the gannets moved elsewhere. In the channel south of Scarp the turquoise clear water revealed the bloated cigar shape of a massive grey seal idly treading water vertically as they do, and scanning the beach. Inexplicably I stood up and waved 'Hi' to it and, as it progressed leisurely up the channel, it surfaced several times with puzzled glances and nasal snorts. It gave that enchanted land-longing look that only a seal in water can give – the nearest thing to which is the sea-longing look in the face of an old sailor – and I thought of the curse of restlessness that is said to haunt the Selkies even in that element which is their home. For the seals were once land mammals – related to dogs and bears – who returned, long ago, to the sea. They retained the need to return to land to bask and to breed, but it is said that the movement of the tides is now ingrained in their souls.

The Selkies – the seal-people – are said to come ashore at midsummer, to shed their sealskins and assume beautiful human forms, and to dance on the beaches under a full moon. If you can steal a skin the Selkie is unable to return to the water and is trapped in human form. Though many a lonely fisherman found himself a beautiful wife in this way – and it may be that they were happy together for a few years – their hearts in the end were always broken when the Selkie, like the seals, at last returned to the sea.

No scientific study can remove the mystery and aura of the seals and their dream-like effect on us land-dwellers. Wherever they have lived and bred we find places named after them, and legends of Selkies and amorous seals play a unique part in coastal folklore the world over. Even today there are places where these stories are not too inconsistent with the unmouthed beliefs of people who know the seals better than you or I will ever do.

Well that was the extent of the evening's unlicensed viewing; it had brought a new meaning to 'what channel shall we watch?' (How about 'the one between Scarp and Fladday'?) and now it was time for closedown. As the universal test card twinkled in the Hebridean sky I curled up in my bag and listened to the sounds of the shore – now just oystercatchers and surf – remembering, just as sleep took over, that I hadn't eaten!

Next morning brought more stormy weather so I proposed, and seconded, an administration session, arguing for its importance to expedition safety. The motion was carried; several maps, pilot books, tide-tables and compasses spread themselves around the tent and began to reveal the caprices of the tides as they related to my routes for the days ahead. I lost track of time but had finished Traven's *White Rose* and George Mackay Brown's *Greenvoe* before the sky began to clear steadily from the west. The tide, on full spring strength, had ebbed to reveal a sand-bar across to Scarp south of Fladday and had reduced the Caolas an Scarp to a narrow burn-like flow. Down on the beach, although I had covered the same ground countless times the previous day in unloading the kayak, the wind-blown sand had erased my tracks and the high-tide had left an immaculate virgin sweep of golden pavement.

Without tracks to explain its existence the kayak would seem to have dropped from the sky and I was loathe to betray my own presence in this virgin world by such mundane evidence as footprints. But I was curious to know whether anything interesting had been brought ashore by the high spring tide of the previous evening. It

The kayak at rest. Port Errol, Cruden Bay.

'Bottoms up!' The author during surf training, Seacliff, North Berwick. (Photo D.MacDonald)

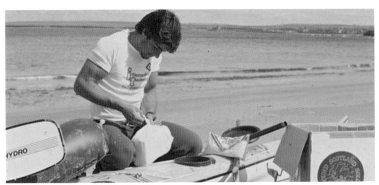

Packing the kayak with supplies for up to one month at a time.

Typical 'one-night stand' camp on the Galloway coast.

West Skye Waterfall: 'an eloquent retort to the bickering assaults of the ocean'.

Puffins, comical sea-parrots of the Scottish coast.

Landing through light surf.

The 'Small Isles' panorama from Sanna Bay, Ardnarnurchan.

'A cross between Ivan the Terrible and Popeye'. Tex Geddes at Elgol, Isle of Skye.

Sunset at Loch Dunvegan, Isle of Skye

Hebridean seascape, west Harris, Outer Hebrides.

Camp above the incomparable machair and beaches
of west Harris.

The kayak weaves among a tangle of islands.
(photo S. Nicholls)

The ancient standing stones of Callanish, Isle of Lewis.

Atlantic storm beach and sea-cave.

'Something had gone from the day and left a porpoise-shaped void'.

Natural Crunch takes on a passenger.

Brian Wilson rests on a
Hebridean beach.
(photo D. Rewt)

Tea-kettle simmering on a
driftwood fire.

North Coast Sunset.

was a clean tide-line such as is found today only in exceptional situations – none of the ubiquitous condoms and apparently immortal plastic debris that are so common on beaches of lesser virtue further south.

I wandered the high-watermark, so clearly defined by small piles of kelp; and the delicate tracery of red carragheen branches amid the foam, skimming pebbles across the smooth sweep of damp sand of the intertidal zone. One apparent pebble of purple-brown kidney colour, about palm-sized, squatly heart-shaped and excellent for skimming, escaped its fate by virtue of its curious lightness. Of course it wasn't a pebble at all, but a large bean known as a mollucca.

I had read of the mollucca bean and at that moment recalled the bizarre circumstances of its origin and journey, for it was a seasoned traveller with a great tale to tell. The seed of a tropical plant, it had begun its life on the distant shores of the Caribbean or the Gulf of Mexico, fertilized by exotic insects and nurtured by tropical soils. In the tale of its journey lie secrets of the complex ecology of the Atlantic, the inhabitability of Northern Europe and the Viking discovery of America! I sat myself down on the warm shell sand to absorb what I could from the saga.

There is a vast artery of warm and foreign water, one thousand times the volume of the Mississippi River, and yet known to the ancients – who feared its currents and malevolent monsters – as 'Oceanus': the 'ocean river'. Today oceanographers write of the Gulf Stream – part of a great system of interlocking currents originating in north equatorial waters – which crosses the Atlantic and whose North Atlantic drift current brings warmth and energy to Northern Europe. Were it not for the influence of this thermal engine the throes of the last Ice Age might still be upon us, and we would share not only the latitude, but also perhaps the subarctic climate, of Labrador. The northward spread of civilizations in Europe (not to mention trees, plants and animals) must have been greatly influenced by this invisible godfather, not only in terms of climate but in many more subtle ways too.

At the bottom of the oceanic food chain are the multitudinous plankton (from the Greek for 'wandering') which multiply or 'bloom' in areas where there is a mixing of waters – such as the upwellings caused by the continental shelves – or where warm waters interact with cold.

By influencing the conditions which stimulate and encourage the growth of plankton, the North Atlantic Drift increases the fertility of the northern seas, regulating and sustaining the life of the Atlantic. For in turn the plankton give rise to rich fishing grounds, influence the migration of the plankton-feeding great whales and basking sharks and their smaller fish-eating cousins, and many other links in the complex chains of marine life.

The Norse who colonized Iceland and Greenland in the tenth century knew little of the Gulf Stream as a carrier, but must have observed its effects in the foreign woods, weeds and seeds which found their way to those shores. In times when the world was not known to be round, and unlimited journeying brought the distinct threat of coming to the edge of the world, it was not pure intuition that sent the Norsemen reeling into the unexplored wastes of the western ocean. Rather the mollucca bean, and others of its kind stirred a belief in unknown lands beyond the seas. Curiosity bred greed, romance and speculation, and seeking trade, reputation and new lands they swarmed down the British Isles and annexed Dublin, the Northern and Western Isles, the Isle of Man and the Norman country of France. Southwards they forged into the Straits of Gibraltar and beyond; and who knows, but for the influence of tropical flotsam, Greenlander Leif Erikson might not have happened upon the western land of North America those five centuries before Columbus.

The Norse were not the only invaders of Hebridean waters; many tropical species find their way north by way of the Gulf Stream. The Portuguese Man o' War is frequently seen; the sting from its trailing tentacles is well known amongst fishermen. Similar to a mild burn it can prove fatal in cases of multiple stinging. This jellyfish may be the natural prey of the large drowsy half-ton turtles occasionally sighted in Hebridean waters. One was washed ashore in North Uist in 1900, to the great bewilderment of local crofters, and another was found at Port of Ness, Lewis, in September 1987. Giant squid, swordfish, tuna and tropical sharks have all been known, along with bamboo stems, sargassum weed, coconuts and exotic wood-species. But it is the seeds and beans which have aroused most interest, and frequently superstition.

One bean known as the Virgin Mary bean was said to change

colour when witchcraft or the 'Evil Eye' threatened and was often worn as an amulet around children's necks. Neither this nor the mollucca are by any means common on Hebridean shores, but the mollucca, being larger was more commonly found, and was often turned into a useful snuffbox. Many fishermen carried them as a protection against drowning and the dishonourable intentions of mermaids.

Far be it for me to discourage the carnal advances of a woman of the sea, but as drowning held no charm I pocketed my bean for the future. I have it to this day and can vouch for its efficacy in so far as neither fate has yet befallen me!

Just as a crimson sunset began to glow in the west, it seemed that its full splendour would be masked by the island of Scarp which occupied the immediate foreground. In 1930 when St. Kilda was evacuated, Scarp became the most westerly inhabited island of Britain, at which time there was a small ferry from Hushinish pier. In 1971, following the trend of depopulation of outlying islands, Scarp too was abandoned. Lazybeds, croft houses and a small graveyard are visible today, and a misprinted tourist brochure I read proudly claims that apart from summer visitors Scarp is now completely UNINHIBITED!

In 1934 Scarp gained the distinction of a bizarre twin childbirth. The mother, delayed by stormy weather in reaching hospital, had her first child on Scarp. It was two days before she could be taken to Stornoway where, on the Monday, her second child was born. Now, Scarp was of the district of Harris, in the county of Inverness-shire, whereas Stornoway in Lewis belonged to the county of Ross-shire. The twins therefore had the dubious but unique honour of being born of the same mother, in different weeks, on different islands and in different counties!

But the story goes on, for in honour of its twin childbirth fame, Scarp was chosen later in the same year for the world's first ever inter-island rocket-mail experiment. Philatelic history was made on 28th July 1934, when Gerhard Zucher demonstrated the capabilities of his prototype mail-rocket. A special 'western isles rocket post' stamp was issued for the occasion, and of course many local people turned out to view the spectacle.

The button was pressed and, with a bright flash, the rocket burst into flames; charred mail was strewn around the island foreshore, and the crowd creased with laughter; Zucher wept.

A second trial in the relative privacy of Amhuinnsuidhe Castle proved no more successful, but the disillusioned Zucher took himself off to Peenemunde where the innocent postal rockets evolved into the slightly less farcical V2s which were showered on London in the Second World War.

The combined fires of many rockets might not have kindled such a sunset as mellowed behind Scarp that evening as I watched.

A Hebridean sunset, like a blazing fire or a beautiful girl, is an event which is particularly difficult to immortalize either on film or in words. As it deepens and matures, perhaps, over hours, one is never sure when it has reached its peak and when it has begun to subside; there is no linear succession of distinct stages which might be captured by a series of pictures, but if you wait too long a unique event has passed – for ever. Yet it is not just a remote event of the external world, for in its apparent welding of heaven and earth it corresponds to a pattern in the human psyche. It is the incomprehensible fusion of spirits made visible, and the mythological Tir nan Og – infinite promise of the west – made plausible. Like the best form of theatre you don't just 'watch' a Hebridean sunset, you participate in it.

The Scarp sunset began to look as though it might just escape from the north edge of the silhouetted island; I was quite caught in the suspense and even switched off Iain Anderson's show on the radio. Then suddenly it was FREE and the cloud-ribbons blossomed with pinks, with purples and with deep blue of a shade I'd never before seen. The waves lapped gently, unimpressed, on the beach, but the ebb flowed peach-coloured through the Caolas an Scarp. At the final curtain I retired to bed, as I hoped to make an early start for the Isle of Lewis. It was to be my last experience of the magic Hebridean sunset, for the weather closed in until long after I had ceased to face westward on the Atlantic seaboard of the Western Isles.

Dragons, Elves and Killer Whales

*'I walked with my reason
out beside the sea
We were together but it was
Keeping a little distance from me.'*

(*'The Choice'*, *Sorley Maclean*)

Like the rings on the trunk of a tree, like the points on the antlers of a stag, or the Queen's telegram in the proud frail hands of an old woman, the dominant rock of an island is the nearest thing to proof of its age. For this reason the Outer Hebrides, or Western Isles, have been called the oldest islands in the world. Certainly they are elder statesmen compared to the Inner Hebridean islands, such as Rhum, Eigg, Skye and Mull – mere upstarts of comparatively recent volcanic activity – and are among the few places on earth where pre-Cambrian rock formations are actually exposed. The Lewisian gneiss of the Outer Hebrides is reckoned to be about 2,800 million years old, 1,400 times older than the primate lineage of man, and among the oldest and toughest rocks in the world.

At one time the gneiss and younger rocks together formed a great landmass reaching out at least to Rockall, two hundred miles to the west of Lewis. As the ice caps melted and water levels rose, the Outer Isles were first isolated as one long island, then as a chain of islands separated by drowned valleys. Lastly came the crafting influences of the ice sheets, scouring smooth all but the highest summits. So, at least, runs the modern myth of the geologists; but science moves so quickly these days that it's perhaps best to keep an open mind about such things.

Scandinavian tradition tells that when the world was young and the Scottish Isles were still attached to Northern France, the acquisitive Norsemen decided to tow this beautiful piece of land home with them. They mustered a fleet of three hundred and sixty-five ships, manned by giant sailors and attached them to an arch in a rocky precipice. The cable was formed from the hair of a thousand maidens, cut by sharp shells and woven by the women

115

who lived in the sea caves of Norway, for that is the strongest fibre known to man. The maidens, for maidens they had to be, were captured and then given their freedom in return for their hair; however by oversight one of them was not the virtuous, untouched damsel they'd assumed her to be and her hair, in consequence, was weaker.

The ships towed for all they were worth but unfavourable seas and high winds caused them to drop some land at Ireland. Then the wind caught on the hills and broke the beautiful land into many fragments of rocky isle until all that was left was the island we now call Harris and Lewis. Finally the flawed strand of hair gave way, weakening the whole rope as it broke and leaving the Islands to flounder where we find them today.

My favourite alternative also concerns maidens, but attributes the primeval origins of the Outer Isles to the slaying of a nine-headed dragon. This dragon had carried off nine maidens to its lair in mid-Atlantic. But he had chosen unwisely, for one of them was betrothed to a young hero who then came in search of the unfortunate dragon. Now this hero was owed a favour by an Each-uisg (water-horse) – which were commoner then than now – for he had spared its life on an earlier occasion.

Together they searched the ocean until they found the dragon, whereupon the hero, safe upon his Each-uisg, cut off the nine heads before stabbing the dragon fatally through the heart.

The giant carcass, being too large to handle, was left for the sea to dispose of, and was nibbled and pecked by birds and fishes until only bare bones remained. These bones eventually turned to stone and so became a refuge for fish and a home for birds. Slowly earth formed on them and, after many years, man too came to live there. Today some of the smaller islets such as Scarp, Taransay, Scalpay and Mealasta are the remains of the heads which tumbled nearby when the dragon was slain, and the fragmented chain of the Isles is the fossilised skeleton itself.

Whichever legend you adhere to, geological or mythological, the joint island of Lewis and Harris is today by far the largest of all Britain's offshore islands. Because, of course, they are different ends of the same island, distinguished historically by the consequences of different ownership, and geographically by a high mountain chain and deep-cutting sea lochs, but one island nonetheless. It is therefore all the more remarkable that their shorelines should be so strikingly different.

Northward of Mealasta Island the Lewis coastline becomes rugged and inhospitable. In contrast to the soft Machair and Traigh shores of West Harris, here are great cliffs of between two hundred and five hundred feet, punctuated only rarely by sandy bays and rocky reefs, broken only at the inlet of Loch Roag, and issuing ultimately at the northerly Butt of Lewis headland where the brewing Atlantic meets the stormy Minch in a perpetual battle of currents. Unprotected by offshore islands, exposed to the full Atlantic swell, the coast here is a frontier of conflict, and possible landing places are few and far between; travelling by kayak, one finds oneself committed to bursts of ten to twenty miles in technically extreme conditions.

Winds from the west have a 'fetch' of two thousand miles or more in which to stir life into the ocean, which is therefore seldom without swell. Low pressure systems, such as that south-east of Iceland, are well-known breeders of storms whose winds whip the sea into great waves. These rollers periodically rise and batter the coast for days on end with damaging surf, making boat handling, landing and launching extremely hazardous.

One doesn't see pleasure boats west of Lewis, nor are there many boats on shore; and if ever there were piers, harbours or anchorages on the western seaboard they are long gone, for the people of the island seldom venture out upon a sea so malevolent and dangerous. For the islanders, at least in days gone by, the sea was an element whose sheer power over life and death bordered on the supernatural. Until comparatively recently (in the seventeenth century) at Eoropie near the Butt of Lewis, regular offerings of ale were made to the sea god Shony, and the islanders still bear an inherent cautious respect for this most unpredictable of tyrants.

The wind was in the south-west and the tide pushing with me as I rounded Eilean Fladday and crossed the sea area called Braigh Mor, leaving Harris behind. In Braigh Mor a large and unwieldy sea was running, but had I been able to foresee my fortunes for the rest of the day the discomfort at that moment would have seemed minimal indeed.

It took only a half hour to cross the four-mile stretch to the narrow Kyle between Mealasta and the Lewis shore where the sea was bottling through in gulps of some ten feet or more. Riding a gulp, I passed through unscathed but well-waterlogged; the spraydeck was leaking again and pints of water already swilled about the cockpit, affecting stability and balance. Very soon it would need emptying but I hoped to reach up past Grenheim Island, only another couple of miles, before going ashore. But with the assistance of a boisterous sea it took so little time to reach Grenheim that I decided just to push on, thinking 'there's bound to be a bay just around the next headland'; and so I headed confidently into the most deplorable blunder of the trip. Weakening from hunger and effort, I was well overdue for a snack-break and struggling to control a seriously waterlogged boat. Most dangerous of all, I had taken an unnecessary risk in paddling beyond the area of Lewis coast covered by my folded deck map; and that mythical bay just never materialized.

Suddenly, off the headland of Aird Brenish, I found myself at odds with a gigantic swell which was actually breaking from a height several feet above my head. With no possibility of turning back – conditions were too severe – and nowhere to go ashore, it seemed that in this recipe for disaster there was no one ingredient in my favour. As the waves hit me again and again, each time harder it seemed, I became very frightened, but there was a primal simplicity in the choice: fight or die.

I was over a mile out to sea, for inshore the waves had the driving power to dash me against the torn rocks and reefs which ringed the cliffs of Brenish. So in every direction the sea was a heaving, seething mass, shaded grey where gradients were sheer on massive walls of moving water, and white where the leaning crests collapsed into tumbling cauldrons of froth. Small steep waves formed on the sweeping slopes of the largest uprisings and called for extra vigilance. It was like a nightmare in which one's capacity to move is restricted, for although desperate to escape from that area, I had to use most of my energy in bracing the paddle against assaults which threatened to capsize or submerge the kayak. Each glimpse shoreward revealed the same angle on the Brenish headland: very little progress; and yet my strength was failing fast. Steadily, water seeped in.

For the three miles around Aird Brenish the thunder of the waves dashing on offshore skerries filled my ears like the rush of blood that is the roar of fear itself, but after an hour I realized with some surprise that I was WHISTLING! In the worst of seas, despite an urgent survival situation and the constant need to respond, my mind seemed to have delegated my body to get on with it, and meanwhile had withdrawn to an inner space where there was music and peace; an automatic-pilot facility and a semi-meditative distance. I'm certain it was a reaction to the fear and stress of the situation, and an automatic buffer against the effects of mental exhaustion which, added to the physical, might have been a disastrous overload.

The final stretch, around Aird Brenish and nearing the sanctuary of Camas Islivig, was the worst of all; a confined area where the swell reflected and broke in several directions, stirred and torn by skerries and Dubhsgeirs. Then, as I lined up on the race which forged dangerously between two serrated skerries, a great heaving 'mother' of a wave picked the boat up and threw me, high and fast, over the skerries and into the sheltered bay of Islivig, only just clear of sharp rocks which would undoubtedly have torn the kayak apart.

Stunned and exhausted, but relieved to be out of the firing line, I bobbed panting in the bay, shoulders hanging limp, forearms leaden. The cockpit was half-full now, but I couldn't go ashore to empty as the shores of Islivig were rough-hewn and bouldered, and lapped with the frenzy of the ocean; I couldn't risk any kayak damage in such a remote area.

I ate four Jordan's crunch bars, changed the map and, sculling for support with one hand on the paddle, I pumped the kayak dry. The map said I'd have to go on; the only suitable landing would be at Mangersta, a further three miles around another wild headland, Aird Fenish. It was the rational rather than the comfortable choice, but it took no self-discipline, no iron resolve of will; my trembling, adrenalin-riddled body just limply obeyed.

Rounding Aird Fenish meant confronting the manic breaking area again, stirred now even higher by an increasing westerly. But with an emptied boat, a brief rest and a bellyful of biscuit-power, it was an easy ride compared to the last battle, and once round the point I could see Mangersta Bay. But my troubles were not over yet; from over a mile seaward the waves were building up and running powerfully towards the beach.

I played cautious, leaning back as the rising shoulder of a wave passed under the boat, and paddling at less than wave speed for fear of being swept shoreward, out of control, by a rogue crest. I needed to reach Mangersta upright and in one piece, with an undamaged boat, otherwise all was lost.

Occasionally an early-breaker would swamp over me, kick me sideways or toss me in its trough, easy meat for the next one. Shaking salt from my eyes and recovering my bearings, I had to act fast to anticipate the onslaught, but at least now it was directional.

Soon I could hear the booming of the surf on the beach and, a hundred metres away, a wide line of froth marked where the sea met the sand. These waves were mature, had travelled long and far for this moment, and on reaching the surf zone began to rear high and steep as though gathering all their strength for the final violent act of their watery lives. Some, passing beneath me, were now so steep that they stood me almost upright on the nose of the kayak, making it all but impossible to lean back out of their insistent shoreward drive.

With a fun-canoe, I'd have paddled hard, caught a wave on the rise and surfed the last eight hundred yards to the beach at exhilarating speed. But I had a heavily-loaded boat of eighteen feet to consider; its back would break if capsized in surf. On the other hand I realized that I couldn't maintain a safe 'sitting on the fence' position for long, and decided to make a run for it on one of the smaller six-foot waves.

Right. Go! Paddle hard; caught it. Brace... Keep it steady. Wooah!... We sped shoreward until, about fifty yards from the beach, I was overtaken by one large wave, a ten-footer, and looked over my shoulder to see the hanging white jowls of an even bigger breaker bearing down on me.

I couldn't surf it! – it would somersault me for sure. I had only time to swing the boat sharply broadside and to plunge my paddle-blade deep into the body of the wave with all the strength I could summon. All my weight and a little more, and the full weight of the kayak too, hung on that paddle, then the wave broke. The world was all white foam which jarred, churned and tumbled the kayak sideways towards the beach. The last of my strength was focused on my paddle-arm, the only hope of stability, in that washing-machine surf. And then ... daylight! As the break dissipated I flicked upright from the hips, and immediately another was upon me, smaller me, smaller this time. I swung the kayak forward and caught the wave under control, steered myself now at high speed towards the beach, finally dodging off and paddling in on a foot-high ripple to beach securely at Mangersta.

On jelly legs I stood ashore, watching mammoth breakers destroy themselves again and again on the sand before me, and was thankful for all the training days I'd spent in the surf of the east coast. Regular surfing in a small canoe, apart from being fun, is probably the best preparation anyone could have for survival in a rough sea. But I knew I'd just survived for over six hours in an open sea bigger than any I'd ever dared to surf in, and reflected with irony that in this case my day's journey had been more than adequate training for any surfing I might care to do in future!

I regretted the stupidity that had placed me in an emergency situation out there, but was pleased at my performance under extreme pressure and was relieved to have been able to handle the situation. The struggle seemed to last forever and it is for the extraordinary demands of an unexpected fight of that sort that one really needs fitness on an expedition.

Nevertheless the day's trial had left me shattered and I lost no time in setting up camp and getting into warm, dry clothes. I was jumpy and reflexive, reacting excessively to minor scares but, camped now above the bay, I calmed myself with some hot soup and croutons and took a walk out to the point at Sheilavig.

A fulmar tipped its rigid wings on a low fly-past and drops of water fell from its tubenose beak. Down on the beach a group of herring gulls stood stubbornly at the wave limit, facing into the wind and spray and awaiting the bounty of the storm as it was churned up at the seaweed line. They looked like bargain hunters waiting for the opening of a January sale.

The tide ebbed, turned and began to surge back, each new breaker expending its energy just that little farther up the beach; it was an old story. As long as there have been oceans their waters must have been stirred by the passage of the winds as they sweep from pressure system to pressure system across the earth's surface. Each wave, as we see it roll in, has its own life history, for some have journeyed across half an ocean before reaching our shores; but as a wave enters shallow water the end of its life is already near. For the first time it feels the drag of a shelving sea floor; its speed slackens; its neighbours crowd in towards it. Suddenly it arches its back, sucks in its chest and, when it becomes one-seventh as high from trough to crest as the distance to the next crest, it begins to topple forwards and collapse in a screen death of foaming whitecaps and crashing noise. But many an old story has a new message when seen in live performance.

The churning of the Atlantic had not eased any, but the distinct, periodic booming had given way to a continuous rumbling roar, increasing and decreasing in volume, like the sound of a busy motorway. And, although I still used city-images as similes, months in the canoe had altered my perceptions; changed the priority of the categories through which I ordered the world around me: I had become receptive to different influences.

The sounds of the sea are not always the soothing paradigm of poetic fancy, but have as expressive a range of vocabulary as any animal. The evening waves in the Sound of Scarp had been the dormitory sounds of deep and noisy sleepers whose breaths swish and echo in an otherwise silent darkness. But today there was aggression in the sea. To me the tones of discontent and malice were unmistakeable; they were of a hungry, wild force which had been cheated of its prey.

In the west white fleeces rose into high cumulus anvils, grey at the edges and occasional patches of sunlight spilt silver across rising whaleback wave-ridges. All was lovely to watch, but I felt no peace. I knew I would have to punch through that surf and fight that swell beyond. Then there was the dreadful prospect of rounding the next promontory and, eventually, the Butt of Lewis and its notorious currents. I was very conscious that the day had been, in its way, an epic. I had confronted, and survived, the Lewis Atlantic under its own rules, and that evening I was a step wiser, a step more cautious and respectful, and a notch closer in spirit to an understanding of the sea itself. But how long could I keep this up? Each day I was confronting and surmounting situations beyond my experience. How long before I put myself in a position I just couldn't handle? Surely it had to come to that. I kicked among the broken fragments of purple jellyfish and the phallic remnants of seatangle 'clubs' that littered the foreshore in deep foamy piles, and thought on how I could so easily have been part of a similar scene of debris on a forlorn beach somewhere; who would have known?

❖ ❖ ❖

Morning brought another storm-bound day, a day off the sea, though not one from which I gained any rest or recuperation; instead it brought an ebb of spirit, courage and enthusiasm. I lay in the tent hour after hour while rain lashed at the flysheet. The light outside betrayed the greyness of mist and cloud, and the endless roar of the sea filled me with fresh fear and dread. The thought of eventually facing it all again was awful; overnight despair, a reaction to yesterday's struggle, had begun to rot my confidence from the inside out.

The idea that morale and emotions tended to operate in cycles was by now familiar; ever more closely my spiritual highs and lows seemed linked to the elements. It was a romantic thought perhaps, but at that moment, in dismal weather with no sign of improvement, not a welcome one!

I made a hasty breakfast then, in an attempt to break the gloom and lethargy with exercise, donned damp shorts and clammy, cold T-shirt and jogged off across the Blacklands (peat hags) of Lewis. It was good to be out of that stale tent air. Heavy rain washed the fire smoke of recent days from my unwashed hair, dripped tar-like down my cheeks and collected in my mouth – a strange tasting mixture of smoke and salt. I thought of the old blackhouses, without chimneys, where the peat smoke of the open fires collected in the thatch of the roofs. A heavy rainfall, seeping through a mature thatch would sometimes leach out the tarry mixture and drop black smoke-clots on the inhabitants. I shook my sooty thatch and laughed at the thought. I was pleased at being able to tackle the rolling hills of Lewis at a good pace; my legs had not become as weak as I'd expected after ten weeks of kayaking, but constant salt-immersion had made my feet soft and spongy and I soon worked up a couple of large blisters. Back at Mangersta I had a quick dip in the sea, made coffee and biscuits and spent the afternoon reading and cowering beneath the majestic Atlantic roar.

The 6pm forecast was for more high winds, and conditions deteriorating in the far north west, with no change in the long-term outlook. Feeling a second wave of depression welling up I went to gather driftwood for a fire and was caught in a heavy downpour that the BBC called a 'moist north-westerly airstream'!

Back at the tent I fell asleep for what felt like hours. When I woke my watch read 8.30 and the surf sounded heavy, the weather still 'moist'. I had mentally condemned myself to another day in the tent, and rolled over to go back to sleep, before I realized that this was the same day – it was 8.30*pm* – I'd only slept for an hour! Totally disorientated and unsettled, this was unlike me. I had begun to act outside my normal sphere of control. The pressure was gradually wearing me down and for a short while I hardly knew where I was.

Loneliness was seldom a problem when at sea, nor when the weather was easy, or things were going well. But when bad weather, bad luck or the constant fear of danger begin to tear at the fragile shell that protects the self, it begins to hurt. Loneliness hit like a cold wave-break and I ached for someone to cuddle, to whisper with in the dark, to reassure me; someone who could lead my mind gently away from the weather, the sea and my chances of surviving the next headland. I drew a picture of Pip as I remembered her, while carefully removing dozens of earwigs from the inside of the damp tent, placing them gently outside, unharmed. Then I wandered several miles to find a phone. I felt emotionally quite unbalanced even before I phoned Fox's biscuits to give an update on progress. Then I heard that the P.R. team who were dealing with my trip had all been sacked for attempting to set up their own company on the side! It seemed hilarious, and alone on the Lewis moor I burst into hysterical laughter. Yet, less than an hour later, back at the tent reading, I was down again. An earwig crawled onto my face and bit my eyelid. It was the last straw. Frightened, lonely, misunderstood even by the earwigs, I realized I was crying.

The following morning brought no change in the weather, but for no apparent reason there was an improvement in morale; perhaps the shadow had passed again.

The surf was still monstrous and the swell beyond marched to the tune of a Force 6 westerly. Mangersta was still dismal and thick but I spent the afternoon sitting on a fishbox, playing my whistle and looking out to sea. From dry paper and wet driftwood I made a good fire and baked some potatoes for tea. I stole a chocolate bar from next week's food pack and felt a warm glow of mischief. I knew then that if I spent another day on that beach, the fear of the Atlantic, that had been growing since my fright around Aird

Brenish, would get a firm grip – that I might not be able to go on – and I resolved that tomorrow, if conditions were no worse, I would move.

Down on the beach at evening there was a young crofter woman watching the waves, her hood up against the wind and rain. We stood and talked quietly until the cold and damp had us both shivering and the light had begun to leave – just the two of us standing close on the edge of a wild sea, on the edge of the planet for all I knew. Suddenly she moved closer and pushed her hood aside to look at me through a damp heath of brown hair. 'The peats have been on all day and I've more hot water than I know what to do with. Would you like a bath?' She said it with a melting smile that felt as good as the thought of hot water itself. There was, in that warm offer, something of a thinly-disguised sexual intimacy that I had desperately needed to feel at that moment. It soothed an area of neglect in me that was itself a large part of my loneliness. And in the symbolic 'me too' of my acceptance was perhaps the reciprocal assurance that she too sought. It was an allegory of the deepest human sharing, already more satisfying and full in its implication, than a one-night stand or casual pick-up attitude could ever be, and as such did not need to become physical.

I had a long soak in a deep bath which put warmth back in my bones; then we chatted by the peat fire till the early hours when I stumbled back across the machair and beach in darkness, and slept recharged.

On the third day the rollers came in regimental rows, twenty feet high and dappled green, white manes snarling from their shoulders, wave faces advancing like great bulldozer shovels until each in turn curled forward, overbalanced and plunged to its death with a booming roar.

Ducking my head, I forged out for the surf zone as though charging towards cannon-fire; I had to get beyond the break-line before the day's journey northward could even begin. At the first attempt I was forced backwards and thought the weight of the break would surely collapse my spraydeck. I tried again and again, built up momentum until *smash!* a new wave would hit me squarely on the face and chest, stopping progress dead or even carrying me backwards, leaving me centred in the path of the next monster. I'd never seen surf this big! Almost Hawaiian in scale. There was only one solution. I paddled hard for the breakline, outstaring, from a long way off, a massive seething crest as it prepared to unleash its life-fury. Just as it broke I threw my weight to one side, capsized the kayak and hung there upside down. The wave passed. Bringing the paddle around in a wide arc, I Eskimo-rolled upright and immediately began to paddle seaward again. I met the next wave just before it broke and repeated the capsize and roll. This time I paddled madly seaward and managed to ride over the third wave before the crest had formed. The next was the same and I knew at last that I was beyond the breakline. It had taken thirteen attempts in a half hour of all-out effort. I was drenched, trembling from effort and the spraydeck had leaked badly. But there was no time to rest and recover for the day's journey had not yet begun. I was heading northwest up the coast with a Force 5 blasting into my face and stirring up a wild sea, but before long I began to feel confident and relaxed. Rollers of horrendous power growled and spent themselves on the many offshore skerries among which I picked, at first, a tentative path. The sea, as it hit shallow water, churned and tumbled back upon itself in a mass of white foam that soon engulfed me. The noise of the continuous sucking and spewing was oppressive but I was filled with the gambler's strange compulsion for risk, the desire to attempt ever narrower, more difficult passages. Passing between cliffs and coastal islands in a heavy sea is always an anxious and exciting gamble and a maze of skerries and slightly submerged reefs at Eilean Molach, filled with surging white foam, tempted a tricky manoeuvre. There were sharp skerries only four feet on either side of a narrow lane of sea and at the speed the water rushed through the passage, a slight brush against the rock would have torn the side from my fragile fibreglass shell. Also like a gambler, I could not now say why I did it, but at the time it was real heart-in-mouth coastal exploration; the nervous tension was severe but, after a couple of days' gloom and fear, the challenge was irresistible.

With everything in violent flux around me; nowhere to focus the eye's craving for stability; a universal 'crashing' louder than any disco, and no refuge save foul rocks and inhospitable cliffs, what, I wondered, would be the consequence of losing my nerve? And would I know in advance if I was going to crack?

Round Ard More Mangersta the Atlantic swell hit north-west

facing cliff-walls and reflected back upon itself to produce the magnified area of wave interference known as 'clapotis'. The sea seemed to have lost all form and became a leaping white field of confusion. Great ridges and valleys kept appearing and reappearing among a range of watery mountains. When two crests met there was an instant thunderclap of force sending columns of white steaming water high into the air; where troughs coincided huge chasms appeared, into which I dropped again and again. I rose and fell at incredible speeds, but seemed to be in control of everything except my stomach, and within an hour of hard work I'd traversed and broken free of the clapotis field. Camas Uig with its beautiful stretch of sand opened to the east; it was time to recompose tattered nerves, empty the boat and take a snack.

It was on this superb traigh that a crofter, walking home along the sands, made one of the most important archaeological finds in Scotland last century when his cow, stopping to scratch with its horn in a sand dune, uncovered a small underground chamber. Peering into the dark opening the crofter could just make out a large group of 'people', only a couple of inches tall and dressed in the clothes of another land. It was 1831 and, being of a superstitious nature, the crofter assumed he had stumbled upon a 'parliament of frozen elves'; he panicked, quickly covered them up and ran home to his wife. She however, being more adventurous, returned to the spot and carried the whole assembly of little people home in a peat-creel, whereupon the local Presbyterian minister appropriated the little figures as Papish relics.

Both the crofter and the minister were mistaken, for in fact it turned out to be an unrivalled collection of excellently preserved chess pieces of Viking origin. Carved of walrus ivory to represent twelfth-century Norsemen, they gave historians valuable clues on the dress, weaponry and customs of the period. Sixty-seven were acquired by the British Museum, and in 1888 the Edinburgh National Museum bought eleven pieces. Subsequently they have become known as the 'Lewis Chessmen' and are the prototype of many expensive modern imitations.

But what if the crofter was right? After all, he did get the first look, and it may have been the sudden daylight and the sight of the cow which froze the little people in action, and I wondered as I walked back towards the boat, how many other little elven parliaments were in session beneath my feet.

To reach the next possible haul out, at Loch Roag, I had to paddle a further four miles up the north-west facing coast. It was not a pleasant thought for outside the sheltered bay I could see that the swell was now even heavier, but I knew that if I thought about it too long I'd lose the courage to continue. If I could only get around Gallan Head, Loch Roag should provide shelter for a day or so.

There was an extensive area of foam chest deep at the breaking point of the rollers in the mouth of Uig Bay, but soon I was beyond it, out in the open sea again, and moving carefully from one area of severe clapotis to the next.

Off Gallan Head, the most exposed buttress on this coast, I could see two thirty-foot trawlers making heavy weather of it. Their great bulk caused them to sway and roll to alarming angles and I would not have swapped places with their crews for anything. In the kayak I offered no resistance to the swell or the great surging lumps of clapotis. I was but a cork on its surface. In an unbroken sea, no matter how rough, if you can only remain upright and retain directional control the chances of comfort and survival are greater in a kayak than in a large vessel. In a twenty-foot open boat, John Ridgeway and Chay Blyth even survived the Atlantic Hurricane Alma where many a large yacht or trawler would have almost certainly come to a watery end.

My deck compass registered east, then south east, and I knew I had rounded Gallan Head. For the first time all day the jagged sea around the cliffs became rounded and regular, and I was at last able to relax, to uncoil knotted stomach muscles and hooked hands, and to eat a few more biscuits.

It had been another difficult day – only fifteen miles in four hours – but again packed with valuable new experience; so I could handle severe clapotis off a major Atlantic headland, and I could negotiate the treacherous passages between razor-edged skerries in a boisterous swell; perhaps then there was some hope for the Butt of Lewis.

The wind reached gale force again next morning and drove rain among the many islands deep in Loch Roag, but sheltered by Pabay and Vacasay, and the mass of Great Bernera, the inner loch and its tangle of islands remained unruffled, misty and mysterious. Working by compass, I crept between the vague forms of Vuia Mor and Vuia Beag and caught a rushing tide through Sruth Earshader under the bridge that links Great Bernera and Lewis.

Gripped by a feeling of pilgrimage, of 'quest by water', almost as much as by the tide race itself, I headed towards the 'pagan wonder of the Western Isles', landed at a bleak rough bay and traversed the final stretch, overland, by hill and bog, to the ancient standing-stones of Callanish.

Two centuries older than the Egyptian tombs, fourteen centuries older than the Great Wall of China, Callanish is unique among megalithic monuments. Only fully uncovered in 1858, it is perhaps the most perfectly preserved megalithic site in Europe, and is the only one of cruciform shape. The main avenue is over three feet long and formed of twenty-five stones; the cross arms are made of 4 stones each, and the central circle comprises thirteen tall pillar stones, the tallest of which stands fifteen and a half feet above present ground level.

It may be that early Christian missionaries added extra stones to form the crucifix arrangement, but the local story is that the stones themselves are the remains of a meeting of heathen giants turned to stone by St Kiaran for refusing to be christened.

The purpose of the site might never be known, but it had associations with various Druidic rites and a cremated human corpse was found within the central chambered cairn. Marriages consummated within the circle were supposed to be particularly fertile, and fertility gatherings are still held at the stones on 1st May, the Celtic New Year.

Many of the stones are weathered and lichened into curious and beautifully marbled patterns by centuries of crotal and erosion, and walking the long avenue alone to stand in the centre circle gave me a strong buzz which made my hackles bristle. But the sense of the primordial, which was just developing, was destroyed when a bus load of American tourists arrived. Not surprisingly, I was an object of curiosity myself, for the sight of a rubber-clad figure, which appeared from the mist at the seaward edge of the marshland and then disappeared the same way, must have been a little alarming! It was a hard paddle on the final five miles up East Loch Roag to Carloway, wasting much energy in attempting to keep a straight tack against a quartering south-westerly wind; but eventually I reached the narrow, serpentine channel of the inner loch and followed it to where the rivers Heidagul and Carloway formed a small bay. The weather was still hostile, but, in a routine which had long since become second nature, I beached, pitched the tent, washed in a peaty burn, changed into warm clothes and had soup and biscuits on the stove, all within an hour of landing.

In a moonless twilight I watched fascinated as a rowing boat pulled stealthily across the bay and beached below my campsite. It had all the potential of a commando raid except that the two boatmen were blind drunk, stumbling and swearing and clad in bright yellow oilskins. They had spied my tent from a distance and, since they were obviously bent on some undercover operation, had come to check me out. As they squatted unsteadily by the tent I explained my journey. 'Man, yer madder than Tom Maclean!' they decided – not a description to be unduly proud of as Tom Maclean, (or Moby Dick as he is known in the north west) was that summer sitting alone on Rockall, a lonely lump of rock two hundred miles out in the Atlantic, on a six-week vigil that was supposed to establish British sovereignty of the rock!

Just then a pair of bright headlights swept around the Point and swung across the bay as a van followed the coast road. 'Eyeball!' cried Jimmy, and when my eyes had recovered from the dazzle my two companions had disappeared! Dark again and they emerged cautiously from behind the tent. It turned out that they were of a breed of men with whom I was to become better acquainted in weeks to come – men who suffered from a pathological inability to distinguish landlord-fish from tenant-fish – salmon poachers. They had originally thought that I was a watcher, an 'eyeball', guarding the loch against their exploits, and were obviously scared witless of the searching headlights of 'the wee fucken yaalow pickup'.

It was a highly risky business avoiding the squads of specially hired heavies who protect the landlord's lucrative interests during the critical salmon months, but satisfied that I at least posed no threat to their nocturnal prowls, Colin and Jimmy stumbled and cursed their rabbit-holed way back to the boat and rowed off to 'shoot their net' under cover of darkness. If caught they risked being charged, fined and severely beaten up, and having nets, boats and vehicles confiscated; they had in fact received a beating and lost a £300 net just the previous week! Yet off they went, heavily inebriated and wearing the most visible of gaudy overalls I could imagine; they thought my journey mad, but I seriously wondered who was taking the greater risk!

After the 12.33 shipping forecast I tried to get some sleep, but about 2.30am there were sounds outside the tent. 'Iss this where the party iss at tonight?' – Colin and Jimmy were back with a carryout, roll-ups and some crisps. Both were weavers by profession – for most of the famous Harris Tweed is actually woven in Lewis, and indeed I had heard the clack and rattle of the looms from the corrugated sheds of Carloway earlier in the evening – and it seems that risk was a part of their daily lives as well. In order to produce enough tweed to make a living the gamblers among the weavers use illicit motors instead of foot-pedals to weave the 'guaranteed hand-woven in the Hebrides' tweeds, and an early-warning system operated in the village to give advanced notice of the arrival of quality-control tweed inspectors.

I learned much from our little ceilidh, but after a couple of hours they left to take in the nets at the turn of the tide, and I never heard whether they were lucky that night for I slept soundly on beer and whisky and was early off next morning.

◆ ◆ ◆

Over twenty miles of rough coastline lie between Loch Roag and the Butt of Lewis, with only a few coarse-shingled beaches to provide a safety net for the committed boatman. The barren moors of Lewis, a wide-open, hill-less, treeless land of peat bog and pools of water-lilies, give way to a single-track coast road along which runs a string of simple crofting townships. The coast is shredded and frayed, and fringed with broken reefs; only the horizon is unbroken and unlimited, stretching surely forever across the wide Atlantic.

It was a long slog up this coast, although south-westerly winds of over 30mph made the passage lively and brisk, fast and furious, in a following sea. I rested where I could, taking advantage of the shingle bays at Dalbeg, Bragar and Barvas to empty water from the boat. Towards the north the jagged coast slopes into the water causing the waves to break fiercely on the shallow constricted area of reefs, a true demolition site which I rocketed through, running a gauntlet of near misses. A goldfish swimming between the teeth of a shark would know the same feeling of vulnerability mixed with insolent exhilaration, but one mistimed dodge could have meant a broken boat and an uncomfortable swim.

My object for the day was to put myself within striking distance of the Butt of Lewis, and after twenty miles in a sea which was becoming progressively unmanageable, I opted for a difficult landing on a steeply-shelving storm beach at Borve, less than ten miles from the Butt. I was knackered, and had collapsed on the huge boulders which comprise the storm-shelf, slowly summoning the strength to haul the boat free of the high-tide mark, when some local kids appeared to examine this strange piece of human flotsam that had been thrown up on their beach. Together we made light work of hauling the canoe; and we shared some fudge and biscuits, watching the peaty burn tinge the breaking waves in the bay with its tea-coloured water.

Full gale warnings next morning deterred me from launching. From the beach I could see an immense break forming, fang-white, all along the coast to the south, and the foam-lined skerries of the bay looked like the gaping jaws of a rabid dog, only it was me who was hydrophobic! The few miles I could have stolen wouldn't have been worth the risk or the effort; it was a day for detailed planning for the Butt of Lewis, my next obstacle. It was the highest of spring tides and, backed with a full westerly gale, the sea would rise well that night. I helped a local crofter pull his heavy wooden boat – the only one I'd seen on the western seaboard – above the highest possible tide line and secure it with ropes. Then we sat in the lee of the wind and watched a large sea-otter prowling and marking territorial rocks around the ruined Borve slipway. I tried not to think too much about the Butt of Lewis. But Alec MacDonald was the typical Hebridean pessimist, giving an initial impression of downtrodden misery and hardship, complaining about the weather, the land, the salmon, the crofters' lot and, of course, the drunken bum of a brother who had nearly drowned them both in the boat last week! I began to think he must be the most miserable man I'd ever met, but it seemed that sharing your grievances rather than your joys was the easiest form of light conversation with a stranger. And all the time he was working towards something, for pessimistic warnings were a paradoxical part of his special brand of hospitality. His tirade turned at last to the sea, 'Of course, you'll not be going around The Butt in a wee boat like that?'

'Well…'

'Man, man don't be crazy! It's the very devil of a place; you'd not get me round there in a thirty-foot fishing boat!'

'Ah yes, but...'

'And look at the weather we've been having! When was the last still day? The sea will not be quiet for weeks.'

'I...'

'Oh, no, no...' He turned his back on me and marched away, mumbling, towards the village of Five Penny Borve.

It was disconcerting, but more than a little interesting too, to come across this attitude. I thought of how successful business and professional men would often say, with doleful regret in their voices, 'If only I'd had the chance...' 'If only I was younger...' or 'If it wasn't for the wife ... the kids ... the job...' and of tourists and friends who almost unanimously encouraged my adventure with elements of 'Good on you!' or 'What a tremendous experience!' But among the people of the islands, the crofting or fishing populations, general admiration, envy and encouragement were largely absent. These people knew the sea; their ideas of romance and adventure were tempered by memories of friends or relatives lost at sea and, most of all, they knew their local patch in its worst moods. My journey must have seemed like an arrogant flaunting of all their worst fears.

Local knowledge and advice is always useful to the traveller in strange and dangerous areas, but it was discouraging to find that Alec's information on local currents didn't tally with my own calculations based on the Admiralty Tidal Atlas and Pilot Guide notes. If I had listened to Alec I would have accepted his offer of a lift by tractor across to the east coast and avoided the Butt altogether. But hadn't the Galloway fishermen laid poor odds on my chances at the Mull of Galloway? Hadn't I come a long way and gained a lot of experience since then? And could the Butt of Lewis really be any worse than some of the conditions I'd already encountered on the Lewis shore?

1 thought about it long and hard, and eventually reasoned that local advice against attempting a dangerous sea must largely be based on the assumption that the brightly-coloured fibreglass kayak was in the same class as an open rowing boat, or even a rubber dinghy. Perhaps they even saw it as a sort of toy; but I knew how it could fight in an open sea, and in the end it had to be my own

judgement which told me whether I could cope with these winds in that sea around this area.

A similar attitude of personal discretion had to be exercised with regard to weather. That night the shipping forecast gave another gale warning for the Hebrides area, but the Radio Scotland forecast gave only 'winds light, south westerly'. Going by local evidence next morning, white-horses churning to the far horizon told of strong and dangerous winds off the exposed coast.

Furthermore as Alec had hinted, the cumulative effect of several days' strong westerlies had left a very heavy and persistent swell along the entire western seaboard; even if the wind did drop today, sea conditions would remain too serious to tackle the Butt.

That evening the sun set on a ragged, storm-tossed Atlantic horizon, and Alec was down at the river mouth with a careful eye for a certain king of fish. 'Ah, it's yerself,' he said. 'Ye'll maybe have seen sense by now.' Without looking at me, he gazed reverently out to sea and I found it difficult to fathom whether he was still searching the bay for rising salmon, or now picturing a small kayak among the currents of the Butt of Lewis. We passed several minutes in silence before I knew that he was even more worried than I was.

'Ach there's nothing to be had here,' he said, then turning to me, a smile ambushing his normal expression, 'Do ye like pop music?'

'What?' But he just nodded and again walked off in the direction of Borve. And so it was: his sister ran a long, hot bath for me, we shared a meal of milk and scones and we all settled down in the tiny crofthouse to watch Bob Geldof's late night Live Aid concert on T.V.!

When I left Alec had been silent and preoccupied; he'd done all he could to change my mind about the Butt, but he'd seen that I was determined to go.

The eastgoing tidal stream from the Atlantic reaches 6 knots around the exposed headland, and an eddy stream runs northwards up the East Lewis coast to meet it at the Butt. During the west-going stream from the Minch a similar eddy runs for some miles west of the Butt, resulting at all times in violent turbulence at the meetings of the eddies and main streams.

The wind was south-west again, light at early morning but expected to strengthen. To have any chance at all I had to reach the Butt before the wind either strengthened or changed direction enough to aggravate any confusion in the area where the Atlantic meets the Minch.

To catch the worst area at the most favourable state of the tide, on the turn, I would have to paddle the first ten miles to The Butt against the flow. It would be tiring work and I hoped a short rest might be possible, at Europie beach in the sheltered embrace of the Great Butt cliffs themselves, before making the final commitment.

I had packed and was ready to leave by 9am when Alec appeared, stony-faced as ever. This time, though, there was no attempt to dissuade me. He helped me carry the loaded boat to the sea's edge then squatted in the sand and opened his sack to produce a flask of hot tea and two cups. After the tea he placed a half-salmon and two sausage sandwiches, still warm, in my hands and said 'It's these ye'll be needing … if ye make it'. He nodded 'Cheerio' and disappeared for the last time over the rim of the storm beach. A lump came to my throat as I realized the depth of his concern for me, even though I had persistently ignored his warnings.

Conditions stayed favourable, the wind at my back gave the pleasant illusion that I was forging ahead with great strength. The Lewis coast sped past and, with my attention focused on the confrontation that lay ahead, I covered the first ten miles with ease. I decided at that point to trust the flow of luck, take advantage of the fair conditions, and make a direct assault on the Butt without resting at Eoropie.

Soon, I was engulfed and flattened under the heavy shadow of the great green cliffs and fissured rocks, a tiny, arrogant speck feeling like a baby in a heavyweight fight-ring; and, almost immediately, strong undercurrents pulled the kayak sideways, westwards, towards the open Atlantic, and I was powerless to do anything about it. This was, however, as I had expected; the tide was on the last quarter of its westward flow and, I hoped, steadily weakening. The wind remained low but the swell was an immense rounded monument to the fresh Atlantic westerlies of recent days; the rollers were large but thankfully docile and regular.

As each ignorant mass passed below me, single-minded in its determination to reach the shore, I would be raised high in the air and, temporarily, all was audio-visual and clear. There were large orange lobster-buoys beneath the cliffs, and an exploration boat heading northwards on the distant western horizon. Fulmars and gulls sharpened the air with urgent cries and ahead the sea was a bright maze of wide spirals of swirling foam which chalked the eddy fringes. Then I would plummet downward rapidly as the great walls of water rose and closed around me on either side. 'No way through,' they said, as the world became muffled and black; the only sound was the water's growl, but through layers of wetsuit, buoyancy aid and jacket, I felt my own heart beating like the engine of a little tug-boat.

Uuuup! again, and the swell was exploding violently off rocks, skerries and buttresses farther inshore, but out where I was the sea rolled and breathed, rounded and unbroken, a tolerant host over which I was able to undulate and progress. The Butt of Lewis Lighthouse loomed into view, high above on a ledge of black gneiss, and then I hit 'spaghetti junction', the meeting of sea and ocean. It took concentration and fast, accurate reactions to stay on course in the confused currents in operation off the Butt. The hieroglyphic spirals of foam made no sense to me, but I soon realized I was in control. The adrenalin began to stabilize; I only needed to keep paddling constantly, carefully, and the day would be mine.

Then, out of the corner of my eye, only thirty feet to my left, came a massive upwelling of water; only it wasn't water. I swung round just in time to see a great piebald giant heave itself effortlessly from the sea. WHALE! Those moments froze as though in action replay as it exploded powerfully upwards, gained clearance of the water and somersaulted backwards in a living embodiment of all the ocean's force. The following splash was immense, and showered over me to break the hypnotic trance with cold, wet reality. I yelled out in instant shock reaction while I absorbed the details. The flash-patches on either side of the head; the white underparts; the great sabre-shaped dorsal fin; it was a killer whale, a large bull, almost thirty feet of him as measured against the kayak, by reputation the most ferocious animal in all the seas of the world. I froze in anticipation as the whale disappeared from sight and passed somewhere below me.

Known as the 'wolves of the ocean,' the killer whales, or Orcas, hunt in packs. They have been known to tip polar bears and seals from arctic ice-floes, grab pack ponies from the shores, and to tear the tongues from the great hundred-foot baleen whales, leaving them to bleed to death.

Tex Geddes had told me of the terrible wounds inflicted on the huge basking sharks, and the stomach of one orca which was found to contain the remains of thirteen porpoises and fourteen seals. They are said to be capable of ceremonial executions, of orgies of wanton destruction, and have been called the 'ultimate enemy of sea creatures'. But surely all these descriptions are highly anthropomorphic: 'ritual killings' and 'wanton violence' are charges more easily attributed to human activities, and the 'ultimate enemy of all creatures' is surely man himself. Despite extensive harpooning, slashes from boat propellers, ramming of their young by boats and hunters shooting at whales for sport, the orca had never been known to retaliate. There is no known instance of an orca attacking man. It is a difference between a race which does not kill human beings although it could, and a race which will kill orcas merely because it can. Still, I wondered whether they might not be averse to the occasional canoeist!

Long minutes passed before it surfaced again on my other side, perhaps twenty feet away this time, and I smelt a stale, fishy breath as it blew with a sound like the air brakes of an articulated lorry. There was eye contact before it wheeled forward and submerged again. But it seemed in a playful mood and repeated the somersault action for no apparent reason other than sheer exuberance and display. There were thunderclapping bellyflops and flashes of tail flukes and shining white patterns on the sleek skin. I 'whooped' and squealed with delight, shocked and hypnotised by this power and bulk of animal life rising so suddenly from beneath an ocean whose surface had, until now, been my only concern. Now it seemed the most exciting dimension of the whole scene was the one I couldn't see!

Part of me wanted to stay, to understand and to communicate; I felt no threat. But this was a potentially dangerous animal, and I was a tasty morsel in charge of a frail craft. In this difficult sea the boat was slowly shipping water and the currents of The Butt could easily carry me well offshore, but this was an unusual form of persuasion and I spent a further half-hour thrashing around in the currents, fighting the foaming waters and waiting to see where the whale would surface next. For me it was an oceanarium display

137

become real, spontaneous, unrehearsed, uncoerced, unrestrained – a quantum-leap, a revelation, and never again would the sea be the same.

But I was being pulled off course. I had to move, and headed for a small beach on the east side of the Butt. Leaping from the boat, I hauled it above the tide, threw off my lifejacket and, grabbing the camera, raced off up the cliffs on foot to the lighthouse point in the hope of some photographs. At sea I had been unable to free a hand from the paddle, and besides that I'm sure that any pictures would have been ruined by the camera-shake of pure excitement.

The whale was still there, only further offshore, and I only saw the great fin rise a couple of times more as he headed slowly out to sea.

I sat for a lunch of fresh salmon, cheese and sausage sandwiches, thought of Alec MacDonald and looked back over part of the treacherous Lewis West that I was now on the point of leaving behind. Then I started afresh down the east coast.

I have always, since then, had difficulty in communicating to others the significance of that experience to me. I did try to, in a magazine article a few months later, but when an unfortunate typing error informed the world that I had been impressed by a flash of yellow-white 'UNDERPANTS', the impact of the moment was somehow lost.

I camped that night a further fifteen miles south at the beautiful sands of Traigh Mor, Tolsta and slept like the dead.

Early next morning, I rounded Tolsta Head and, avoiding the great dead end of Broad Bay, headed for Tiumpan, the extreme point of the Eye Peninsula, en route for Stornoway.

Tiumpan Head was a déja-vu experience of high cliffs, lighthouse-crowned and turbulent below. But this time a sabre-fin rose about twenty metres from me, three feet high, followed by a broad, smooth black back, and disappeared with a smart rolling tail-flick. An electric ripple twitched my nerves but I paddled on, scanning the water on both sides and behind. It appeared again, only this time I saw the thin edge of the fin. It was moving towards me fast! Another killer.

I stopped paddling, wondering if it was aware of my paddle splashes, or even my hull, and this time I did feel frightened. Again it surfaced and I saw another fin cut the surface to my right; two more on my left were cruising at speed together. This was no playful display; I had blundered into the middle of a hunting pack of killer whales fishing the rich waters below the headland. They were less energetic than my friend at the Butt, and a little smaller, but I reached over my shoulder and withdrew a hand-held rocket flare; a bump from a cruising back or a flick from a tail, to say nothing of a friendly nibble, would do my chances of reaching Stornoway no good at all. But it was fascinating to be among them, almost one of the pack and before long the rolling fins seemed to move more to my left and I breathed easy as they headed for the deeper waters of the Minch. Alone again I pushed on south.

Flanking the east side of the wide entrance to Stornoway Bay was a chicken, one of the oldest chickens in the world, a great chicken of Lewisian gneiss. The headland is known as Chicken Head because of this convincing thirty-foot rock stack which could almost have been carved for fun by some ancient coastal sculptor. But there were still five miles to Stornoway, and the boat needed emptying; the only choice was an extremely tricky landing near the Chicken on a shingle beach banked at about 40 degrees and with a heavy dumping surf and treacherous undertow on it. The surf was too agitated to ground the boat in; if I came in forward the nose piled into the shingle, and if broadside the undertow trapped me down in the path of the next wave. The last resort was to detach the spraycover, paddle in close to shore and dive for land, grabbing the boat and then dragging it clear of the danger area. But the boat was too heavy, my legs too weak from prolonged sitting and I shredded my finger badly on landing. The kayak filled with water within seconds the breaking waves found the open cockpit. Full, it was almost impossible to drag clear up that shelving beach, but I managed to tip it sideways enough to lighten it and, with a last effort, hauled it out of the water. Exhausted, I collapsed on the shingle, tied the boat to my arm and slept until the surf began to lap at my feet.

Shivering now I refuelled on Kendal mint cake and biscuits, bandaged my torn finger and performed a life-boat launch from the steep beach. The kayak slid down the shingle at speed, submerged and surfaced about twenty feet out, heading across the five miles of open, choppy water to Stornoway.

Landfall was at Mol Sandwick, the east end of the town, at the end of another long, hard day. After three weeks and a hundred and seventy miles, it was the final camp of my sojourn on the 'Long Island,' and I couldn't help feeling just a little relieved for I was now past the halfway point of my journey. But the rain came down in buckets. Someone was emptying the bilges of heaven and paying little heed to my private triumph.

It was still raining next morning when I walked the two miles to Stornoway to make some essential visits. The first was to the Coastguard Station which had been so helpful in providing forecasts and keeping track of me while on the island. I dripped all over the floor of the Operations Room, sipped their coffee and gazed, fascinated, at the efficient set-up: radio operators, radar screens, and a pretty redhead in a tight uniform. 'Oh, you're the canoeist', she said as she turned and stretched on tip-toe to reach the Butt of Lewis on a wall-sized chart of the Islands. 'I'll just move your little flag.' And sure enough, among all the coded markings, there was a green pennant to represent my movements!

The *Stornoway Gazette* did a quick article on my progress and I made an appointment to visit the BBC's Radio Nan Eilean office next day.

How difficult it was to recollect the order of events. Even yesterday's whale adventures had faded into the general tapestry that the recent months had become. I had been accustomed to anticipating, forward-planning, rather than recollecting and reminiscing. God, it was difficult! Where was I a week ago? A month ago? Then it all came flooding back and there was so much to say; had all those things really happened to me? Surely no-one would ever believe it!

So next morning from Radio Nan Eilean I did a link-up with 'MacGregor's Gathering' on Radio Scotland, a rushed, last-minute spot, but I was taken under the wing of Neen MacKay, another stunning Stornoway redhead. Neen compiled a Gaelic music programme while I sat and drank coffee. She then switched to a lilting English for my benefit and we did a friendly, chatty interview before heading to the pub for lunch. Afterwards, I couldn't even remember what I'd said, and hoped only that they wouldn't edit out my thanks to local people and to the coastguard.

After a day's absence, city-struck and in love with Neen, the coastguard girl and the Stornoway Gazette receptionist, I returned to the camp at Sandwick to find my tent flattened by the gales of the previous night. Anchored by only two pegs and a guy rope it flapped horribly in the wind. The rain, driven under the blowing flysheet, had soaked my sleeping bag and all that was in the tent, and the forecast was for gales continuing.

As I packed the kayak roughly I kept an eye on the sea. The gale funnelled into the bay, pushing walls of unwilling water through the narrows between Arnish and Holm Point. It must have been in conditions like this, on New Year's Day 1919, that the H.M.S. Iolaire went aground on a submerged reef known as the 'Beasts of Holm' near the entrance to the harbour, in the most tragic disaster ever in the Western Isles.

Of the 260 naval ratings returning to the Islands for New Year leave at the end of the War, 205 perished that night within two miles of Stornoway and home. The lifeboats were smashed to pieces in the storm and at dawn only the masts of Iolaire showed clear of the water, a half-frozen survivor clinging to one of these.

Scarcely a home in Harris or Lewis was not touched by some bereavement, and January lst 1919 will always be a particularly sad date on Lewis gravestones.

Few people appreciate the devastating conditions caused by a strong and prolonged wind blowing into an enclosed area of sea such as a steep shored bay or a harbour. But it can be illustrated very easily: sit in the bathtub and blow, medium strength on the water in front of you and ripples and small waves will form; but get out of the bath and blow similarly in your teacup and watch the difference: instant chaos, and don't burn your nose! For the same reason, surviving the two-mile paddle into Stornoway, in the thrashing waters of the harbour, was a greater ordeal than the tortuous passage around the Butt of Lewis. I bounced and tossed on the multiple clapotis from the outer harbour walls, spun the boat on a wavecrest, my jaw and hands locked tight in concentration, and squeezed between a Dutch merchantman and a French Navy boat. Amused sailors cheered me on as I skidded up the shingle beach and hauled the boat up a flight of stone stairs.

With more gales forecast, the stormy waters of the Minch between Lewis and the mainland, another restricted body of water, would not be safe for many days yet; so I had no qualms about taking the Calmac Ferry for Ullapool where I would find my next supply box and begin the fourth stage of my journey.

It was the third week of July and, just before leaving, I saw a copy of the *Stornoway Gazette*. The heading read 'Round Scotland Canoeist is Mainland Bound'.

Turn Right at Cape Wrath

'Through cruel harbours his men did sail,
His ships on mountains of ice did fail,
Only the eskimo in his skin canoe,
Was the only one that ever came through.'

('Lord Franklin – Trad.)

The town of Ullapool in Scotland's north-west was planned and built in 1796 to exploit the seemingly endless shoals of herring which appeared each year in the Minch. Those shoals were severely depleted by the early years of the nineteenth century and the railway from Inverness was never extended to Ullapool. But even today, in the multinational bustle of Ullapool, where the Fisherman's Mission has bibles printed in Russian and Bulgarian, and where the street corners are said to bristle with eastern bloc spies avoiding immigration checks, the common unit of currency is still the fish. 'Klondyker' factory ships come from all over the world to churn Ullapool mackerel into fishmeal for cattle feed and fertilisers. But non-EEC countries are not allowed to catch fish within two hundred miles of British territorial waters so there's big money in it for the Scottish purse-seine boats which scoop up to a thousand tonnes at a time to sell to the incomers. When the mackerel are gone there's always the sand-eels, sprats and other industrial species, but that's another story; in 1985 the fishy gold rush was ON.

The safest place in town, I reckoned, must be a fish storeroom, so I left the canoe under lock and key among crates of pink, wriggling prawns in the store by the pier and wandered off in search of somewhere to stay. Behind the Fisherman's Mission kitchen counter there was a vast beer-belly, and then there was Bill Jones, a mammoth of a man. Looking more like a bodyguard or bouncer than a mission domestic, he stood there incongruously, dish-towel in hand, deftly juggling tiny pieces of crockery. His first 'HALLOOO!', loud and extravagant, suggested that there was a boisterous character to fit that swaggering bulky container.

'I may not be a clergyman,' said Bill, 'but I'm certainly a "man of the cloth"!'

During my short stay in the Ullapool Mission my acquaintance with Bill was to unfold significantly and this first impression, the paradox of 'Big Daddy and the Dish-Towel', expanded into one of the most moving encounters of my journey. Meanwhile, however, Bill went fishing in the bay and I went lighthearted into town for a drink before bed.

Next morning I collected my supply box from the *Ullasport* Outdoor shop and, between showers of rain and cups of coffee, was able to load it into the boat inside the prawn store. Everything went smoothly. The Neats, at their *Ullasport* shop, had received a strange parcel for me, all the more surprising as it was addressed:

Brian Wilson,
c/o 'Nevisport',
Ullapool
Isle of Skye,
Scotland.

Full marks to the G.P.O. for decoding that one! It turned out to be from Dawn Gray, an Australian who'd befriended me in Uig, Skye, when my portage trolley had suddenly collapsed under the strain of the newly-loaded kayak. It contained an inflatable P.V.C. roller for moving boats on shingle beaches. When deflated it was A4-sized; inflated it was a four-foot sausage. Could this be the answer to my portage problems? I was dying to try it out!

The afternoon passed in conversation with (or rather 'talked to' by) Bill. It took the form of a series of gruesome confessions relating to past phases and incidents of his life – violence, degradation, crime and destitution. At first I couldn't understand why he was telling me all this; he almost reached the point of boastfulness, but when I met his eyes there was no egotism, only tears of regret.

Bill loved the outdoors. As a caver for many years when younger, he'd had aspirations towards doing a major expedition of some sort, but drink abuse had always prevented him from crossing the commitment line, and so he had done all his expeditioning in books. Beside a photo of his wife and kids, who had long since left him, were piles of books on mountaineering, survival and exploration, and the thought of my own journey filled him with excitement. But it also caused him remorse, a renewed awareness of his wasted chances and his hopes of reform. Somehow the bizarre circumstances and

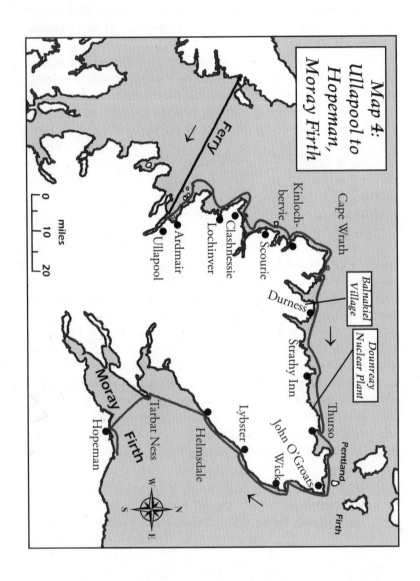

Map 4:
Ullapool to
Hopeman,
Moray Firth

manner of my arrival had inspired Bill, made him believe that I was significantly different from other people, and allowed him to talk frankly and openly. In fact he fully believed that I had been 'sent' to help him along a certain stage of his rehabilitation! 'Put me in your book too' said Bill, 'Don't make it all about winners.'

Time after time, my journey seemed to powerfully affect certain people. Like Herman Hesse's wanderer Knulp, it seemed to bring 'a little nostalgia for freedom into the lives of ordinary men'. I was always unsure whether to be proud of this; sometimes it made me very sad, and certainly it was becoming a real responsibility. But I couldn't turn my back on Bill. There was much in him that I liked, and that inspired me in return. From a life which had revolved around drink, sex and violence, he had salvaged a surprising amount. He wrote jotters full of poetry, social commentary and folk song lyrics; he was into ham-radio, played the bodhran drum, and had found a certain niche in the local community. The least I could do was to listen, to chip in the occasional helpful comment and to nod encouragement, so that eventually he felt that I had understood what he had struggled so hard to say.

When I left Ullapool next morning there were cameras and people. Captain Jennings, of the Mission, came to wave me off with a push, a blessing and a New Testament inscribed as a souvenir of my stay. I knew why Bill was not there, and understood; but two months later he sent me a donation for Intermediate Technology: 'Enclosed as promised ½ my weekly wage – £20!! – It's a pity I don't earn £500 per week!!' 'He may not have seen himself as a winner, but against the heaviest of odds Bill Jones had at least managed to resist becoming a total loser.'

❖ ❖ ❖

On a wild and overcast Tuesday, just as the morning tide reached Ardmair pier, I started out along the Coigach coast, inside Horse Island to Badentarbat Bay. It was time for biting off a chunk of the north-west coast and for digesting a bellyful of miles in a long day's paddling. The old rhythm returned within the first half hour … Reach, pull with the blade, push the upper hand, tighten the stomach, a quick flick and repeat with the other blade. Each stroke was a flowing amalgam of push and pull round a central unmoving point on the paddle-shaft, forcing the narrow boat forward to cut a furrow through the chop and surge of the noon tide, and almost subconsciously correcting the direction by tiny variations in width, strength or duration. Paddling, after three months, had become like walking, jogging or cycling, an activity fuelled by feelings, directed by a desire to create distance and by an interest in the area passed through. By travelling on a unique perspective, at a limited speed, your perceptions are focussed upon a multitude of objects and events which are somehow appropriate to that framework. On a high-speed train, for instance, you see only the station of departure and the station of arrival, places appropriate to the concept of hasty commuter travel from A to B. From the closed cocoon of a car, the appropriate experiences are those framed by the windscreen and road verges, and insulated by the roof. Put another way, the tortoise can tell you more about the road than can the hare.

This was Sutherland, at five knots from sea-level, the 'south-land' of the Norsemen, a much-carved land of mighty headlands and deep fjord-like sea lochs, tantalising clouded hints of spectacular views over Inver Pollaidh, Ben More Coigach and the hummocky wastes of Assynt. The mountains of Sutherland – Suilven, Cul Mor, Canisp – dodged and dipped in a game of hide-and-seek whose rules were mist, rain and the winds of the west, for from this perspective the weather itself was a real and important variable. Here were great Celtic sphinxes, lying dormant and yet influencing all that falls within their sundial or rainshadow, thrust skyward by great upheavals of the adolescent earth and battered earthward again throughout her decaying years.

I surged through the bouncing mercurial waters of Badentarbat Bay and close inshore of Tanera Mor, the largest of the Summer Isles where pioneer ecologist Frazer Darling lived and farmed, putting into practice his philosophy of conservation by regeneration and proving that the devastated lands of the West Highlands could, given care and attention, be revitalized.

The first stop of the day, for a snack and a bailing session – for the spraydeck was still leaking badly despite resealing – was on the beautiful little Isle Ristol, where the curve of a petit beach reached out to embrace the approaching kayak in a shingly grin. Here were the rudiments of rest and refreshment in a spirit of abundance without ceremony, from the free-spirited streams to the always-islands which soften the horizon and bring comfort to the eye. It would have made a wonderful camp, but I had come only ten miles and was good for a few more yet, heading north, away from the sheltered jigsaw pattern of the Summer Isles.

It was low water in the bay at Old Dornie; small boats slumped sideways in the muddy anchorage awaiting the support of the returning tide, and Caolas Eilean Ristol was so shallow that only a duck or a kayak could have made the passage. I squeezed through, pushing off rocks and easing myself along punt-style to the deeper water beyond the island shallows. A further five miles in a gradually building swell took me around the headland of Rubha Coigach and immediately there were spectacular views deep into Enard Bay, to the wide skyline display of Inverpollaidh and its isolated sugar-loaf mountains. Although still largely under cloud, even the suggestion of this fantastic panorama was quite stunning, as seen from the stilled, shining surface of Enard.

I headed north east now, six miles across the bay to where my deck map showed the town of Lochinver should be, but nothing was visible from the sea save a barren and beautiful coastline and an oily, cloud-reflecting well. Clouds rested their sagging paunches on the hills of Sutherland, but out in the bay the evening was tranquil and open. A steady 'putt-putt-putt' drifted across the elongated swell as two fishing boats headed home to Lochinver on the evening tide. A large orange sun sank in the west and I had to shade my eyes to follow their line, to pick out the path which led between the islands to the entrance of Loch Inver. But it was no good; far across the bay the two boats faded in a haze of orange and the secret of Lochinver lay safe.

A further hour of steady paddling took me to within sight of A'chleit and Soyea islands. Still the entrance to Loch Inver remained hidden from sight, but on the light offshore breeze of evening there were other clues: the unmistakeable smells of diesel and fish! I had to be on the right track. Thinking of the old Shetland seamen who could navigate the waters around their islands in the dark by sense of smell, I rounded an anonymous point of land and opened, into deep Loch Inver, at the head of which stands the busy fishing village of the same name.

Now my nose was really twitching, for suddenly I could smell trees! It had been weeks – no, months! – since I'd had contact with trees in any quantity, and the pure fragrance of pine across the loch hit me like a Bisto vapour-trail. Sure enough, the map showed, around the Culag area, a little oasis of green in the midst of a topographic desert of rock and water. Instantly succumbing to its seduction I turned my bow from the diesel and fish aroma I presumed to mean Lochinver harbour, and headed inshore to a small wooded bay south of Culag.

The mighty peaks of Suilven and Quinag, still clad in shredded cloud, now aglow in the sunset, showed above the forest canopy like a scene from a South American rain-forest. I hoisted the boat up the shingle and unloaded on a mossy bank where the forest met the beach. The inflatable roller worked well; placed under the hull it saved the boat from any scraping at all and made light work of what was normally a strenuous haul.

I changed into dry clothes and followed the sound of tumbling water to a fresh spring to fill my gallon container. Then it was only a short walk to Lochinver where I bought bacon and eggs for morning, and an excellent black pudding supper. Back on the beach I sat happy in the company of trees, sharing their breath. I leant back against warm rough bark and watched the light fade in its own time across the bay before spreading my mat and sleeping beneath an open sky.

I woke refreshed, cooked a good breakfast on a fire of cones and dead branches, and set off to round the headland at Point of Stoer, ten miles north. Alone on the sea I enjoyed the restless conditions and the feeling of confidence in coping with them. Those nightmare days on Lewis had vaccinated me against worry on any but the largest and most dangerous seas and I now gained a lot of pleasure from steady progress over what would once have seemed a very hostile sea indeed.

It was a good trip around Cluas Deas lighthouse point and the Point of Stoer itself. There was the great pinnacle of Torridonian sandstone, the Old Man of Stoer, which had remained unassailed until climbed by Aberdonian Dr Tom Patey in 1966. Conditions were too rough to allow the photos it merited, but mentally I recorded a beautiful set of high cliffs, and colourful scores of puffins which bobbed on the water or flew to and fro on whirring clockwork winglets. Then, like a vast cold shadow or a premonition of evil, a large skate at least ten feet across, and longer than the canoe from nose to tail, passed slowly, hearse-like, only feet below me.

◆ ◆ ◆

I left Clashnessie Bay in sunshine and a brisk wind, skirted the coast and negotiated the narrow channel inshore of Oldany Island, sheltered from the strong winds. But out on the open bay of Eddrachillis my cover was gone. The sea was broken and churned white by the animal passage of a very strong northeasterly whipping its savage way out to sea.

My compass bearing to Scourie, eight miles north east across the bay, took me into the very teeth of the gale and constant paddle splashes and wave spray were hurled cold and hard in my face. I paddled with eyes narrowed, head down and fought hard; tried to dodge waves which hit me from all directions, but inevitably they found their way through my defences, breaking over my head and sending icy torrents down my neck to chill my body. Thinking miserably of the beautiful bay I'd left behind in sunshine and fine sand, I battled on through the truncated, frantic area of sea which had jammed itself between the islands of Meall Mor and Meall Beag halfway across the bay. It was a trial by wind, a wind of 35mph or more, but the sea was fast becoming unmanageable and I was virtually exhausted. Scourie suddenly seemed an impossible target, so I accepted the comfortable proddings of common sense and headed instead for the sheltered archipelago which lies off Badcall Bay, hauled out at a small jetty and, with drooping eyelids, ate Fox's biscuits almost whole and barely unwrapped. It had been a hard day.

Like Lochinver, Kinlochbervie was located from two miles off by sense of smell, this time diesel fumes and peat-smoke, but there was an element of Polynesian navigation as the wooden and plastic flotsam on an outgoing tide were a dead giveaway. One fishbox, like a floating signpost, actually announced 'Kinlochbervie'. Such are my memories of days and sea-miles on the north-west coast, until one night I found myself camped above beautiful Polin beach near Oldshoremore, a bay enclosed by two long and rugged arms of hummocky Archaean gneiss where one could comfortably sit out many a storm in solitude and peace. But my days in the west were drawing to an end, for at last I was within striking distance of Cape Wrath, the massive buttress that is the north-west corner of Britain and after which 'all routes lead east'.

As such it was well known to the Norsemen who called it Hvarf, meaning 'turning point', and a greater landmark could not be imagined for here, at Clo Mor, the sea cliffs rise sheer to a thousand feet, the highest of mainland Britain, overhanging the sea that thunders and screams at its foot. And although Wrath is but a corruption of the Norse Hvarf, the word is nonetheless appropriate, for when the winds from the west meet the cliff walls, they surge upwards in freak, inverted squalls strong enough, say fishermen, to pluck a thirty-foot boat from the water and send it out of control to be crushed at the cliff foot or swamped in the monstrous swell.

I searched my soul for the confidence with which to meet the Cape and, despite all I had already been through, found only raw nerves. Large coastal obstacles and difficult wind-thrown seas had become almost routine, and yet somehow it didn't leave me feeling ready to confront Cape Wrath. Perhaps, I thought, that confidence just never comes; perhaps the preliminary stage-fright is somehow necessary? Cape Wrath was an unknown, another genuine challenge. And the true nature of a challenge must be that you don't really know what's required of you until you meet it. How then could confidence be anything other than false and dangerous?

Despite rationalizing I slept only one hour that night and rose unrested, determined to overcome the nerves enough to make an objective estimate of the situation. There was no doubt that the day was suitable: a period of late neap (gentle) tides, medium visibility and only slight winds; the forecast was for little change. No one could predict when the next suitable day would be, perhaps tomorrow, perhaps next month. Objectively, everything pointed towards having a go, but immediately I regretted being objective, because it was obvious that I had a deep subjective resistance to the whole idea!

At Polin, I was still a full fifteen miles from the Cape itself, so the first step was to break camp and paddle round a small headland, up past the pear-shaped rock pinnacle known as the Buchaille or 'guardian', and so to the picturesque and sweeping sands of Sandwood Bay to rest and eat before tackling the Cape.

Sandwood, often considered the finest beach in Britain, is accessible only by sea or by a long walk on a rough track. It was here that a local shepherd, Sandy Gunn, had a famous encounter with a mermaid on 5th January 1900. But the deep sense of oppression

I felt at Sandwood was due not to a mermaid's presence but to the fact that, despite a grey cloud cover sneaking over the northern sky, Cape Wrath was now visible across ten miles of sea.

Shivering with cold and apprehension I ate lunch in a light drizzle; the plan was already formed and I would stick to it: Leave Sandwood at 12.30; paddle close inshore where there is a continuous north-going eddy; reach Cape Wrath (ten miles) by 2.30 – slack water – minimal turbulence; carry flood tide past troubled areas and fast east along north coast. That, at least, was the dryland theory version; the saltwater reality was to prove slightly different. But before I set off there was a simple modification to make.

The spraydeck, a double-sealing variety, which had started the trip entirely watertight, was now highly inefficient due to constant chaffing of the waterproof material against the small of my back, and a replacement sent on to Lochinver hadn't arrived.

What worried me most was the problem of carrying a lot of water while trying to handle a rough sea; the moving ballast makes the boat heavy, unpredictable and unstable, and could be a fatal complication in an already severe situation like Cape Wrath.

I did carry an essential spare spraydeck in case of loss, but it was a loose-fitting, old-fashioned kind, of limited use in a breaking sea, and was stowed way up front in the never-never land of the kayak's narrow nose. Suddenly it occurred to me that, fitted in addition to the leaking deck, it could provide the waterproofing that the other lacked, while still being collapse-proof and worthy of a breaking sea. Keeping water out around Cape Wrath would be a high priority and it had to be tried.

The weather, which I had been watching closely for any sign of deterioration, remained apparently settled. But almost as soon as I was beyond the grey surf of Sandwood and heading north, the wind increased and the sky darkened dramatically. Hard clouds scudded across the sky throwing rushing shadows on the angular sea like the climax scene of a disaster film. At that moment I knew it had been a conspiracy! The wind and sea had plotted to seduce me into believing there was a chance; now they had me where they wanted me and, almost, I considered turning back. Only the momentum from the 'objective' decision kept me on track until, not long after 2.30 I reached the cliff shoulder at Am Bodach. Over the great cliff the tip of the Cape Wrath lighthouse was now visible, and around the next corner I was committed to the flight; now there was no turning back.

Close inshore south-west of the Cape was the continuous north-going eddy I had used. East of the Cape is an almost continuous west-going eddy stream. Where these meet with the main tides they form exceptionally heavy turbulence and a dangerous sea that runs for a considerable distance seawards; too far seawards to be avoided by kayak.

Even as I rounded Am Bodach I was on the edge of a growing swell that was sending enormous terraces of water into the oblivion that lay ahead; and suddenly there was a sea on a massive scale, so huge that even after the Lewis Atlantic I could not have anticipated it. The chasms between waves plummeted, wave-top to trough, to a shadowy thirty feet surrounded by almost vertical walls of grey water. There was none of the small-time bucking and tossing I'd become used to in the Hebridean waters of past months; this was a different league.

Rising high on the crests of wave mountains I became conscious of a Cairngorm landscape of watery mounds over whose foaming pinnacles the lower parts of great cliff buttresses were intermittently visible. Almost endlessly the cliffs extended upwards, sloping out over me in an implied, but almost unbearable, weight of form, and their shadow added to the dark terror of that sea. At times the light disappeared as I was hurled at breakneck speed down the 45-degree faces of wave-slopes to the forgotten chasms and valleys that succeeded the water-mountain upheavals.

I paddled only for support, and yet was conscious of moving at a fantastic speed at all times, and so huge were the masses of travelling water, that I had the distinct impression of paddling over rows of houses, into the streets between and up again, over the next block!

Beneath those cliffs in that massive sea I was acutely conscious of my own vulnerability and insignificance, pitted somehow – for some purpose I'd forgotten – against a monumental concentration point of raw environmental power such as I could never conceive in my waking hours. It was the stuff of fever and nightmare. Had those walls of water which towered above me broken into roaring waves I would have been crushed like a grape and known nothing about it; but although white-capped the swell remained rounded and unbroken. Obviously it wasn't a nightmare! I was still awake, still upright and had a chance.

The adrenalin that burned through my tissues flooded my consciousness with the need to fight, and provided images which helped to combat the insignificance. Here I was off the extreme corner of the country I'd lived in all my life. Once again I'd pursued the kayak beyond the previous limits of my world, geographical and emotional. I had flattened a barrier of personal terror and was filled with an elation which annihilated fatigue and melted the entire experience into a valuable episode. A final image occurred to me, in which I pictured myself as a flea on the rump of a great bull elephant in the midst of a herd orgy.

And as I came round at last, under the lighthouse point, the sky began to lose its grey and heavy burden of cloud and opened blue to the east. With the suddenness of a curtain's sweep I stumbled upon an apparently infinite view of headland after headland receding eastwards along the northern coast of Scotland. So this was the tempestuous north coast, whose sea channel was the most feared in Europe; around each of those beautiful stark fingers of land, reaching out for Orkney, ran a fierce tidal race culminating eventually in the Pentland Firth. It had for me the quality of a vision, a glimpse into the future of my journey. I felt beauty, privilege, and all the conquering awe of the first primitive seafarers who, also in manpowered boats, challenged these grim northern seas, and must have been rewarded with a view little different to this.

I felt like a true adventurer! The heavy clouds and oppressive sky of late morning were now only a mist evaporating steadily eastwards as sunlight bled upon an expanding panorama and warmed my fear-strained, salt-crusted face. Of course a heavy and serious sea persisted, but I was untouchable; I had inoculated myself with the temporary immunity of a hero and was borne along on the tumbling swell as if on the shoulders of a triumphant army. But the almost incredible scenery unfolding ahead made me determined to find some way to land and photograph the great moment, and I dodged out of the main race into the fierce clapotis which blasted volcanic under the serrated cliffs and geos east of the Cape. There was a small jetty, marked on the map, in a shallow geo at which I thought I might just be able to haul out. Walter Scott, in 1814, wrote of his journey around 'This dread Cape, so fatal to mariners…'

and also mentioned this same geo: 'There is no landing, except in a small creek about one and a half miles to the eastward. There the foam of the sea plays at "long bowls" with a huge collection of large stones, some of them a ton in weight, but which these fearful billows chuck up and down as a child tosses a ball.'

Because of the direction of the swell the geo had become a frantic mass of exploding water, the clapotis of the cliff-foot was magnified within the confined walls. The cove was backed by Scott's 'Long Bowls', a rough bouldered area pitching at an impossible angle out of viciously dumping surf, and the stone-built slipway was submerged dangerously in the churning confusion. I approached gingerly to the surf-line but saw it would be impossible to reach the shore without smashing the boat to shreds. So, holding the boat stable on one paddle I hitched off one spray cover and jettisoned my ammo-box which held the camera. Then I threw my paddle towards the surf churning on the rocks, manoeuvred closer by hand, hitched off the second cover and tumbled into the wild water. I swam clear, surfaced and grabbed the bow ropes, touched rock and hauled the boat ashore, gently as I could, over man-sized boulders and safely above the reach of a fast-rising tide. The paddle and ammo-box were rescued, unharmed, from the surf.

From the Cape Wrath cliff top, sea conditions a thousand feet below looked disappointingly docile, but wild spiralling foam eddies gave hint to the scale of turbulence and sea-anger that continued at the cliff-foot. The eastward view, however, was improved with the height and I spent some time just staring in amazement. To the north the sea stretched, uninterrupted save by Iceland, to the Polar Icecap.

❖ ❖ ❖

Following the eastgoing tide, now in full flow, I passed beautiful sets of smaller cliffs with stacks and rock pillars galore, and a gorgeous uninhabited house at the sandy bay of Kearvaig. But all this was a restricted area for the Cape Wrath peninsula, the Parbh as it is known, is yet another chunk of spectacular coastline which has been annexed for naval bombardment, research and testing by the Ministry of Defence; three per cent of Scotland's beaches are now used for military purposes. I remembered my delays at Mullock and Luce Bays in Galloway, and thought bitterly of the island in Wester Ross whose Gaelic name 'Gruinard' has all but been superseded by the sinister label 'Anthrax Island'. The Cape Wrath land-sea gunnery, at 8,308 acres, is the largest of its kind in Europe, and occupies a key designated Nature Conservation Review site of major ornithological interest.

That the Ministry of Defence were among the biggest landowners in Europe, I knew. But not until I saw Garve Island did it occur to me that the MOD is probably also the most active force of geological erosion since the last Ice Age! Like much of the nearby mainland cliffs and adjacent moorland, Garve was in poor condition, its magnificent cliffs crumbling badly all round and huge rock faces hanging ready to fall in the next gale; the top quarter of the island, where there would normally have been some greenery, had been reduced to rubble. Lying half a mile offshore, Garve is a demolition site which might as well have had concentric rings painted on its side, for the fighter planes and artillery boats, which approach from seaward, home in on Garve and, with missiles whose explosions rock the village of Durness five miles distant, gradually reduce the island seaward.

The bombing has caused extensive damage to the sea cliffs and seabird breeding sites, and the noise levels alone have had devastating effects on the wildlife. Auk species (guillemots and razorbills) have been deserting nest sites, and dead guillemots have been found with evidence of concussion and haemorrhaging in their chests and heads. And one wonders what untold damage such activity could be doing to the whales and dolphins whose hearing is known to be ultra-sensitive. In the past, the area around Garve Island, with its fast tide race and rich feeding, was especially favoured by dolphins. But dolphins in captivity have been known to die even because of construction noise in nearby tanks! And noise pollution caused by boats is thought to be one of the reasons why whale and dolphin species have all but deserted the southern North Sea. How much more devastating then must be a full-scale bombardment? Ultimately, we are in danger of driving these creatures from our shores for good.

The 8-knot current, so loved by the dolphins, pushed me through between Garve and the mainland and I was soon heading across the wide Kyle of Durness to Balnakeil Bay. It was a teased-out end to a strenuous day and I was groaning loudly on each stroke long before I reached the shore. My shoulders ached like never before and my bum was cramped painfully on the hard seat, but not without cause; it had been an epic day in which I'd covered over thirty miles of sea, rounded the Cape and left the west coast behind; on landing at Balnakeil a new phase of the journey began, along the 'Roof of Britain'.

◆ ◆ ◆

Next morning, with evil weather making a forceful comeback, I lay exhausted long in my bag until late morning a big face and a small face peeped cautiously round the tent flap and introduced themselves as Ludo and his son Rowan from the craft village.

Above the bay at Balnakeil a derelict MOD Early Warning Station was taken over in 1984 by a group of craftsmen and women and made habitable. Today there are sixteen independently-owned businesses operated by craftspeople from all over the world, and within this small nucleus one can find candle-making, metalwork, weaving, pottery, printing, painting and picture-framing, photography, stonework, knitting, wood, bronze and aluminium sculpture among a growing range of crafts.

Ludo, a thirty-year-old Belgian, was the gardener at the village, and the proud owner of an Umnak sea kayak. Seeing my kayak upside down on the beach he had decided that chance and the tide had at last brought him the ideal friend. Up at the village he introduced me to his Scots wife Ishbelle and baby Rhiannon, and after a meal of grains and vegetables we went next door to visit Alan Harman, Balnakeil's woodturner and poet, and one of the founders of the community. His was the kind of workshop I could have browsed in for days; outside, a shell of sterile, MOD concrete; inside a hive of interest and creativity. There were life-sized wooden sculptures, toys, windmills to generate electric light and, most interesting of all, fishbox furniture and driftwood sculptures. Late into the night we browsed through books, and chatted over esoteric ideas of 'life-themes' and journeys. Ludo, it seemed, was keen to travel with me for a day and we discussed plans to go round Faraid Head together, the next peninsula on my route east.

4pm. The tide was ready for us; I had packed up and was all set to launch when Ludo appeared over the brow of the hill cycling a grocery bike and towing his kayak behind. He rumbled down at amazing speed, scraping his boots on the tar to gain control, and swung to a halt, undamaged, by the beach.

Tidal streams run fairly strong off the headlands of the north coast and there was bound to be some turbulence, but the weather had settled and things were looking good. Around the point conditions were choppy but not serious and the swell was unbroken. Despite confessing that he'd never been on anything so frightening before – in fact he'd never been out of the bay! – Ludo handled it well. He was happy to have someone to paddle with, and I to have someone to talk to at sea. East of Faraid Head we picked our way carefully through the rough section between two small islands beneath scores of foul-smelling seabirds. All around, the sea was dotted with the tiny, comical puffins. Quite suddenly Ludo yelled, retched and began throwing up everywhere. I caught up with him and steadied his boat in the swell. 'Just feeding the puffins,' he said with a ghastly, green smile, but I was worried. It could have been the tension and fear, a form of seasickness, or even the piddly smell of the bird islands, but a weakened paddler in a rough sea is a serious situation and we made for a direct landing at Sango Bay.

But the surf was pounding heavily on the steep beach and Ludo, it seemed, had never made a surf-landing before. Trying to go ahead and choose a line, I looked over my shoulder to see poor Ludo in the gathering area of a huge breaker that was piling up behind him. There was nothing I could do for him and soon I was engulfed in it myself. Through the white foam I reached him and we landed successfully on Sango beach but in the panic to secure Ludo I had lost my deck map and its waterproof holder; such was the undertow that it was sucked away and never surfaced.

Once rested and calmed, Ludo continued the paddle, undaunted, along the coast and past the amazing Smoo cave to finish our trip at Cannabienne beach, where again those heavy white lines and roaring din meant a problem surf. But a stream flowed out of the bay at a corner where, along the cliffs, the tidal outflow also channelled its way back to sea. This, at some stages of the tide, would have been dangerous in itself, but at full tide merely inhibited the surf and made for a convenient passage to the beach, giving Ludo and me a dignified end to our trip. We shared biscuits and coffee and parted, as friends should, grateful for each other's role in an unforgettable few shared hours.

❖ ❖ ❖

The north coast is a rugged succession of long headlands and a particular brand of rock-fringed, surf-laden beaches, and the area between Cape Wrath and Whiten Head, a distance of about twenty miles, has been called 'the most desolate sub-arctic landscape in the British Isles'. But as I crossed wide Loch Eriboll, the views out to sea were limited by heavy weather and my full attention was focussed on the head itself which, in terms of geology and coastal sculpture, was anything but desolate.

Crumbling quartzite rock gave the 'Whiten' effect on the upper parts of the cliffs, and all around the headland was an amazing display of geological diversity, almost a safari-park collection of erosion features, due entirely to the sculpting effects of moving water. Sea caves are literally blasted from the cliffs by waves pouring into crevices and forcing them apart by hydraulic pressure. Within the caverns the weight and hydraulics of water and trapped air in an enclosed space may continue excavation upwards until eventually a hole is torn through the roof and a spout forms. Natural arches are carved on narrow promontories and later, after years of erosion, the arch may fall leaving the seaward mass of rock to stand alone as a 'sea-chimney' or rock stack.

At Whiten there were sculptured cliffs of almost nine hundred feet, rock stacks of infinite variety, massive geo-fissures and high, muddy waterfalls. But particularly impressive were the caves, many of them larger and more interesting than the famous Smoo cave, and only accessible by sea. I paddled right into a large cavern mouth where the booming and roaring of the sea was magnified and echoed by the natural acoustic structure of the cathedral-like chamber. Deeper and darker, I tried to pass beneath a low rock beam and enter an unknown, pitchfork chamber. But the sea was too jumpy. I took fright and turned around carefully towards a patch of light that indicated another exit from the great warren. So I emerged again further eastwards, but still amid arches and stacks and the swirling turbulence that rings all the headlands of the north coast. Eventually the Head opened eastwards on the Kyle of Tongue and the Rabbit islands. I was overflowing with electricity after another rough and exhilarating trip, but was more than ready for that camp at Talmine.

It was towards the Rabbit Islands that I headed next morning, crossing the Kyle of Tongue quickly and easily. The strong tide which rushes through Caol Raineach, the narrow channel between Eilean Nan Ron and the mainland, boosted the kayak to around 8 knots, but I was surprised when I caught up with a yacht which had left Talmine at least an hour before me. The yacht, a beautiful three-masted sixty-footer, had slowed to a drifting pace with only a small sail up.

As I approached there was a loud 'AHOY!' from the deck, and although I was to regret it later, I responded to their 'What say to a tipple?' in the affirmative, tying the kayak to the inflatable dinghy they towed behind and climbing on board the yacht pirate-style.

In response to the usual questions, I explained concisely about the journey, and at more length about the Intermediate Technology charity, then recoiled under the sudden wave of plastic admiration. 'Laudable' and 'Wonderful' were bandied meaninglessly around by the party seated on deck while some grinning females reached over to prod my biceps as though I was a racehorse or something they'd just reeled in on a line from the sea. It was obvious that they had no conception of what my journey meant; they couldn't remember exactly where the Pentland Firth was, had no conception of Cape Wrath, and had turned their fabulous ocean-going yacht into a Talmine Bay Gin Palace. They even thought my ammo-box was a container for collecting money and began to reach in their pockets for cash!

Holding glasses steady without a spill seemed to be the onboard pastime as they passed around gooseberry and elderflower wines, moving on to the rums and gins around lunchtime. I joined them by accepting a beer and some sandwiches, but as most of them were already more than a bit 'tidal' I spared myself any further elaboration of my trip.

The yacht cruised now at a steady 5 knots away from land, apparently unnoticed by skipper Rupert, who introduced himself as Roop, sank a gin and almost stumbled into the hatch that opened to below decks.

Two women bickered over the merits of different shooting dogs, and 'don't you find labradors just terribly ... SQUODGY?' while another explained that I 'simply must' call on her divorced friend in Thurso. The house? Of course it was the one with the horsebox

159

in the driveway and the Range Rover outside. There might also be a Golden Labrador in the car... I had no time to ask if it was a 'squodgy' one because Roop had forgotten he had an eighteen-foot kayak in tow and unleashed another large sail.

He shouted at the top of his plummy voice 'Heave to!' and 'Prepare to gybe!' and, with a sudden lurch, the yacht moved off in a surge of great speed. The little kayak strained at its leash as it swung sideways, and water poured into the cockpit alarmingly. It struggled for dignity, bravely resisted capsize for several minutes then began to list helplessly to one side, unused to being restrained at the nose with a half-load of water in. If it turned over, or filled up, the rope would snap and there was every chance that, under Rupert's command, I'd lose it for ever.

Yelling abuse at Rupert I grabbed my ammo-box and leaped over the side of the speeding yacht, landed (luckily!) with a leg in the dinghy, dived for the canoe and drew it close to me. To my amazement a girl appeared by my side, the only one who had not been drinking with the others and who seemed awake to the danger of the situation. I held the kayak tight as she emptied it using the deck pump. Almost incredibly the giggling and 'yaahing' continued on board, oblivious.

In the cowboy film this was the scene where the cowboy climbs from the runaway stagecoach to the bolting horse's neck; balancing the paddle across the two tossing boats, still being trailed through the ocean at speed by the yacht, I swung my legs into the kayak, tucked the container between them and clipped one spraydeck over the cockpit. The girl crouched in the dinghy, held tight until I was ready then untied the rope, blew me a kiss and set me free. I smiled and was grateful, safe at last as skipper and crew of my own boat, as Rupert's Madhouse gybed again back towards Talmine Bay.

I was about five miles further seaward than I should have been, but located the distant gleam of Farr Bay and headed off on a compass bearing. An hour of hard paddling took me back inshore where, approaching the headland, squally showers created chaotic pictures on the sea, like part of a living, moving paisley pattern.

Around Farr Point to Armadale Bay, I pitched camp by the Armadale Burn, changed quickly into thermal trousers and a woolly jumper and cooked a good meal. The old routine was back; I could laugh at the incidents of the day, but something was troubling me. I went down to the Strathy Inn for a drink and a phone, and suddenly incidents started to gel and become clear.

Tomorrow I was due to round Strathy Point and to pass the Prototype Nuclear Fast Reactor plant at Dounreay. Potentially far more devastating than the oil installation it had superseded the 1950s experimental fast reactor and was now the site of a proposal to build a £300-million reprocessing plant, ten times the size of the present plant. If it goes ahead – against the protests of many local people, the Orkney and Shetland Islands councils and the voluntary environmental organisations Greenpeace, Friends of the Earth, S.C.R.A.M. and others – ships carrying plutonium will battle through the Pentland tide-races, around Cape Wrath or lay up in the Orkneys; highly dangerous re-processed waste will be flown out an estimated two hundred times per year and the coastal pipelines will disgorge an even greater volume of radioactive waste into the sea than at present.

Already there was controversy over the local levels of childhood cancers which even the government's medical statisticians discovered to be nearly ten times greater than expected. Five cases of leukaemia occurred locally between 1979 and 1984. With similar leukaemia clusters and childhood cancer incidences around the plant at Sellafield in Cumbria, the arguments which say that there 'can be no proof' or that there is 'no conclusive causal link' are as spurious as those which claim there is no 'proven' link between smoking and lung disease.

By pure coincidence the book which had surfaced the previous evening from my random collection of paperbacks was *The Fate of the Earth* – Jonathan Schell's study of apathy and its effects on pollution and the environment. And that night I met Maggie, the proprietress of the Strathy Inn who also mobilised local anti-nuclear support! By a third coincidence the T.V. was showing 'Threads', the film about nuclear holocaust which I watched with Maggie and her children. Maggie knew that film well, and had a row of vodka glasses lined up in front of her, chain-smoked as the film became more gruesome, horrific and realistic, and strategically sent graded sizes of kids off to bed as different scenes loomed!

Was synchronicity again trying to tell me something? Next day along the Reay coast I paddled close to the power station to get some pictures of the infamous dome as it hummed and buzzed beyond the breaking waves. I was loathe to stay too long, but then there was no VISIBLE pollution. What does one do? Like the average man in the street I knew little about the specific dangers of nuclear discharges; the industry itself seems guilty of ruthless application, on an unprecedented scale, of only partial knowledge, especially in the transport and disposal of waste. But if the leukaemia clusters are merely coincidental then perhaps it was also coincidence that from four months of photography, only my film of Dounreay was seriously overexposed!

❖ ❖ ❖

The sea of the north became increasingly interesting and complicated as I proceeded eastwards. Though the wind remained only Force 4 or less, the waves smashed regularly on the rough shores of Caithness flagstone, bringing to that deep northern blue a fringe as white as gull feathers. There was a different feel to the sea, as if its behaviour was governed by something I had not yet understood. And then it clicked, the sea here was not just the product of an ocean swell, but also an offshoot of the great Pentland current that surges twice daily between Orkney and mainland Scotland.

Offshore, occasional rogue breakers caused by large waves passing over slightly submerged reefs, broke fiercely and suddenly in localized areas. Usually these danger areas could be identified well in advance and avoided, but when smaller wave-patterns passed over the same area the traps remained invisible, and several times I narrowly avoided being caught in the rapid building and destruction of these huge lumps of water. One particular reef area whose presence had not yet been revealed by a large enough wave, I paddled right into and was caught with my trousers down. In what felt like slow motion the huge wave sucked its bulk from under me and, like a man pulling in his stomach to swell his chest, drew itself up to three times my height and tottered there uncertain. I was paralysed, helpless as it poised with a roaring hiss like a mythological serpent about to strike. For a second it held, but – all the time body-building – it was ultimately unable to sustain its own mass and leaned over ready to collapse. There was nothing I could do to avoid the inevitable blitz, and only thought 'Oh shit!' as I thrust my blade like a harpoon into the smooth hard flank of the great water monster. Thanks to the slow motion I had just enough time to throw my weight into the water on the breakside before the great 'BOOOMMM!' It wasn't a surfwave, simply a massive, short-lived phenomenon of amazing energy. It dumped, spent and disappeared and, remarkably, I found I was still in the cockpit, still holding the paddle and the shell of the boat seemed undamaged. Amazed the boat hadn't been smashed in half, I flicked myself upright, shook water dog-like from hair and eyes and paddled free, giggling nervously, into a sea which seemed to deny that such a monster could possibly have existed. But I knew it was there; I knew it had towered over me like the eternal Hokusai wave, grinning at my futile efforts at defence, and I knew it had let me off lightly.

A little shaken, but highly relieved, I sought the first possible refuge for a lunch break; a sheltered cliff ledge reached by a rope ladder whose real purpose I couldn't guess. From the cliff I could see again the distinctive reactor dome of Dounreay far to the west and felt comfortable to be creating distance in the opposite direction.

At Brinn's Ness I met the first of the Pentland races, caused here by a 3-knot current forging over uneven ground. A long barrier of heavy broken water, tumbling viciously back upon itself like a vast river-stopper, operated loudly along the reef which stretched seaward as far as I could see. Luckily, for I would not have willingly challenged that race, there was a narrow passage of unbroken water just between Brinn's Ness point and the race itself, and although reaching it meant almost being drawn into the race, it brought me safely to a gentler area closer inshore.

From Brinn's Ness to Holborn Head I made slow progress, labouring against an eddy formed inside the main Pentland Flood stream. There were so many caves beneath Holborn Head that the great cliff seemed to stand on little legs like a massive oil platform, and little waterfalls tumbled from its clifftops, vaporizing long before they reached the sea. But I was too tired to take full pleasure in these things, and paddled on doggedly, head down, glad at last to see the lighthouse at Scrabster and to make a hasty camp nearby.

I was totally worn out and, even in the luxury of dry clothes, the fact that I'd just completed the fourth stage of my journey made little impact on me. But it had been a fast passage along the north coast. I had caught up to only a week behind schedule and, given a fast run down the east coast, could finish the next section around predicted time.

163

❖ ❖ ❖

From my camp high above the beach at Scrabster I watched the breakers lapping at the rim of Thurso Bay. Orkney drifted in and out of sight but, eight miles across the bay Dunnet Head, the most northerly point of the British mainland, remained a massive presence; it stands sentinel at the south-west entrance to the Pentland Firth, the most feared and treacherous tideway in all Europe, where the waves have been known to toss boulders aloft to smash the windows of the lighthouse, a mere three hundred feet above water level!

There followed an exceptionally rough night during which gale-force winds threatened either to rip panels from my tent or to heave it bodily off the cliff edge, only two feet away. Rain soaked me several times as, between anxious bouts of studying the tidal atlas of the Pentland Firth, I paid worried visits to the shore below to check that the storm-lashed tide had not yet carried off my newly re-loaded kayak.

I was camped not only on the brink of a cliff but on the threshold of a question which had persistently been asked of me by those who know Scotland's seas, and always left open: 'What are you going to do about the Pentland Firth?' I had always answered in terms of 'cross that bridge when I come to it' and put it largely to the back of my mind, unwilling to give it anxiety time when it was by no means certain that I'd even reach this far. But I had not been entirely lacking in foresight; during the distant days of security-watch in Aberdeen I had crammed five pages of A4 paper with detailed notes on tidal anomalies, hazards and warnings, and I carried a full Tidal Stream Atlas which outlined the crazy behaviour of the area over a twelve-hour period.

With neap tides continuing for a few days yet I could afford to wait for an improvement in wind conditions, but when the time came I would have to be prepared to go. Plotting and planning in the tent I stored up nervous energy against the Pentland Firth. I became a campaign general in charge of a commando assault and immersed myself in the timing and tactics of the next manoeuvre; there would be no margin for error.

The *North Sea Pilot* of 1875 contained a warning to mariners that is repeated unchanged in modern sailing directions:

'Before entering the Pentland Firth all vessels should be prepared to batten down, and the hatches of small vessels ought to be secured even in the finest weather as it is difficult to see what may be going on in the distance, and the transition from smooth water to a broken sea is so sudden that no time is given for making arrangements.'

Through the Firth, tidal streams run stronger than anywhere else in Britain and encounter various obstructions in the form of islands, reefs and headlands, any of which cause eddies and races which, in restricted passages, become particularly violent. In some places the transition from the eddy-currents to the main stream can occur almost instantly and even in calm conditions heavy turbulence occurs in the races. But the most terrible forces of all are unleashed when the tidal currents cross the paths of moving waves or a ground swell, or are opposed by strong winds. At such times, according to the *Pilot* again, 'a sea is raised which cannot be imagined by those who have not experienced it'.

The greatest danger for me lay in being drawn into one of the major races by the tidal streams which sweep towards them at a rate of 10 knots and more, far in excess of even my most desperate paddling speed!

Slowly, by matching the coast and distances shown on the O.S. map with the tidal constants, speeds and directions of the flow, and the experience I'd gained of sea/weather interactions, I began to grasp the situation.

I resolved not to attempt the passage on spring tides, with a wind or awkward ground swell opposing the tide, or with a wind over Force 4. By keeping to the Inner Sound, the narrow channel (one and half miles wide) between Stroma and mainland Scotland, I could avoid the Pentland Skerries and the great whirlpool known as the Swelkie. The Inner Sound was described as 'navigable with extreme caution', for its hazards included Dunnet Head, the race known as the 'Merry Men o' Mey' and the great 'Bore of Duncansby'.

I then did some calculations concerning the timings of the flood and ebb streams and, feeling far more in control of the situation, I walked into Scrabster, to the Fisherman's Mission, for a shower and a cup of tea.

It was a typical Mission, filled with cases of old paperback books, and black and white photos of the Queen looking younger than me.

On the wall, next to a nautical version of 'The Lord's my Shepherd', was an ornate three-foot list of sailors who had lost their lives in the Pentland Firth. I left feeling insecure and apprehensive about that list of names: there was plenty of space left at the bottom!

Down at the pub I sat in despair and confusion after a chat with local fishermen had almost entirely contradicted my own calculations based on hours of poring over the Admiralty information.

, The most worrying discrepancy concerned the very first hazard, Dunnet Head itself. 'Ye'll hae ta tak 'er on the flood, boy – there's mountains o' watter come aroon' on the ebb'. My *Pilot* notes read categorically, 'Avoid Dunnet Head on the Flood'!

It may be, I thought, that they were having a little joke, or just plain didn't like me. Either way, even in the light of local advice, I couldn't bring myself to abandon the style of calculation and tactics that had got me this far. As usual I would have to 'paddle my own canoe', but would have given much for a definitive schedule that I knew was the right one to follow. The following day was the last of the neap tide run, and a low wind was forecast, so I walked back to the tent to finalize the plan and to prepare for an early morning start.

A great mass of water swirls around Dunnet for six hours, in both directions, twice a day. It would be impossible to paddle against it (the fisherman's point), but folly to go with it due to the turbulence and the chance of losing control (the Admiralty point). But if I could reach Dunnet on the early part of the east-going (flood) stream and pass close inshore I might just avoid the stampede further offshore to my left. But the timing for the Dunnet Head section also had to be co-ordinated with my passage through the next obstacle six miles further on at St John's Point, the most violent of the whole Firth, the race called the Merry Men o' Mey. Normally it spanned the whole of the Inner Sound in a violent barricade of standing waves which would certainly engulf me, but during the final two hours of the west-going stream it becomes detached from the mainland side and can be passed with care in a small boat. So if necessary I could wait eight hours for that chance, and if that went well I would be approaching the next race, at Ness of Huna, at its least violent – that is during the west-going stream. Of course I wanted to be heading east, but a strong westerly stream such as the Pentland creates a fast eddy in the opposite direction and, as long as I could avoid the conflict points between eddy and main stream, I could travel eastwards on that.

Fuelled by a Mission bacon sandwich and pumping adrenalin like a hydraulic ram, I set out early across the eight miles of Dunnet Bay towards Dunnet Head, my heart restrained only by the lifejacket laced extra tight. It was, in a way, the ultimate challenge of the journey and yet, strangely, I had felt more nervous and insecure at the Mull of Galloway. As I crossed Dunnet Bay I never really credited the possibility that I might not make it; through the boat I felt a supreme confidence, but together we were prepared for some frightening water.

It took me two hours, exactly as planned, to reach Dunnet Head where, under massive black cliffs I hung close inshore on a ribbon of lumpy but manageable water. This was big motion, but the flood had started and, as I rose on the waves I could see, to seaward, exactly what I was so carefully avoiding: the main rush forged like a breached dam, an inky undulating torrent, eastwards beyond all control.

Having edged safely around the cliff headland I stopped for nothing and bore out across Brough Bay, where I fought against wind and an eddy stream to reach Longeo Skerries below the Queen Mother's Castle o' Mey. It was a wet and exhausting crossing, for the eddy was unusually powerful, and on two occasions the wind almost caught me off guard; but on reaching the skerries I ate lunch very happily. Within three hours of leaving Scrabster I had penetrated the outer defences of the Pentland Firth; so far so good, although the next section would be the most serious. Conditions were good and I decided not to wait for the tide to reverse, but to go right ahead. After a lunch of mackerel steaks and biscuits I blazed forward, paddles flashing, on the strength of the flood tide, ready to meet the Merry Men o' Mey on their own terms. I knew I had them off guard, for they are at their most powerful during the west-going stream, and charged onward full of confidence.

At the corner of my eye I caught coastal features roaring past at an incredible rate as I added my most powerful paddle strokes to a 10-knot Pentland tide. The feeling of superhuman power was similar to that experienced when you run up an independently moving escalator, and it filled me with potent fire. I let out a yell as I approached the race and saw its bowed shape stretching out toward Orkney. It would not detach from the shore for another six hours yet, but there was no going back now and my heart missed a beat as, with a sudden sickening jolt I hit the race and dropped three feet in level. With any opposing wind or swell I should have been immediately swallowed up and possibly transported, underwater, northwards; but it didn't swallow me, and on that day the turbulence resembled little more than a Grade III river rapid. I remembered to start breathing again, and before I really knew what was happening I had fought my way out of the hollow and was being swept rapidly on to the race at Huna.

Huna, I caught dormant and unawares, playing with her vast eddies and domed upwellings as though she was about to release a submarine from her ocean depths. I was heaved gently sideways in an unnatural shunting motion, but long before the race could muster full strength I had punched my way across the troubled water and was heading for John o' Groats. Beyond Groats lay the terrible Bore o' Duncansby race, already visible as a white crescent extending northwards but wheeling gradually anticlockwise. Its fury would not subside until the tide turned westwards, so with a long, tense but successful day already behind me I decided to pull into John o' Groats for a black pudding supper, a pint and an overnight camp.

John o' Groats was bubbling and swirling with tourists like a major whirlpool in its own right. Gift-wrapped girls and souvenir hunters thronged around the signpost-photo booth and the 'last house' in Britain, and the canoe, drawn up on the sand at the harbour edge, provided yet another curio for sensation-hungry tourists. I quickly adopted anonymity in land-clothes and sat on the harbour wall with a can of lager watching them hover around it like a flock of vultures, tapping it with their feet to see if it was dead, unsure whether it might jump up and bite them. Craning their necks to read what was left of the stickers, they seemed genuinely puzzled as to where it had come from. I had seen it all before and wanted to avoid questions. I was extremely weary, but after three of the Pentland's worst obstacles, was also full of relief and a glowing contentment. There was a colourful sunset back towards St John's Point and a view across Duncansby to the light and raised horizon at the Pentland Skerries. Closer than South Ronaldsay and Swona of the Orkneys, marking the opposite edge of the Inner Sound, was the island of Stroma, off whose north shore runs the whirlpool called the Swelkie. Here according to legend a giant salt-grinding quern once ground so much salt that it sank the boat on which it was being carried and so the sea became salty. Both the Swelkie whirlpool and the continued saltiness of the sea are fair evidence that the Giant Pentland quern grinds powerfully even to this day.

I camped within sight of the seething progress of the Duncansby Race, but felt no fear of it, only a peaceful indifference; surely it was all downhill from here?

Foul of Eastern Promise

'I met a herring fisherman-
A leader of his class,
Who many weeks had feared
What now had come to pass.
You want to know the cause, said he;
I'll tell you straight and square
We did not catch the fish, my friend
Because - They were not there!'

('The Reason Why', W.R. Melvin, 1931.)

On Thursday 8th August the sun shone in congratulation upon the 270-foot cliffs at Scotland's north-east corner. The Bore o' Duncansby, the final race of the Pentland Firth, had been safely defused in the early hours of the morning, and my wet paddle blades flashed mirror-like as I rounded Duncansby Head and, for the first time on the journey, began to head south. This part of the Caithness coast is a geological feast of caves, cliffs, stacks and – perhaps the most distinctive feature of the Old Red Sandstone cliffs – the magnificent, deep-delven rock fissures known as geos. As high and majestic as the great cliffs themselves, these geos transform the coastline into a natural wonder which far outranks the greatest cathedral; and the sea, glass-calm as I had never before seen it, allowed the kayak to explore this wonder to the full. There was 'Fast Geo' and 'Thirle Door' – a two hundred-foot-high entrance to a sultan's palace of silver rock – and 'Wife Geo' with its two entrances, one a tunnel, the other a skylight opening to the south. If architecture is 'frozen music' then these cliffs were fossilized symphonies, and I moved among the orchestration like a conductor's dream.

As I wove and dodged between and behind the famous Stacks o' Duncansby, a young kittiwake fluttered weakly from the cliff and landed in my lap! I placed her gently onto the raised deck on top of my map and there she sat, apparently quite contented, a comical figurehead as I paddled past the Stacks. And so we forged south in *Brian's Ark*, an eighteen-foot banana boat with a human crew and a feathered skipper, lazily paddling in calm and sunshine, soaking up the landscape, the compass registering a steady 'S'.

Scotland's east coast is quite markedly different to the west in many ways. Most obviously it is much lower, less mountainous, and is a 'single' coastline, lacking the island fringes of the west and north. Unlike the west, which is cut to ribbons by innumerable sea lochs, the east has only five major indentations or firths, of which only the Dornoch Firth is in any way comparable to the sea lochs of the west. But the sea itself felt quite different to what had gone before. As yet I was unable to put a finger on the difference, but perhaps it would come to me as time went by.

Meanwhile the bird and I moved southwards, she strangely docile and I suddenly responding to the company with an endless stream of nonsense conversation. It was nice to have a companion but she (for I always think of the gentle kittiwakes as feminine!) was obviously unwell and I didn't really know what to make of her situation. Hopefully she'd stay for a while, accept some food, perk up and fly off. The wind inevitably increased and the glassy sheen left the sea's surface. Off Skirza Head there was light turbulence and we took a few waves on board, but a kittiwake is no stranger to sea-spray and, bracing herself, soon developed her canoe-legs. Nevertheless I got a cock-headed, one-eyed frown whenever I was clumsy enough to allow a wave to break over her – she was female right enough – and soon I was leaning over or slowing deliberately to avoid bow waves as much as possible!

With our seafaring partnership cemented by our first headland together, I decided that lunch was in order and pulled in neatly at the tiny Skirza pier as though it was a transport cafe. I ate my usual pepper-pâté and hard biscuits, but the 'delicacy of the month', salmon spread, was donated to the bird who was now showing yuppie inclinations by perching on a nearby cabin cruiser. Through tweezers from my first-aid kit she readily accepted half a pot of salmon.

Lunch over, we headed across Sinclair's Bay to Noss Head, but within minutes of a rising wind the bay became rough and we changed course inshore towards Ackergill Links; and we almost made it. Only a couple of hundred yards from shore she lay back against me and seemed to lose strength; her legs stretched out stiffly and a wing flapped in a sort of spasm. Her head cocked limply to one side and I realized she wouldn't last long now. I put on a last sprint for land, but arrived with her dead on my lap. She remained unnamed and I'd never know the cause of death, but at least she didn't die hungry, and in her final hours had brightened ten miles of travel for a wandering canoeist. The limp body on my beached canoe attracted the attention of a little girl on holiday, who poked at the bird and squawked 'It don't work no more!' in offended Cockney. I wanted to explain why it was there, and where it had come from, but it sounded too 'Snow Goose' to be credible.

By the following morning the brief respite was over. Somehow, despite constant deflation of hopes, I still believed that eventually there would come a month when the weather would be sunny and windless; but the familiar pattern of high winds and heavy seas that had dogged me throughout seemed determined to reassert itself. In fact my journey down the east coast was to become a month of meteorological bedlam in which I was to experience everything from thunderstorms to sleet, and winds peaking frequently at Force 9, in what was later rated by the Met Office as the 'worst summer in eighty years'. The challenge was to become as stubborn as the weather itself, and to continue to force progress where possible, in short powerful bursts. But not today.

I looked out from the tent across the sandy beach to the largest bay in Caithness, where Tang Head and Noss Head, with a fierce race around each, enclosed a corall of 'white horses'. The radio warned of 'SEVERE GALES (F9) IMMINENT', and as if to make me feel better about being landbound yet again, confided that ferries on north and west coast routes had also been grounded.

Beyond one of the massive 'blow outs' – where prevailing winds had broken their way through the dune system and spread sand slowly inland – was a great, steep-sloped dune gushing thick smoke like a volcano about to erupt. I assumed at first that someone must have lit a driftwood fire in its lee, but there was no one around, and only later did I realize that I was watching a 'sand-spout' in action. The wind, funnelling up the concave dune-face, was whipping dry sand off its peak in a smoke-like wispy stream. Impressed, I sketched the scene, then took the chance to reseal the tent which had become distinctly less than waterproof during the last month. It was also an ideal day to give the sleeping bag a much needed airing.

It was days like this, with strong winds funnelling off the sea and over the berm – that part of the beach above normal tide level – that made it possible to see how the dunes form, travel, collapse and reform, for they are only another form of wave. Sand dunes are classified into different 'species' according to where they occur, but they are all wave-like in character, ranging from overgrown ripples to the mountainous Saharan 'whaleback' ridges of up to two hundred miles long and seven hundred feet high. Some are described as transverse, parabolic, sigmoidal, all terms also used for waves. Others are shaped like stars formed by variable winds, or crescents formed by constant trade winds. Star dunes remain in one spot, but most dunes are mobile according to the prevailing winds. The coarser grains roll themselves up the windward slopes and over the crests with the main gusts, while the finer sand floats off with the gentler side-eddies of the main wind, forming and maintaining the dune's shape and character as it moves.

Along Scottish coasts 'foredunes' sooner or later become 'reardunes' moving inconspicuously but relentlessly inland. Marram and other grasses and coastal plants may stabilize and reduce sand movement to a certain extent, but in many areas dune-shifting and blowouts deposit so much sand over coastal farmland that expensive artificial erosion control and other conservation measures have to be implemented. But we should think ourselves lucky; the seasonal dunes of south-east Asia reverse themselves twice a year under monsoon windshifts, and the fast moving dunes of the *barchan* in Africa or the *medano* in Peru may travel at up to a foot a day!

❖ ❖ ❖

Next morning, bright and fresh with the wind again rising fast, I made an early start, reached Noss Head by 9.30 and covered the eight miles to Wick Bay in one and a half hours. Fantastic geos again added a touch of the sublime to the trip, with waterfalls tumbling from a hundred feet and yet never quite reaching the sea. I even saw one powerful cascade blown back up onto land by the wind funnelling up the cliff face. Here again were arches, weird sea-stacks and caves that could have swallowed a trawler. Outcrop after outcrop, mile after mile, green-topped, white-sided cliffs raced me south like an endless train that was always keeping just ahead of me. I could see its carriages snaking off into the distance, and after a further two hours the scene was still largely unchanged. But now on the horizon stood two oil platforms, and beyond them, low and hazy, fifty miles or more to the south-east, was the Moray coastline.

After noon the sea shed its choppy, agitated morning costume and it was pleasant paddling into a bright afternoon sun. Reflecting on the water it burned my face and I squinted constantly to protect my eyes, yet every time I opened them there were still caves and cliffs, cliffs and caves.

Occasionally there was a dull, weighty 'thud' as my paddle hit one of the plate-sized, brown Lion's Mane jellyfish. There were hundreds of them, some up to two feet in diameter; they give a nasty sting and I consciously kept my hands out of the water, but I loved their peaceful meditative presence, like floating Buddhas enjoying the sun. But further on there was a more sickening presence, herring, gulls, black-headed gulls, kittiwakes and auks – also in their hundreds, all dead, and spread over a large area. I counted sixty on the narrow path of my kayak alone, yet there was no visible pollution such as oil or sludge; my 'layman's' conviction that 'pollution' meant something dirty, smelly and sticky was being challenged.

By 5 o' clock and with over eight hours on the water, I was growing weary and my nose and eyelids were burnt raw by exposure to salt-wind and sun. Where at last the cliffs seemed to die away to the south I sought refuge in the tiny harbour at Lybster. The east coast, I'd decided, was not less beautiful than the west, although the scenery didn't have its stark and self-sufficient grandeur. Part of its beauty lay in the settlements, tiny picturesque villages and solid little harbours of local rock, tucked in the most unexpected corners of a daunting coastline. Like so many others that I passed or stopped at, Lybster seemed to grow unobtrusively from the powerful timeless rocks. Monuments to man's craving for sanctuary on the weather-edge of the North Sea, these clinging rock villages have the charm of well-thumbed but well-produced picture history books, giving an insight into the prosperous but short-lived days of the east-coast herring fleets.

Until the late eighteenth century the Scots had no boats equipped to catch or transport, nor the means to process or preserve, the vast shoals of migrant herring that arrived in Scottish waters each year. But by the 1790s merchants and curers were setting up contract systems with Scottish fishermen; the framework of a gutting and salting industry was being formed onshore, and by 1800 over two hundred Scottish boats were involved in the two-month herring season. By 1820, a thousand boats could be seen congregating in the Moray Firth for the season and numbers continued to grow until the early years of the twentieth century, when some ten thousand boats were involved.

Chasing the 'silver darlings' was no longer seasonal or local; the fleet, followed by itinerant curers, coopers, merchants and fisher lassies, followed the shoals clockwise around the coast to meet the huge market for the herring.

After the Russian Revolution of 1917 the Russian market collapsed, and after World War I the Germans, Dutch and Norwegians began to develop their own fishing industries; in addition the herring were thought to have moved further north with the Gulf Stream and by 1934 the herring catch was less than half that of 1913. The fleet rapidly diminished and the industry became concentrated on the larger ports.

At the height of the herring boom Lybster had been the third largest fishing station in Scotland, after Wick and Fraserburgh. Today it is a quiet harbour with only a small traffic of lobster and crab boats; a peaceful town where one could spend a dreamy night undisturbed.

Early evening, two young fishermen came down to 'my' shingle beach for a chat. One of them worked on the famous Wick fishing boat the *Boy Andrew* which, he boasted, had consistently landed more fish than any other boat in Scotland since 1977. The largest in Wick's fleet, at eighty-five feet, it won the 'Top Scots Boat' award in '82 and '83 and probably landed more fish than any other boat of its size in Europe. The other one explained that he, too, worked in Wick, the large town fifteen miles north, so I asked what brought them both to sleepy Lybster for a Saturday night.

'Fanny!' he replied, and waved to a couple of strangely half-dressed but amply upholstered girls on the harbourside. 'Dolly's nae wearin much tonight, boy' he said, his eyes lighting up, 'and she'll be wearin' less later on if I've onything to dae wi' it!'

Apparently young people regularly take taxis the fifteen miles from Wick for the Lybster 'nightlife'; what's more, there was a wedding on in Lybster, and it would be a wild village that night! So much for my quiet evening; even after three and a half months

I'd learnt nothing about first impressions!

With a parting nudge and a smile probably born of a few days at sea, Iain the fisherman implied that the Lybster 'fanny' was of exceptional quality, that I'd be welcome at the celebrations and that I could 'use' the fishing store-house afterwards if I liked. 'Ye'll be a' right with her on the nets, boy, and I should know!'

I crouched for a couple of hours on the shingle and read Clare Francis until the warmth of the evening had gone, then wandered up the hill to the quieter of the two village pubs. The pub was busy with pre-reception drinkers, and Iain introduced me to the local curiosity, an old man who had, he said, spent his life at sea. In fact he talked as if he was a boat and was known as 'The Ship'. Swaying from side to side on his seat, as though rocked by a restless tide, he clutched his head in his palm and declared that he had 'a sair prow tonight'. We chatted away about Caithness and the novels of Neill Gunn, who 'The Ship' claimed to have known, but revelations of undoubted wisdom such as 'There's more brass on the winch than on the keelstone' went way above my head.

'How're ye doing, Ship?' shouted someone across the bar.

'Oh, going like a battleship!' said he, and made the appropriate chugging sounds. He swayed around the tiny bar as though he was navigating a small harbour, threatened to torpedo some young 'bloods' who were baiting him, and all the time poured back black rum like red diesel.

After a hard day's paddling and a couple of drinks the soft nets of the fishing store sounded even more appealing than the Lybster 'fanny'. Iain slipped me two bottles of Guinness 'for the road' and shook my hand as I left. Touched and a little drunk, I was stumbling down the road in pitch darkness looking for the store when the second fisherman drove slowly past me to demonstrate that he, at least, had 'secured the company of a young lady'. He sounded his '4th of July' airhorn and roared away with her to the harbour before I could see if it was Dolly or judge whether she was in fact wearing any less than before.

I slept well and long, curled up among lobster-creels, nets and ropes coiled like great anacondas, on the floor of the fishing store, and woke to the sound of harbour gulls. Back down at the beach the gulls had been in my hatch, opened and shredded my food bag, and eaten all the chocolate-chip cookies that were to be my breakfast. So with only a cup of coffee I sat on the shingle and waited for the tide to rise.

Again I set off on a long cliffside journey, flowing south with them and bouncing echoes off their walls, but after about two hours' paddling I passed into the entrance of a massive archway, through which I could just make out light at the end of a tunnel perhaps a hundred yards long. The entrance was so huge – perhaps thirty feet wide and seventy feet high – that it felt like entering Tolkien's great tunnels of Moria. Suddenly I gasped sharply, and in blind panic began to back-paddle as hard and as fast as I could. I was perched hopelessly on the brink of a steep slope of water rushing downward to the tunnel exit in the dark distance! Instinctively I threw my weight backwards to escape the forward thrust, but fully expected to feel myself plummeting down, out of control, any second.

Of course, nothing happened. Water just doesn't form hills, nor does it stabilize with a height difference between two points a hundred yards apart! Soon I calmed down enough to see that the water wasn't even moving at all, but still I was the victim of an extraordinarily powerful and vivid optical illusion on a huge scale! Far more effective even than Ayrshire's famous 'Electric Brae'. After some minutes I concluded that if the water was level, then the strata of the rocks within the tunnel must be angled slightly upwards away from me. The roof perhaps sloped slightly downward to the smaller exit arch, and the tunnel effect itself-looking through the gloom to the brightness of the exit-enhanced the illusion. It was all very unsettling and if I had had a handbrake no amount of rationality would have persuaded me to release it, for that tunnel still looked and felt like the slope of a ski-jump. Slowly I edged through it, my heart unsteady, and was eventually able to look back uphill from the bottom. Shaking my head in puzzlement I passed out into a blinding sunlight knowing that, in all my journey, the 'electric arch' had been one of the most bizarre and impressive of natural phenomena.

I wove the kayak carefully through a maze of sharp skerries, hauled out on a large rock platform and walked across a bridge-like tidal reef to have lunch in a cove almost inaccessible from land. Surrounded by sheer cliff walls, it was a perfect suntrap, and a haven for seabirds. The shingle was coated white with guano and the piddly aroma of a high-rise bird colony was strongly present. But there was also a smell of death. Along the lower section of the beach hundreds of birds were stone dead, and many more stood dazed, apathetic and bedraggled on rocks near the tides' edge. The worst affected seemed to be fulmars, gulls and terns, but there were also shags and guillemots, and an otter, dead but still limp, which had perhaps been feeding on the dead birds. The stench of death in some corners, magnified by the midday sun, was overpowering.

Immediately I thought back to the scene at sea the previous day, and to my passenger from the Stacks o' Duncansby, and it worried me to be amid such a powerful death force and yet be totally ignorant of its cause. There was no more than the usual litter on the shingle shore, and no oil or any obvious form of conventional pollution. But then with many modern contaminants, only their damage is detectable by human nose or eye, by which time it is probably too late. The story of present-day pollution, exploitation and mis-management of the North Sea is a sickening one, but bears a little exploration.

Each year in frightening quantities the products of our increasingly industrial and sophisticated society find their way into the North Sea. Giant ships, specially built for the purpose, dump over 5 million tonnes of industrial waste, 100 million tonnes of dredge spoil – the highly contaminated sediment from industrial ports, harbours and canals – and about 6.2 million tonnes of sewage sludge every year. Sewage sludge is a mixture of organic matter, heavy metals, biocides, detergents, petrol and other hydrocarbons, which contributes to a shortage of oxygen in seawater and sediments, a reduction in species diversity and an increase in fish diseases. Persistent toxic substances accumulate in fish and in seabirds, and many North Sea fishermen are already reporting deformed and mutant fish among their catches.

In 1988 Britain was the only country dumping sewage sludge in the North Sea, and in 1990 was the only country, bordering the North Sea, committed to disposal of waste by dumping at all.

And, sadly, dumping is not the only source of North Sea contamination. Pipelines around our shores pump huge quantities of industrial effluents, heavy metals, treated and untreated sewage, and of course liquid radioactive wastes into inshore waters.

These pipelines rely on dispersal and dilution to reduce the levels of toxicity in the waste; but, as many substances persist in the food chains, and accumulate, 'dilution as a solution to pollution' patently

178

does not work. Some shellfish, such as mussels, seem to thrive on their industrial diet, but concentrate pollutants within their own bodies. These are then passed on to species which eat the shellfish, such as seaducks and waders, and already seafood from the Firth of Forth is considered unfit for human consumption.

Heavy metals, acidic gases, airborne pesticides and other substances also reach the sea via the atmosphere, although it is not yet known in what quantities, and river-borne pollution has reached a significant and worrying level. New synthetic substances, sometimes even known biocides, are continually being discharged via rivers, and in many cases the substances are so new their effects on the environment are uncertain or unknown. Some of these man-made organic compounds, being non-biodegradable, will remain and circulate in the ecosystem indefinitely. The highly toxic PCBs for instance, being insoluble in water but highly soluble in fat, will accumulate in the body tissues of animals and circulate in the food chains.

Perhaps the most horrific source of all is ocean incineration. 90,000 tonnes of highly dangerous waste is incinerated at sea each year where it is difficult for authorities to control and monitor operations. Ocean incineration involves an enormous risk even in the loading and transporting of such devastatingly toxic substances, and the consequences of a major spill hardly bear thinking about. But most shocking of all is that toxic wastes are not totally destroyed when burned and some escape as dangerous pollutants into the atmosphere. Others – like PCBs again – can even be converted by incineration into new, even more toxic, compounds like dioxin, which remains in the environment indefinitely, and is known to cause horrific birth defects. *The North Sea in the mid-1980s was the only sea in the world where waste burning on a commercial scale was permitted.*

Quite apart from chemical contamination, the widespread disposal of plastic garbage from ships and via rivers is also harmful to living organisms, either by entanglement or by ingestion. Beachcombing along the North Sea shores reveals plastic bottles, plastic sheeting, polystyrene foam, glass bottles, cardboard milk cartons, metal drums for petrol and diesel, lavatory cleaner bottles, plastic crates ... most of which have been dumped indiscriminately from ships. A recent examination of fulmars found dead on Dutch beaches revealed that 92 per cent of them contained plastics, at an average of twelve plastic objects per bird. The birds had died of blockage, or of ulceration of the gizzard.

❖ ❖ ❖

In geological terms, the North Sea is relatively 'young'. A young and developing ecosystem will often tolerate substantial disturbance without irreversible change, and by the same token might have considerable powers of recovery once any deleterious influences are removed.

Had this not been so, perhaps the North Sea would already have been poisoned forever beyond hope. Even given its vigorous, developing nature, there is now serious concern among scientists that we are approaching, or have already exceeded, the North Sea's capacity for assimilation of our waste. Other states have already adopted major precautions with regard to North Sea pollution, but UK authorities – using infallible logic without even a hint of wisdom – have concluded that because causal relationships are hard to demonstrate there is no proof of any inability of the North Sea to assimilate pollutants.

The saddest fact of all is that the techniques are available to treat effluent of almost any origin. Much of it could be recycled and used as fertilizer – but there is always the overlying imperative to seek cost effectiveness. Ocean incineration and dumping are cheap. New standards of environmental protection could be achieved, but the level of public demand must balance the cost of the treatment; only then will we begin to influence the policy makers.

We tend to forget that the sea is not merely a highway, a playground and a dump, that it is also our larder, the home of other creatures, part of the heart and respiratory system of the world, and that it is only plundered at the cost of future problems. The North Sea and its natural resources constitute an irreplaceable environment, but while we remain short-sighted, dirty and thoughtless neighbours, every sullied wave is a crash of guilt on the shores of Earth.

❖ ❖ ❖

Camped on a grass verge above the steep shingle beach at Helmsdale, my canoe-gear dried on the fence of the main railway line from

Inverness. Comfortable in dry clothes with coffee and a cigarette at the end of another long day, I could relax and think in general. Progress was good; the daily mileages were picking up and I was enjoying the Caithness coast. The inflatable roller had proved to be the perfect answer to my portage problems; unlike the portage trolley, it took up hardly any of my valuable storage space, weighed next to nothing and could be used on almost any terrain, avoiding only sharp rocks, broken glass and nailed driftwood.

Why did the sea feel different? Of course it was a SEA rather than an OCEAN, a relatively confined, shallow basin which could never develop swell or travelling rollers on the scale of the Atlantic. The tide flowed slower and more evenly, unrestricted by islands and channels, and obstructed by fewer massive headlands. There was a different weather regime too, different wind patterns, different sunpath and no seaward sunsets; was that it?

My mind drifted. I didn't get so lonely these days; tired – yes, melancholy – occasionally, but I was generally far more able to channel the negative moods into different forms of energy. Part of the change was due to the fact that there was no doubt now in my mind that I could complete the trip; the end of the expedition was now mentally graspable and less than three hundred miles away. But a part of it was also due to a growing philosophical attitude of acceptance that I was proud to recognize. A far healthier attitude towards hold ups and weather problems was even more important to me than any improvement in canoeing skills. However, the vague feeling that the real challenges of the trip were over, that it was only now a matter of time, was utterly mistaken!

By evening the radio forecast could do little more than confirm the conditions which howled outside the tent. The cloud-base had descended and the first fronts of a depression were stampeding across the North Sea. Looking at maps inside the tent, it seemed the most plausible next move would be down the coast to Golspie, make a ten-mile crossing of the Dornoch Firth to Tarbat Ness, followed by a fifteen-mile crossing of the Moray Firth to Findhorn. This meant that the Nairn/Banff coast lay at least three days away.

But on Monday 12 August the surf beat manically on the rough coast and the onshore wind whipped spray from the sea two hundred yards to my tent. I donned waterproofs and walked into Helmsdale town; there was no possibility of going to sea. The front page of the P & J newspaper seemed to sum up the weather situation.

'STORM HITS FASTNET RACE'
'AIR POCKET SAVES SIX AS YACHT CAPSIZES'
'MAN DROWNED AS BOAT IS LOST'
'Storms have ripped up 100,000 tons of seaweed from the Channel... The piles of weed are now up to 6 ft deep from the high tide to low tide marks.'
'POP STAR CHEATS DEATH' (Simon Le Bon had a close shave as his yacht capsized!)
     and more locally:
'FIVE PLUCKED FROM BUCHAN ROCKS'

Severe gales (F9) were forecast again, and I had no trouble in justifying my decision to stay onshore.

I read in a tourist brochure that near Helmsdale, at Baille an Or, ten miles up the Strath of Kildonan, was the site of a great Gold Rush in 1868 and 1869. Apparently more than four thousand ounces of gold were found over four years and there was supposed to be more yet. Gold in Scotland! The whole idea struck in me, as it has in many others, a deep romantic note, and I wished I could find out more.

As it happened, I was down in the pub that evening and fell in with a gang of swaggering, unshaven, rough-cast drinkers who claimed to be gold prospectors!

They didn't exactly have gold dust among the stubble, or 'Clementine' tattooed on their forearms, but in torn shirts and heavy boots they certainly looked the part of modern day Klondykers. One produced, from his hip pocket, a small phial of what looked like brass filings, slapped it on the bar and boasted that it was in fact two ounces of pan-collected gold, worth well over £400! When another clenched his hairy fist at my chin I prepared to order a round, but he was merely displaying a solid ring of 22-carat Kildonan gold. 'Plenty of that left in the hills, if you know where to look – there's even nuggets if you're lucky. And that's just the run-off. No one ever found the Motherload'. 'Aye; there was an Irishman found the Motherload, but he was killed in a brawl before he could tell!'

Kildonan gold has found its way around the world in brooches, rings, and even forms part of the British Crown Jewels. Now this was getting interesting and, over another couple of rounds, I found out all I could: Were there really nuggets? What size? How does the 'panning' process work?

My prospectors had set up a panning camp at Carn na Buth (Hill of Tents) near Baille an Or (Town of Gold), ten miles up the Strath into the hills. Keen to take them up on promises to show me the techniques of simple panning, I accepted their invitation to join the rest of the evening's revelry back at the camp. They all seemed strangely insistent that I should join them, but for the moment I thought nothing of it. So we headed into the back of a pickup truck, drunk and garrulous, and rumbled and swerved along a winding road which carved its way uphill through the night. Half an hour later we tumbled out at Carn na Buth. The sky was clear and full of shooting stars skitting across velvety black, and the cold night air had begun to sober me up: there was only one tent!

A Tilley lamp threw flickering silhouettes against orange cotton and the tented scene, from outside, seemed Bacchanalian and raw. Hoarse male voices roared and shouted and cigar smoke reached me on the night air. Then someone shouted 'Come on in, we're opening the bottles'. There were two large bottles of malt and we were off again – bawdy jokes and trinket wisdom, displays of whisky knowledge and, even for a drunken night, an exceptional level of friendliness among these men. They rested leaning on each other's laps, sat with arms linked and generally touched more than I'd noticed down at the pub. Just for the slightest moment again it seemed like a strange set up – ten guys together in one tent – but the thought passed as the bottle reached me yet again. I began to feel tired, my head spinning, and I asked where I should sleep.

'Oh, there's only the one tent, you'll be OK in here with us'. A roll of laughter went up as a curtain was pulled back to reveal a cramped awning with sleeping bags lined up edge to edge as though for the seven dwarfs, and a couple of them already 'crashed out' at one end, their arms tightly round each other. 'Yours is the one in the middle; the zip doesn't work, but you'll be warm enough'. Another roll of laughs!

Now I began to worry; ten guys choosing to sleep together, two in the corner cuddling, and me in the middle! But I was absolutely 'steamboats' like the rest of them, I hadn't a clue where we were, and was dependent on them for a lift back to Helmsdale next day. It was time to play my cards carefully.

I crawled into the bag, removing only my jumper for a pillow, declining the offer to share that of my neighbour, and stretched out to sleep. 'Perhaps I'm being too suspicious?' I wondered. 'Maybe they're related, or just very good friends?' and I began to relax and doze off. Then I felt it, quite unbelievably at first, then more obvious, the rasp of rough skin against nylon and the pressure of a heavy hand searching for my tenderest places.

Hell, what do I do now! I'd never been faced with such a blatant sexual challenge before. Could I just go along with it? How do I *really* feel about homosexuality? Was this the time to experiment? No one else need ever know… But no, I genuinely couldn't face it: the idea was too sudden, the situation too sordid; it turned my stomach. Quickly I rolled over to turn my back to him. Then I realized that might be interpreted wrongly and pretended to be fast asleep! Of course now I'd rolled over to face the others. It was awkward. I didn't want to create a scene by telling the guy to 'F-off' or starting a fight, besides where would I go? Equally I needed to make it clear that I wasn't interested! Minutes later a hand crept towards me from the other side, feeling for an open zip! This time I growled loudly, flipped onto my front and continued to 'sleep', all the time cursing my stupidity in falling into yet another ridiculous situation. There were muffled rhythmic movements and bouts of laboured breathing from parts of the darkness around me, but soon, under the influence of the malt, I found it impossible to remain awake any longer and, ignoring the lingering pressure of a heavy hand resting on the sleeping bag above my bum, I drifted off to sleep.

I woke early and uncoiled myself from the arm of my sleeping neighbour, and got up to explore the river. The day felt clean and healthy after what seemed like such a bizarre and tainted night. 'But nothing happened,' I told myself, and yet I knew that something had happened. I had been in a situation of opportunity, had thought about it, decisively refused it, and yet been unperturbed enough to sleep in the midst of it all! I'd learnt something about my own attitudes. But I didn't learn anything about panning for gold, and if anyone ever sings 'Oh my darling Clementine' I'll laugh, for on the whole it had been an experience, a bit of fun, and a tale to tell. Back on the beach at Helmsdale, physically unaffected but emotionally wobbly, I made breakfast, broke camp and was glad to find the company of a young girl. She was picking her way carefully towards me, stepping tenderly and gently on the large rounded shingle with bare feet. With fair, almost white, hair hanging to one side of her shoulders, I thought she was very probably a mermaid. The accent said otherwise, just a lonely Swiss girl out for a morning stroll. She told me that the reason she had been walking so slowly and carefully was that, sitting low in the shingle with my wetsuit, she'd thought I was a seal! We shared our shattered illusions with a laugh and some biscuits; after all, the only thing more paradoxical than a kayaking seal is a *Swiss mermaid*! After last night's experiences I was temporarily muddled as to what I really was, but as the morning grew warmer my mermaid hitched up her T-shirt and stretched back on the shingle with a sigh and a dreamy look in half-closed, heavy-lashed eyes, and I was in no doubt any more. I lay back too and we chatted and watched the tide filling the calm inshore bay like a great basin. But the basin was the wide Dornoch Firth and, brim-full, it was ripe for the long crossing.

Standing up to her knees in the water, my mermaid pushed the kayak out, smiling. For a brief moment I hesitated, then waved and paddled on. The sea felt so right that morning that I turned my bow from Brora and bore out directly across the Firth towards the distant, invisible peninsula of Tarbat Ness. The land-based attraction had almost held me and yet I had turned back to the sea and was happy on it. Perhaps I really was a seal, or at least a Selkie! But the mysteries of human sexuality paled into insignificance as I gathered momentum and reached out, always seaward, into the Firth.

Shifting clouds allowed brief but brilliant shafts of light to spill over the long low crocodile of Banffshire; By the time I looked back I could not distinguish the Helmsdale shingle, and I knew she could no longer see me; but you never can tell with mermaids, so I waved again.

An hour to sea and all was peaceful, muffled and still, save the familiar swish and trickle of my paddles. The land came and went in caprices of low cloud, leaving me well out of sight of it for long periods while my steady, gentle rhythm made itself known upon the still noon tide, bringing Tarbat Ness ever closer. Often

I stopped paddling to glide, to drift and, finally, just to float – to savour that silence that is not an absence but a positive and tangible presence, and is too seldom a part of contemporary life. So often had solitude made me miserable, longing for company; now I could feel it enriching me, pruning back my dead branches and encouraging healthy new growth. I soaked up the goodness of utter silence, and floated some more.

And then the shroud was torn, the airwaves shattered and, through their ragged remnants the vandals appeared from the east. Jet fighter planes seared through the sky, banked steeply, circled and doubled back, slashing the clouds and towing an evil growl all the way down the Tarbat Ness peninsula towards Dornoch. The noise was horrendous, unchallengeable, and was repeated, with slight variations on the manoeuvre, regularly for the rest of the afternoon. Sometimes they came across the Firth so close and so low that I could see into the cockpit, and with a volume which pressed me down into my seat and reduced me to a cowering, unbalanced wreck. I thought again of the whales and dolphins who perceive their world through such an exquisitely sensitive sound system. It is thought that the chemical fouling of the seas, man's greed for fish, and entanglement in nets and dredges, have been largely responsible for the virtual disappearance of these species from the southern North Sea. But with sound travelling four times faster in water than in air, and the proliferation of power boats, planes and missiles, man is surely guilty of polluting their environment in the most diabolical way of all – noise.

Sometimes the jets became muffled as the planes disappeared behind great cloud-banks in the depths of the Firth. Then I would hear a dull but definite 'thud', and a puff of smoke would rise like a balloon from the low grey shadow that was MOD land near Tain. It became clear that they were flying a pattern – different speeds and heights, banking, circling in – and bombing the hell out of something. Again! and Again! And Again!…

All the time I slogged onwards until the fighter plane circuit lay well to the back of me. Now the land had become bold enough to sneak out from the cloud for longer periods, and rhomboid rain-shadows gathered and rumbled at speed across the Firth to dump their loads on land, much as the jets had done.

And my head remained craned upwards, for there was a third

form of aerobatic manoeuvre to capture my attention on that long afternoon crossing. Silent this time, but not without its element of hooliganism and raw injustice. A tiny, delicate tern dodged and wheeled its way frantically through the skies, desperately trying to dodge the persistent and calculated teamwork of the two skuas that hounded it.

These skuas, or 'bonxies', are the arch fish-pirates of the high seas. Dark brown with white flashes, as big as the largest gull, they are professional hook-billed predators specializing in offshore aerobatic harassment of smaller birds. They weren't hunting the tern itself, but its last catch of fish. Nevertheless, it was a vain, losing battle for the tern as the skuas worked coolly in tag-rota. Relieving each other in an intricate, weaving flight which slowly but surely wore down the skill and stamina of the tern, the skuas rested alternately and so remained fresh and composed. The tern became distressed and twisted and shrieked in a flight of helpless determination, one skua shadowing its every manoeuvre effortlessly, the other occasionally making short bursts to keep the tern from heading shoreward.

The noises of desperate appeal and fear were heartrending, and the pursuit so full of suspense, lightning action and dazzling flying that even I was quite exhausted when it was all over. At last beaten, the tern ejected its fish and flapped wearily shoreward. One skua caught the morsel of fish before it hit the water, and both winged lazily off to seaward in search of more sport. I had seen this form of predation before and was always captivated by it, but miles out to sea, in all that great arena, happening right above my head, that was perhaps the most vivid show of all and reminded me that a well-planned open sea crossing is one of the most special of kayak experiences.

So engrossed was I that I nearly blundered into a massive grey seal, fast asleep in mid-Firth. In direct contradiction of the common belief that seals always haul out on the rocks to sleep, he bobbed in vertical position in the light swell, snoring soundly with his large-snouted nose held skyward and the big V-shaped nostrils flapping open and closed with each deep breath. His eyes were closed, and their sight is poor anyway (many blind seals live an apparently normal life), but hearing and sense of smell are acute, so I approached carefully from downwind. With a couple of long silent strokes I was close enough to touch the massive head, and out of sheer badness I stroked its sensitive whiskers with my hand. Immediately the eyes opened, and after a blank, disbelieving stare the seal exploded into action! Accelerating with a massive pull of the front flippers and a great commotion of spray he thrashed, dived and disappeared, almost capsizing me in the process. It would have served me right, and as I refound my compass bearing and paddled on, a gruff, indignant head surfaced a short distance to my left. If seals could talk, I'd have learnt a few choice words that afternoon!

One of the saddest sights on a long crossing is the number of burnt-out bumble-bees flying aimlessly and exhausted in a zig-zag path out to sea, or floundering helplessly in the water. I have heard no adequate explanation for this phenomenon except that it may be a navigational mistake caused by magnetic influences that sends them off course to die at sea.

My own navigation, however, was on form, and soon I was approaching Tarbat Ness where the candy-striped lighthouse stands proud and exposed on the long rugged promontory. The rain I'd watched playing across the land all afternoon eventually caught up with me, or perhaps I caught up with it; either way, a dark swollen cloud was pricked by the sharp eastern point of the compass and rain poured over the sea. After staying dry on a 17-mile open sea crossing, without so much as a wave-splash all day, it seemed incredible, but I was drenched within minutes.

At first I was annoyed and uncomfortable, but heavy rain, in a small boat at sea, is a game in itself. I found myself suddenly deluged and paddling across pockmarked water, the heaviest beads of rain resting momentarily, like mercury upon the brine, until the surface tensions evened and the salt engulfed the fresh. It was fascinating to watch, beautiful to be among, and all the caked salt of the day, in its marbled white patterns, was washed away in seconds.

At Rockfield, on the southern edge of the peninsula, I landed after four hours, eighteen miles of paddling, and camped exhausted by a lone phone-box on waste land overlooking the next target, the wide Moray Firth.

❖ ❖ ❖

'Get up you fat bastard, it's 6.30!' I woke with a jolt like an electric shock, but it was just a fisherman's 'dawn chorus' to his reluctant mate. As the mists of sleep shifted I focused on a large spider clearing debris from a beautiful web on the upper corner of the tent. With crossbow technique, by delicate movement of its front legs, it was actually 'firing' the garbage into space, systematically clearing the entire web. The wind was forecast Force 6 easterly, and the Firth lay wide open to the east, so I was reluctant to break camp. But this stalling was just part of the morning routine that ensured that the dreaded moment when I left my warm cocoon to don cold, wet shorts and tee-shirt, and a salty, festering wetsuit, was postponed as long as possible. Eventually, breakfast, forecast, planning all over, unable to prolong the wait any longer, I would make an iron act of will and spring, naked and screaming, out of the tent to the rear flysheet and pull the whole lot on while a tight grimace contorted my face. Then I'd stomp around, felling the tent and packing the boat until the damp had again soaked into my skin and my body-warmth began to fight back inside that reptilian hide.

I wriggled into the slipper-fit of the kayak cockpit where at least my lower half was out of the wind, hauled on the double spraydeck, then it was out of the frying pan and into the Moray Firth.

I headed south east into an immediate world of chilling wind, perhaps not yet Force 6 but – with a heaving sea of white crested grey and plenty of flying spray – a good Force 5 at least. It was a dismal seascape with visibility down to about six miles in the heavy rain; the distant Banffshire coast would not be visible for a few hours yet.

My growing confidence in the boat continued to amaze me. This could be over five hours of difficult paddling in a fierce wind and angry sea, working on a compass bearing, but even in these conditions I knew I could manage the twenty-mile crossing. I pushed on, determinedly at first, and then cheerfully aggressive, as I settled into my stroke.

The Pilot notes warned to 'avoid Guillam Bank' eight and three quarter miles due south of Tarbat Ness, where there were dangerous overfalls and confused seas especially in conditions like these. But I had calculated my course to pass well to the east of the bank, and the tidal movement out of the Firth would serve only to increase my safety margin. Safety was still paramount. I had telephoned the coastguard before setting off and would phone in when I arrived on the other shore. My back pouch was full of assorted rocket and smoke flares in case of trouble, and for the extreme contingency, the Sarbe radio distress beacon, programmed to transmit a signal on aircraft and ship frequencies, was tucked beside my seat.

The crossing proved long and arduous. The danger of the wildly breaking sea was much reduced by its regularity and predictability, and the rain subdued the swell slightly, but I was constantly drenched by waves which ploughed spitefully over the boat. The wind had its usual devastatingly tiring effect on me, and the bones of my bum became sore quickly – a bruised legacy of yesterday's prolonged sitting.

Uncomfortable from the start, the pains in my bum and lower back grew worse, but I forced myself past the two-hour mark before allowing the 'luxury' of a half-bar snack of salt-soaked fudge. By this time I reckoned that, despite wind hindrance, I should be roughly half way across the firth; but the target coast was not yet visible, and behind me the Tarbat Ness coast had also disappeared. I was in a viewless bubble of weather, adrift and alone far out to sea; the nearest land was ten miles away in two directions, twenty-five miles in a third and the fourth was open North Sea to Norway.

There was again that very special, though queer and daunting, feeling of being far beyond any sight or sound of land, that I'm sure very few people ever have the chance to experience. Certainly those who have will never forget it.

It would have been comforting to know for sure whether I had crossed the half-way mark, for my bladder as usual had begun to nag, my bum ached and my mind was tired from concentration on the waves and from strict adherence to the compass bearing. And hunger was setting in! Nevertheless I enjoyed the rhythmic discipline of the prolonged paddling situation and pushed on, artificially motivating myself with squares of fudge at half-hourly intervals in much the same way as one would coax a young child up a mountain. I set my watch to 'bleep' regularly, and studied its face – as it passed on every other stroke – with salivating anticipation like one of Pavlov's dogs!

Occasional RAF hooligans still hogged the skies, but not so many as the previous day, and now their noise was drowned by the louder – yet less oppressive – roar of the sea. This was bottle-nosed dolphin territory and I was delighted at one point to see the tumbling gait of wheeling greybacks travelling alongside me. They didn't stay long, but it was more than enough to send my spirits soaring, and I 'whooped' involuntarily as a four or five-footer leapt clear of the water ahead of me. As it dived again, the whole group seemed to move off, presumably to find a faster and more agile companion than this plodding human.

After the dolphins the seascape remained blank until well beyond the three-hour mark when the coast at last appeared as a distant tea-stain on the otherwise unblemished horizon. If the darkest point was Culbin Forest near Findhorn, my bearing was accurate and I stepped up the pace a little. But it took another two full hours before I beached; my 'forest' turned out to be a stretch of dark cliffs, and I'd drifted with the tide almost eight miles farther east than I'd calculated and so given myself a longer crossing.

Dragging weak and wobbly legs, and still wearing my wetsuit, eyes half-closed and salt-crusted, past caring what anyone thought, I wandered into the sleepy Banffshire village of Hopeman for some groceries and a black pudding supper, and to phone myself wearily but safely off the water. I remember little else about that evening except that my 'wonder-roller', which had served so well, burst irreparably along a seam, and it looked as though the boat would be in for a hard time on the rough beaches of the east coast unless I could come up with some alternative.

When I landed at Cullen the following evening it was with another hard fight behind me; twenty-three miles 'all out' in another Force 6 easterly. To save putting the tent up I settled into a gorgeous deep cave in a grassy mound overlooking the rocks to the west of the town. On the map it was called the Black Lady's Cave, but unfortunately there were no Black Ladies in it these days. After a quick search to make sure, I lay at the cave mouth and wrote in my log until the light was gone, then settled back with a coffee to watch the darkness fall. There was a light breeze from the sea and several bats darted around the cave mouth catching insects I couldn't even see. Periodically a row would break out from the gull and shag flocks on the rocks at low tide. It's a good coast for seabirds, and many have local names: the kittiwake is simply a 'kitty'; the razorbill is a 'coulter'; the guillemot a 'queet' and the little puffins are 'Tammi Norries'. I suppose that somewhere, sometime there were reasons or stories behind the names, but there seems little reason or sense

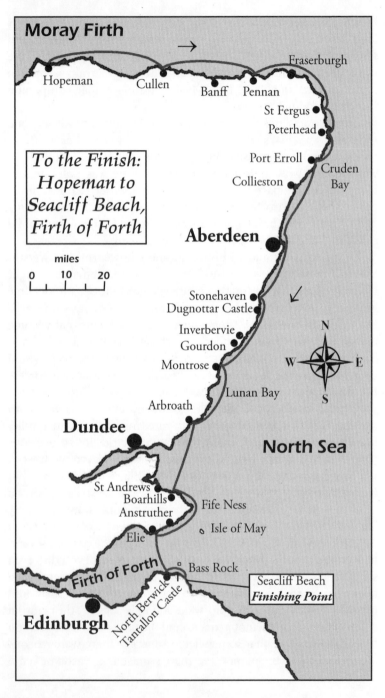

behind this anonymous east coast poem about the shag:

The common cormorant or shag
Lays eggs inside a paper bag
The reason you will see no doubt
Is to keep the lightning out
But what these unobservant birds
Have not noticed is that herds
Of wandering bears may come with buns
And steal the bags to hold the crumbs.

Deep within the cave itself I heard drips of water tapping steadily, melodically, different notes from different corners and they lulled me into a gentle sleep, but above me it remained dry all night.

Early next morning a little girl, out for a walk with the family, ran ahead and peeped into my cave. She was standing, staring in silence when I lifted my head in the half light to look at her. She turned tail and ran away as fast as she could and I heard her trying to explain to a sceptical father, 'But Daddy, there really is a man asleep in that cave up there!'

The following night I was re-civilized in so far as I was living in the tent again, at a tiny cove near the picturesque village of Pennan. But it had been another twenty-two cold and windy miles of many chilling splashes and my sphincter muscles had several times given up the fight to contain the bladder-flow. Now at the day's end – totally beat yet again – I was too tired even to bother washing properly. But apart from a brief note in my log commenting on 'personal standards going downhill fast', I didn't care much.

My mind flashed back along the day's shore of sandstone cliffs, caves and blowholes; the towns of Portsoy, Whitehills, Banff and Macduff, harboured and nestled, greystone amid green-capped red-grey cliffs; the great swelling of Troup Head rising from the hollow at Gardenstown. It was good going; despite wind at above Force 6 I had paddled my way off three O.S. maps in two days, and the next map would take me round the Fraserburgh/Peterhead corner to Cruden Bay, virtually home territory.

'To hell with the weather, I'm still moving,' says the log. I felt unstoppable and realized that the wide crossings of the firths, and hard paddling along the Banffshire coast, had significantly reduced the schedule gap.

Next day of course I was 'stormbound' again. 'So much for my relentless progress!' I thought as I listened to a Force 8 gale and watched it shovelling the sea in great lumps. I'd been out in an '8' before and will never forget rising on a steep wave to have my bow caught by a gust and flipped into a backloop! That had been a long time ago in Galloway, but I wasn't yet ready for a second bout. Maybe a rest day wasn't such a bad idea.

Dismal grey weather as usual eventually infected my spirits and it was a day of accident after cock-up after calamity after disaster. First I tried to have a wash at the shallow edge of the steep shingle beach, but stumbled and fell headlong into deep cold water, almost giving myself a heart attack into the bargain. Then I spilled rice over the inside of the tent and knocked a mug of coffee into my sleeping bag. I exhausted myself by jogging over the hill to Pennan in search of a telephone and some entertainment. The phone was broken, but there was a local showing of the film *Local Hero*, scenes of which were actually filmed in the village – that would have made a nice end to the afternoon if it hadn't been sold out!

Obviously it was a jinxed day, so I supposed it was better at least to be on dry land. Back at the tent I cut and fried huge 'steaks' from a giant mushroom – bigger than a dinner plate – which I'd found by the roadside, and gazed, unthinking, out across the shingle to the great cliffs at Troup Head.

Suddenly a fast car swung into the bay, screeched to a halt, and several figures tumbled out onto the steep shingle beach. There were four young lads with two air rifles which they began to fire rapidly. At first I thought they must be shooting at the canoe, and jumped out of the tent wearing only my thermal trousers. But it was the birds they were after, firing wildly into the gull flocks and kittiwake ledges on the cliffs.

I shouted, but as I expected they paid no attention; so I went to my B.A. pocket and emptied its contents quickly on the grass – a collection of marine pyrotechnics that would have made Guy Fawkes tremble – and selected a giant, red, rocket-flare. I shouted one last warning to the 'hit squad' then, with a bang of the palm and a twist of the wrist, released the rocket with a loud 'BOOMFF' to scream over their heads and smash in red flame against the cliff! Before they could reload I had another flare cocked ready and aimed at their car. They got the message, grabbed the guns and fled, wheelspinning away as suddenly as they had arrived. I could hardly have asked for a more instant cure for potential depression, nor a more interesting end to a dull day, and chuckled as I crawled back into my coffee-lined sleeping bag; Dirty Harry eat your heart out!

❖ ❖ ❖

By the time I reached Fraserburgh a dense sea-mist had rolled in from the east and swallowed the bay in a blanket of wet, white silence. This was the famous North Sea Haar; a notorious east-coast shipping hazard born of the rapid condensation of warm, moist continental air masses as they travel across the North Sea.

Crossing Fraserburgh Bay, a bustling centre of fishing traffic, was a frightening and cautious manoeuvre, like paddling upside down in a murky sea. Visibility, in feet, was down to single figures, and even the tip of the kayak seemed a distant object. I pulled on my hi-glo hat and carried a white collision flare in my hand as a 'comforter' and paddled as quickly as possible, for other boats had to be located by sound alone. Massive iron hulks cut through the mist, sometimes only yards from me, moving slowly and cautiously on their own radar-assisted courses, entirely oblivious of my tiny presence. Slightly farther away, dark looming shapes would almost materialize, and then dissipate again like Captain Kirk having 'beam me up' problems, and I dodged their paths on the basis of sound directions which I well knew to be deceptive anyway! My deck compass was set for the lighthouse across the Bay at Cairnbulg Point, but I'd twisted and woven my course so much that I no longer trusted the bearing. Surely I'd crossed the bay by now? Was I off course, or perhaps heading out to sea? Suddenly the light tower was dead ahead of me and a nasty-looking sea was breaking, without volume, on the bar to the south of the light. Caught on the rushing tide I rounded the Point at speed, compass registering south east, then south. Still the Haar thickened and began to distort, even to magnify, things. My eyes are not reliable at the best of times, but as I came close inshore a group of gulls on the beach looked almost ostrich-sized. In fact, for a moment, I thought they were cattle.

Now well out of the traffic of the bay, I had no way to pinpoint my position in the Haar. For all I knew, the rest of the world had been taken by the goblins, but for sure Rattray Head was still there, its presence to the south revealed by the occasional deep-bass of a double siren. But how far away? I couldn't tell, but I remembered from the ever-pessimistic *Pilot Notes* that, due to strong tidal streams and an uneven sea bed, dangerous seas and sharp reefs were to be expected off Rattray Head.

No matter how apprehensive I was about meeting hidden trouble in the mist, it seemed never to come any closer. I checked my watch – one hour from St Combs, at 4 knots – I should have passed Rattray by now. Then, just as at Cairnbulg, out of the Haar, only fifteen feet ahead was the great light-tower of 'the Ron', surrounded on all sides by a churning sea.

Looming mysteriously high above was the red-painted siren, in a narrow circle of tunnelled vision, like the 'pipes at the gates of dawn'. I heaved in a nervous sea as the strong afternoon tide swept south, around Rattray Head, towards Peterhead. 'HMMMOOOOOO' bellowed the siren at my back as I forged south west hoping for the security of seeing the coastline again.

No landmarks, nothing to pinpoint where I was, I'd had enough of this and was ready even for a damp night in a soggy tent. As I rose on a wave I saw a cluster of white-washed cottages on the shore and headed in. Again I was the victim of a mist-mirage, but only after going to great lengths to beach in the heavy surf of a steep-shelving beach did my white-washed cottages take wing and fly away – a group of resting gulls!

The salt rinsed from my wetsuit as it hung on a barbed-wire fence in heavy rain, and the tent was still soaked from the previous night. But the evening brought a brief clear period when the North Sea Gas terminal, behind the dune-slack pools at St Fergus, blossomed in beautiful colours across a small reservoir from my camp. Despite the wet tent I slept thoroughly and hoped to reach Cruden Bay next day. In fact next day's effort – a furious and protracted battle through atrocious conditions and past several dodgy areas of water breaking unpredictably on jagged reefs – gained me only 5 miles south to the massive breakwaters of Peterhead Harbour.

Peterhead was 'Eastern Promise' in a nutshell; now the principal fishing port in the whole of Europe, it bulged to the seams with a lively fishing trade as well as vessels serving the offshore oil industry. I wove carefully past huge trawlers, Russian Klondykers and under the mammoth anchor-chains of outsized container ships, along a line of identical rig-supply vessels, each with its helipad, and finally through the ranks of yachts and small pleasure craft to a sandy shore to the south west of the bay.

The rain persisted down as I dragged the boat ashore and changed my clothes under the veranda of a golf-club pavilion. My towel, having been drenched for days, was useless to me, but I put on my clothes anyway and was never more glad to see those thermal trousers. Someone stepped up the rainflow like gunfire on the pavilion roof and the boats in the harbour faded into hazy grey shadows.

To the south the granite cliffscape is generally hardwearing and uniform in character, but many stacks, caves and inlets have been gouged by the sea and by glaciation along the easier-eroded dykes of dolerite. At the spectacular Bullers o'Buchan are stacks, blowholes, arches and rock-arenas among some fine cliffs. Then Slains Castle appears, high on a precipitous cliff where between 1893 and 1910, the arch-vampire Dracula inspired Bram Stoker to write his horror tales. The coastline fragments into rocky outcrops and small inlets with the delightful local name 'Yawns', before it opens on the wide sandy beach at Cruden Bay.

Pippa and I had spent many happy weekends here with a tent and canoe while I trained for the journey in the winter surf and along the rocky shore. I camped, as usual, at our craggy knoll overlooking the Port Errol Yawn, where a tidal burn flows out through a winding passage between cliffs, where there are views of the castle and its rocky drop, and where the lobster fishermen always wave 'hello' on their morning creel-checks.

But next morning I missed them for I set off early, initially against the tide as far as Collieston, to reach Aberdeen, 20 miles south.

Across wide Aberdeen Bay I could see the familiar skyline of home and knew, without maps, where to find the harbour, but the journey seemed to drag on and on. Helicopters plied back and forth to the oil platforms on the North Sea horizon like pollinating insects, and a huge tanker and several smaller supply vessels moored off the harbour awaiting servicing.

While still well out to sea I had to bulldoze my way through two very heavy sudden squalls which could easily have capsized me had I been unprepared. But I had become an avid, if subconscious, weather watcher, unusually sensitive to subtle signs and changes long before they hit me. Squalls are short, powerful, localised windstorms, often taking the form of a sudden violent rain blast in a heavy downdraught of cold air. I had seen these squalls passing over the land as deep grey shadows and then watched them wheel out to sea and approach my path with gathering speed. In the final moments the sky darkened as the heavy cloud came skimming across the sea towards me. Beneath it the grey blur of rain reached down, like the strings of a puppet, to a mass of frothing sea. I braced myself as the wind leapt from about 15 to about 40 mph, shook me and then disappeared just as quickly seaward, leaving me ruffled and wet to continue on my way. After a total of four hours from Cruden Bay I entered Aberdeen Harbour at almost exactly the estimated time.

I rounded the harbour wall and stemmed the outflow of the River Dee, watching the cirque of tall, glassy oil-company office blocks that meant 'home'. There were fishing boats, patrol-boats and cargo-ships, and as I entered the main harbour the huge blue and white P & O Ferry St Magnus steamed out past me on its way to the Shetlands, dwarfing my tiny kayak and making good footage for the T.V. film which showed my 'homecoming'. At the lifeboat berth I hung up my paddle for a couple of days, for I was back on schedule; but in the end it was just another stop before the final push south.

Coasting to the Finish

'*Four strong winds that blow lonely,*
Seven seas that run high,
All these things that are constant, come what may.
But our good times are all gone,
And I'm bound for movin' on;
I'll look for you if I'm ever back this way.'
                              (**'Four Strong Winds'** – **The Seekers**)

With a wave from the harbour control tower and a friendly salute from the pilot launch which crossed my path, the little kayak glided out of Aberdeen Harbour on the flow of the Dee and 'crossed the Bar' on the final leg of its journey, a hundred miles south to North Berwick.

Offshore a row of large vessels waited patiently for admittance, servicing or guidance from the busy pilots, while to my right, above the cliffs, fast trains thundered southwards along the coastal route to Dundee. It was a journey I had made countless times over the last ten years, following a stunning coastline of fragmented cliffs and jutting, recessed headlands, punctuated at St Cyrus and Lunan by great sickle-shaped sandy bays, and more frequently by innumerable coves and shingle inlets. Seen from an early morning train, it was perhaps one of my favourite pieces of coastline with a mist on the sea and the sun on colour-graded headlands, but only now – paddling south with the O.S. map in front of me – did I realize just what daft but picturesque names attached to these same coastal features. There was 'Tilly Tennant' and 'Blowup Nose', 'Doonies Yawn' and farther down the coast, the 'Three-Storey House' stack, 'Dickmont's Den' geo and the 'Mermaid's Kirk' blow-hole!

Fourteen miles south across Stonehaven Bay, beneath the perched ruins of historic Dunnottar Castle, the cliffs changed colour from grey to a deep red-brown until the tiny harbour-village of Catterline offered a chance to stop and snack-up. Then it was southwards past the lighthouse point at Todhead and the impressive red-cliff section known as 'The Slainges'. At Bervie the rock became a stiff black and shelly clay and I was ready to call it a day. Though only twenty-five miles from Aberdeen by my deck map, it was the result of seven hours' paddling, much of it against the tide, and so to camp.

I beached carefully at a small, shingled gap in the reef-fringed shore and made camp on a bank of grass overlooking Gourdon, Doolie Ness and the sea dashing on the broken teeth of many skerries within Bervie Bay.

This was the kind of shore that took chunks out of the fibreglass of a kayak dragged, but since the roller had burst in Hopeman I had been working on a new portage technique. The most common items to be found all along the coastline were wooden and plastic fishboxes – it made sense to use them. The theory is that if you are going to have to drag the boat ashore, then to drag it over smooth wood or plastic will do less damage than boulders or shingle. Two or more boxes can be used to create a conveyor belt, but in fact one is sufficient.

I rested the nose of the kayak on the box and pushed it along until it balanced midway, then I walked to the nose and pulled until the kayak had traversed its whole length along the box. That meant I'd crossed eighteen feet of rocky foreshore with minimal wear and tear to the boat. The efficiency of the 'fishbox system' was improved by wetting the boxes, or even laying seaweed across them to create an almost frictionless surface; a little bit more bother than the roller, but a good second best, and perhaps it would see me to the finish.

As night fell on Inverbervie, some heavy cloud spread across the full moon, a wind rose from nowhere, and suddenly things didn't look too good for tomorrow. For a long time I stayed awake enjoying the crashing of the sea on the rough shore and wondering whether the high spring tide would reach my boat, but for the first time amid impending weather and severe conditions I felt a profound calm. Four months of weather frustrations had taught me how futile it was to feel angry or thwarted; now it was accepted with a shrug; it no longer mattered.

The high tide came and passed at 2am, and at last satisfied that the canoe was safe for twelve hours I rolled over, zipped the bag and slept soundly. At 6.30am I popped my head out to meet a dark leaden sky and a cruel sea speckled with the flying manes of innumerable white horses. Spume and spindrift rose from the sea crashing on the reefs and blowing over the tent.

Later there was no change; the day stayed rough and I stayed put, warm and snug; my rhetoric and persuasion in a 35-mph south easterly were very effective! All day the sea was frantic, and noisy as hell, as I worked out a projected schedule, wrote a brief Press Release for Intermediate Technology and phoned Fox's to announce the finishing date as Wednesday 5th September at midday. With a date set the race with the calendar was on, and with the weather still proving obstinate, meeting that date would be the final challenge of the trip.

There followed a second rough night when I feared damage to the tent in severe and regular squalls, and there was little improvement next morning. The sun broke the cloud cover but the wind remained above Force 6 and the sea churned white all around.

I wove gingerly out from the beach, dodging reefs and swelling surges which threatened to dump me upon jagged rocks. Along the coast it was hard going. The wind raised a large white-topped sea which broke up on the shallows inshore and sent salt spray steaming across the swell. Paddling initially against south-east Force 6 and a 2-knot tide, this was the kind of day that tests equipment and experience to the full. Thankfully both were still in good nick for it was an exhausting trial. Off Johnshaven the sea became, for a brief stretch, especially dramatic as the wind climaxed with a sharp thundering squall before returning to Force 6.

For two and a half hours I fought southwards spitting salt spray from my mouth, and narrowing my eyes against enthusiastic, wind-blown waves which broke boisterously across my forehead, before impending exhaustion forced me ashore to find a landing on the extensive beach at St Cyrus Reserve.

At one point the wind whipped the paddle blade from my hands, but I had it tied to my wrist, as usual in such conditions, and pulled it back from the water before I hit the first wave. Then there was the large surf to crash through before beaching beneath the dunes. This was wild!

Moving quickly to ward off cold and wind I dragged the kayak up the beach, unpacked lunch and high-tailed it into the dunes for shelter like a frightened rabbit. On the beach I had been unable to face the wind for the stinging pain of the wind-blown sand against my salt-swollen face; my eyelids hung heavy, red and raw as though from a boxing match. But out of the wind the sun was pleasantly warm and soon raised a steam from my damp kit. Parched and ravenous, I demolished two Mars bars and twelve Jordans bars straight off. Constant salt spray had swelled my lips and gummed my throat and, having no fresh water to drink, I opened a 2-litre bottle of wine saved from Aberdeen and gulped half of it down almost without stopping! It quenched the thirst but stung my swollen lips and throat, and knocked me unconscious for perhaps a half hour under the sun.

I woke, feeling dazed and drowsy, to the same bright, fresh, fast-forward, starkly blue-and-white day that I knew spelt a hard fight at sea. Forwards, sideways and eventually backwards, it took me many attempts to crack that heavy surf-line, but there was none of the sheer terror of the Atlantic seaboard, just teeth-gritting hard work. I was determined, refuelled and, with the help of liberal dowsings in cold water, soon restored to full consciousness.

Still the wind howled from the south east. Often as I powered over the crest of a steeply rising wave the wind would whistle up its forward face and catch my bow from beneath. Then with a couple of strong strokes I'd launch into take-off, aqua-planing temporarily before plunging downward under the sheer weight of my equipment. This inevitably meant a steep dive, a deep entry into the trough, and a thorough soaking. But it was pure exhilaration, kept me wide awake, and made sure there was very little danger of overheating!

The afternoon's campaign took me south past Montrose, and across wide Lunan Bay until the sun had taken an evening position in the sky and, after eighteen miles, I began to feel truly done. I groaned, stretched my back and changed my deck map, groaned again and struggled a final five miles around the red sandstone cliffs to Auchmithie, a remarkable little cove with a cluster of whitewashed cottages atop an exposed and barren cliff.

Here eighteenth-century fishermen lived extremely comfortably from smuggling, for the red sandstone cliffs are honeycombed with caves and are ideal for hiding contraband goods. I had 'nothing to declare' other than my remaining litre of Aberdeen wine, but the sheltered caves above the little harbour offered a welcome alternative to pitching the sodden tent again.

Physically and mentally drained after the sixteen-mile wind-journey, I climbed the steep cliffside stairs, one hundred and fifty feet to the village, and treated myself to high tea at the café. The large bouldered beach at Auchmithie was reckoned to be excellently adapted, in times past for the drying of fish. Split and filleted they were laid out on the stones, in the sun, to dry before smoking, and it was here, not Arbroath, that the world-famous 'Arbroath Smokies' originated.

I was served a magnificent meal of smokies by two pleasantly dotty old waitresses, and all the helpings seemed huge. The main meal was followed by two pots of tea, two racks of toast, two sets of scones and butter and two vast slabs of cake. I ate until I could hold no more, popped a couple of buttered scones into my pocket for breakfast and returned to the beach. Only later did I realize that I'd been given two high teas! With duplicate helpings of all but the main course the ladies must have forgotten that they were both serving the same customer! I accepted it with a smile as the reward for a hard day, and spread my bed at the cave mouth, drank some wine and let my eyes wander.

There's not much to Auchmithie harbour today, but there had been a thriving fishing community in this extraordinary cove for hundreds of years. In the early days the boats were dragged up the beach and secured to iron rings above the tide, much as I had done, but the harbour was built in the 1890s and in its prime thirty-three boats fished out of Auchmithie. Ancient customs and traditions were strictly preserved, and until very recently, the menfolk were always carried through the surf to their boats on the backs of their women, to save them wetting their feet! But during the Second World War a stray German mine floated into the cove and blew a large hole in the harbour wall; the harbour has declined in use ever since.

I relaxed quickly as the warm food mingled with the wine and the tensions of the day left my body. I watched birds and bats on the cliffs above me and the stars appeared shyly as the late August sky darkened into black velvet.

❖ ❖ ❖

With no tent to pack I was on the move early, and with as settled a day as I'd had since Duncansby in the far north I branched out southwards and eighteen miles across the wide firth for the crusty, rusted outline of the Fife coast. My initial plan had been to cross the inner Firth from Carnoustie, a mere twelve miles, but it felt like the ultimate in freedom to be able to alter course with a sudden change of weather and a twist of the compass dial; to take life and adventure in the same hand and to run with them far out to sea. I knew by now that these long, open crossings were taxing and dangerous, but also that they offered the special rewards of a unique small boat experience: the feeling of powering across a vast stretch of open water, miles from land and entirely self dependent. Just set your rhythm, choose your song and away you go:

'Freedom's just another word ... for nothing left to lose.
Nothin' ain't worth nothin', but it's free ...
Feeling good was good enough for me
Good enough for me and Bobby McGee'

and although it felt like longer, the crossing took under three hours to reach well south even of St Andrews. I came ashore at a sand patch among reefs at a pretty little spot called Pitmillie, and sat behind a tuffet, sheltering, for the wind was on the increase again. Cracked sharply on a stone, a boiled crab I'd been given in Auchmithie opened to provide about half a pound of meat which was good with biscuits after the long, hungry crossing.

There followed a wild night of hammering rain, thunder and lightning and next morning the sea bucked like a spooked stallion in a ring. As canoeing weather it was far from ideal, with the Fife shore wide open to a Force 5 easterly, but I hoped to reach Pittenweem, a mere fifteen miles around Fife Ness. The battle was on.

Just north of Fife Ness Point are several dangerous reefs known as the Tullybothy Craigs, or Balcomie Brigs, and with the wild water ricocheting off them conditions were pretty bumpy. As I rounded the point, travelling at speed and fighting for control among random reflected waves, I had an audience of scuba divers resting on the rocks below the coastguard centre. No one on shore could have known how my heart thumped with apprehension as I bounced through the rough, so I surfed forward on wave surges and rode the choppy swell as stylishly as I could before disappearing, a further four miles down the coast, for lunch at the picturesque East Neuk village of Crail. Later the wind rose to Force 6 and I bounced past Anstruther on harsh, crashing waves, stunned into almost constant reflex actions by cold soakings. While my energy lasted I laughed inwardly and enjoyed the sheer flying sport of it, but by the time I reached Pittenweem and negotiated the awkward swell pouring into the harbour mouth I was cold and tired.

Leaving the canoe on the harbourside, and my wet tee-shirt and shorts hanging to dry on a boarded window I went off in search of my friend Iain Macaulay whose studies of the Anthropology of Scottish Fishermen had required him to set up home in Pittenweem; for, almost unique among the villages of the East Neuk, Pittenweem can still boast a fishing fleet and a thriving fish market for local catches.

My hope was to finish the journey in the next two days by paddling out to the famous Isle of May Bird Sanctuary, eight miles out in the Forth Estuary, as a 'stepping stone' before crossing finally, via the Bass Rock, to Seacliff Beach near North Berwick. But next day, Sunday 2nd, there was a warning of Extreme Gale Force 9 IMMINENT – surely a day to explore the East Neuk on land! Monday 3rd too was extremely rough and I accepted the cumulative persuasion of the coastguard, the harbourmaster and the wind itself, that the Isle of May trip had to be abandoned. The old irrational feelings of frustration and disappointment reasserted themselves for the briefest of moments, but were soon submerged under a flood of passive acceptance, and I went down to the harbour content just to steal a few miles down the Fife coast.

The last thing I expected was to lose the canoe, but it was gone! There was no sign of it at all; even the clothes I had hung up to dry had disappeared! A small fisherman who saw me running around in frantic circles, fretting and searching, himself became worried and spoke of a spate of thefts in the harbour area recently.

But who would steal a canoe? What had I left inside it? Was I covered by insurance for theft? Were the contents covered? And what do I do now?

Swim! Dammit, I'd be unable to make the final journey to Seacliff; unable in the end to finish the trip!

Still, I'd got most of the way there... It wasn't my fault if the boat was pinched... And I'd almost talked myself into a miserable acceptance of the whole situation when the harbourmaster arrived, put two and two together, and relieved my worries with an explanation which, in retrospect seems quite bizarre. Apparently some 'helpful' locals, worried about finding a canoeist running about Pittenweem without his shorts and tee-shirt, had carried the canoe away and locked it safely in a storeroom along with the offending shirt and shorts!

Reunited with my boat, frayed nerves spliced with coffee and biscuits, I headed down the East Neuk coast in stormy and unpleasant conditions. The day was dark and unnaturally dismal, and even when sheets of rain joined the strong wind by mid-afternoon, very little light filtered through those enormous cloud ranks. It was the kind of day when things inevitably go wrong, and I breathed a sigh of relief when I beached safely, although only a few miles down the shore, by the ruined 'Lady's Tower' at Elie. It was named after a renowned local beauty, Lady Janet Anstruther, who used to bathe unrobed from it after sending a bell ringer through the streets to warn people to keep away! At least in those days royalty didn't fly around in helicopters catching nude bathers unawares!

With the end of the trip near I had become slovenly in my packing and had generally allowed strict routines and systems to relax; suddenly it seemed that everything was falling apart. Stupidly I had packed the various components of the tent in different places, which meant an upheaval of some dry gear while I tried to locate them; I even managed to lay my camera down in a saltwater puddle! Tired and hungry, shivering and wet, I pitched the tent on lumpy ground in the driving rain and was looking forward to getting dried, changed and into my sleeping bag, out of the damp with a cup of hot chocolate. Carrying very little food now, I had abandoned the use of waterproof sacks on the rear deck and stowed my dry clothes inside the hatches instead. Now I found my woolly jersey, in the rear hatch, to be damp and assumed the hatch-cover must be leaking a little. But when I went deeper to reach the sleeping bag it was absolutely drenched. It was pointless to lift the heavy, sodden object and wring it out, so I just left it there washing about in a great bath of feathery water in the rear hatch. I knew now there must be a serious leak, most likely somewhere on the hull again, and the sleeping bag, being down-filled, might well be permanently ruined. John Hodgson's repair, in conjunction with the 'wonder-roller' had seen me through over a thousand miles of turbulent waters and far-from-gentle shores, and only now, on the second last landing of the journey, required new attention.

Strangely enough I didn't stomp or swear, or even tut (for

tantrums are wasted unless you have an indulgent audience) and just resigned myself to a long night in a wet tent, wearing damp clothes, with no sleeping bag, in a howling wind and driving rain. To crown it all the BBC forecasted a continuation of rain and gales next day. I began to wish I'd just kept on my wetsuit!

I made that cup of hot chocolate, but the top part of my stove, rusted through by four months of salt air and rough-packing, broke off in my hand and couldn't be fixed. I tried to read but the torch packed in and I was out of candles; then halfway through a discussion the radio died, and I was out of batteries too!

What next? I thought as I wrapped myself in all my damp clothes, spread my cagoule over me and huddled on my mouldy karrimat, a book for a pillow. Roll on morning! One thing was certain: I wasn't going to stay in that miserable place. Tomorrow, Tuesday 4th, if at all possible, I'd strike out across the Firth of Forth, for only then would I know for sure that I'd make the finish by the pre-arranged Wednesday lunchtime.

I listened to the unhappy sea sucking at the muddy foreshore pebbles and thought of the long cold paddle across the dismal, leaden Firth that lay ahead.

Not surprisingly it was a sleepless and uncomfortable night and I was up at 6am to catch the tide, but for once it was no hardship to drag myself out and don the lurking pile of sodden gear for there were no comforts to forsake that morning.

The morning forecast wasn't good; a large ocean swell was reported, with winds already Force 5 or 6 northeasterly out in the Firth. Gale Force 8 expected 'later'. There were ten miles of open seaway to cross to reach North Berwick – a busy shipping channel for merchant, military and fishing traffic – and visibility was atrocious. What's more, despite a temporary repair patch, the back hatch was badly damaged; to start shipping water in the rear in mid-Forth would be awkward to say the least!

There would be massive oil tankers navigating by computerized radar, unable to change course even if they could see me; assault boats and minesweepers from the naval shipyards at Rosyth, moving in and out of the Forth and large, fast, modern trawlers, constantly changing course due to the nature of the work. This congested community of the open water co-exist at a safe distance from each other by radar screens and radio contact, but none of them were likely to notice me passing beneath their iron bows.

This was my normal rhetoric pattern before tackling a big problem. I would present the drawbacks and paths to disaster all the more convincingly in the full knowledge that I was going ahead irrespective!

The problem of bad visibility would be met with my usual token gestures of hi-glo hat and white collision flares, but it was my responsibility to dodge the other shipping, not vice versa; visibility did not compromise my meetings with the giant tanker and container ships or the speeding navy vessels as they wouldn't see me even on a good day. It would just have to be a two-hour dash of high tension and finely-honed awareness.

The weather pattern of recent days had been one of heavy winds and rough seas, but seldom reaching their worst before midday. A two-hour dash across the Firth should, I reckoned, be more than adequate to outpace the approaching gale which was, after all, only forecast 'later'.

It was 8am, with the tide already on the retreat before I had phoned the coastguard and was fully ready, and there was a twenty-yard drag to the water's edge. But soon I was bobbing off from Elie and into that vast body of water that is the Forth Estuary. All was grey and the edge of the world was at fifty yards.

Ten minutes out from Elie and already vague misty bulks were just discernible through the dense low cloud. What I originally took to be distant Craigleith Island began to move steadily, suspiciously, eastwards across the horizon. Twenty minutes from Elie and another hulking mass grew from the mist on my port side; it increased in size at an alarming rate accompanied by a rumbling ominous belly roar which I'm not sure if I felt or heard! In no time at all it had assumed mammoth proportions – a looming grey berg with a white-capped bow-wave which alone would have made confetti of my boat. The noise was intense. Was it coming towards me? The noise increased still. An urgent decision: it was heading across my path. I stopped dead to let it pass rather than attempt to dash across in front of it, and was instantly confirmed in my decision as it rumbled determinedly by like a rogue elephant within twenty yards of me at around 25 knots, a giant container-ship. Totally oblivious of my prudent, timid courtesy, even if it had crunched me beneath its bows it would have remained for ever as blissfully unaware as the man who, rushing home, treads on an ant.

Interpreting the vague and changing shapes of ships' hulls was, for a non-expert, a tricky business, and yet an essential skill in making a vital decision. Would it pass in front of me? To my right? My left? Will it cut behind? Should I speed up? Slow down? Is it coming for me? The decision must be instant and certain, for if they are bearing towards you they arrive with frightening speed.

At one stage there were six distinct but hazy hulls within range, and each required mental plotting! The trick was to paddle on a fixed bearing, a straight line, swerving for nothing, and so keeping track of the shapes and relative directions of each, trying to gauge at the first possible moment if any of them were coming towards me, and how fast. Increase in size, noise and the changing profiles of the hull were all I had to work with.

With 9am came the realization that I must have crossed half the Firth, and it seemed that I must also be outside the major shipping lanes by now. But I had forgotten about Rosyth. Almost immediately, a regulation grey naval power-launch roared out from the inner Firth passing well behind me but at an incredible 35-40 knots. I heaved a chuckle of relief that I didn't have to sit calm and gauge the course of that one!

A large, maroon, tanker-like vessel passed to my left, heading well out to where the North Sea meets the Forth, and I recognized it as the *Gardyloo*, the boat that dumps Edinburgh's sewage and sludge weekly at sea. And ahead lay 3 stationary tankers. No ... not tankers ... islands, at last! Slowly emerging from the mist I recognized Lamb, Fidra and Craigleith, ghostly volcanic sentinels of the Forth.

South now and I headed behind Craigleith Island to North Berwick beach. It had taken only an hour and a half from Elie, and as yet there was no sign of the gale. I had beaten the weather and completed the last crazy adventure of the journey a full day ahead of the scheduled reception at Seacliff Beach which lay now only three miles to the south east.

I booked into a guesthouse, ran a long bath to warm myself up and dispel last night's damp, then simply read and slept the day away while the gale outside searched the Forth for any sign of me. It was hard to believe that, after a hundred and twenty-eight days and nearly 1,800 miles, the whole thing was coming to an end. I didn't know how to adjust: I'd be giving up my daily routines of tidal calculations, weather battles, coastal camps and living with the sea. How do you neutralize four months of experience of that sort and make it compatible with living ashore in a town or city again? And what was I going back to? As for four million others, there was no money and no job.

There would be no more creeping down the coast, stealing miles against the weather, coasting from village to village and getting near the finish. This was the finish. Tomorrow I'd climb out of the water, turn my back on the Bass Rock, and on my four-month expedition, and look to the future.

Because I'd spent my last cheque on the room, but also in a slightly pathetic attempt to cling to what was so fast slipping away, I cooked the last of my dehydrated food using the last of my fuel on what was left of my stove as the rippled ebb sands reflected the kaleidoscopic golds of the evening sky.

I left North Berwick early on the Wednesday morning, paddling not for Seacliff Beach but for the Bass Rock itself, a four hundred-foot plug of grass-topped volcanic rock lying three miles offshore.

Perhaps the best known landmark of the Forth, the Bass was first inhabited by St Baldred but was later used as both a fortress and a prison and even featured as Jamie Balfour's prison in R.L. Stevenson's *Kidnapped* story. One of the largest and earliest recorded gannet breeding sites – an important source of eggs and oil in times past – it lends its name to the bird's scientific designation *Sula Bassana*. So many seabirds nest on its cliffs, including 14,000 pairs of gannets, that the naturally black rock appears from a distance as it if were chalk from the white guano.

For me it symbolised much. As a student in 1980 it had been the target of my first offshore kayak journey, and later became the focus of regular Wednesday afternoon journeys and an escape from studying. Groups of us would paddle out from the surf at Seacliff Beach to explore the bird cliffs and seal caves of the Bass, often returning just as the sun set over the ruins of Tantallon castle. And it was also a symbol of improvement, for I could remember the early days when the thought of capsizing in the open Forth, or in the swell behind the Bass, used to fill me with dread!

Today it was the final personal focus of the journey and the only thing I dreaded was a mass reception and fuss. I realized that I owed a certain amount of flourish and publicity to Fox's, and that it would be good for Intermediate Technology too; but I had chosen Seacliff as a finishing point not only because it was a personal favourite but because I thought its remoteness might prove slightly prohibitive to an overly large gathering of onlookers and newshounds!

It was a bright fresh morning and I reached the rock easily in half an hour and paddled round it to the big cave entrance. A tunnel, just passable at extremely low tides, runs through the rock with a cave entrance of about thirty feet on the other side and a hundred feet high on this side. Paddling round the rock you see the highly segregated seabird sectors, a guillemot-ghetto, a shagsville and several gannet-towns, and beneath the tidal zone is the true colour of the dark rock, washed clean by the sea.

Within the great cave seals swam beneath my boat and echoed their eerie cries from deep within. Before long there were bobbing heads all around me, where I too bobbed, sheltered from the roughest water by the vertical cliff walls, playing penny whistle to the seals for over an hour.

The wind, from the north, brought thoughts of recent weeks and a flood of August's memories ran through my mind like double-exposed photographs: Pittenweem and the caves of Auchmithie; helicopters over Dracula's castle at Cruden Bay; dolphins and the North Sea Haar; long open crossings and my kittiwake passenger. People, places and events concerted themselves at sea for a last time and I'd have gladly turned around and headed north again. Instead I paddled around the Rock once more and headed ashore.

As I approached Seacliff figures were gathering on the beach. There were reporters and photographers from Scottish papers, Kenny MacIntyre from Radio Scotland, and the Fox's PR girl with her own photographer. I recognized two suit-clad Fox's managers clutching a champagne bottle, and the President of the Local Council was there with some henchmen. The indomitable Richard Crane of Intermediate Technology arrived with plans for an appearance on 'Blue Peter' and for a publicity RUN around London with the kayak. Three coastguard officers fired maroon rocket-flares in triumph, and Pippa was there to take me home.

But paddling those last few yards I felt like an escaped convict who was at last giving himself up to the authorities – 'you can't run forever'. There was a hint of autumn in the air as, riding that last wave onto the beach, a weary kayak surrendered the freedom of solo travel and traded the sea for the shore.